New York by Gas-Light

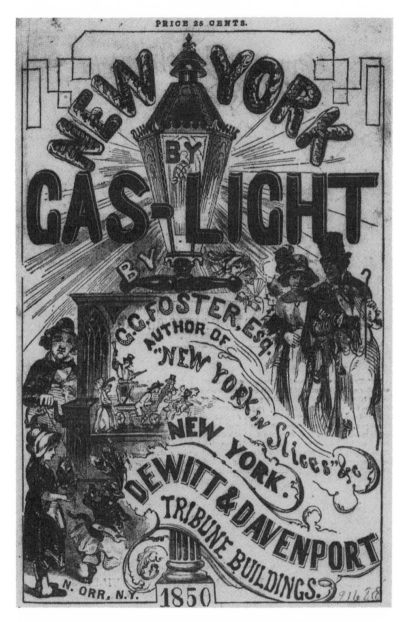

Original cover, *New York by Gas-Light*.

New York by Gas-Light

and Other Urban Sketches

by *George G. Foster*

Edited and with an Introduction by
Stuart M. Blumin

UNIVERSITY OF CALIFORNIA PRESS
BERKELEY   LOS ANGELES   LONDON

University of California Press
Berkeley and Los Angeles, California

University of California Press, Ltd.
London, England

© 1990 by
The Regents of the University of California

Library of Congress Cataloging-in-Publication Data

Foster, George G., d. 1856.
   New York by gas-light and other urban sketches / by George G.
Foster : edited and with an introduction by Stuart M. Blumin.
      p.   cm.
   Consists of the author's New York by gas-light, and selections
from his New York in slices, and Fifteen minutes around New York.
   ISBN 0–520–06721–5 (alk. paper).—ISBN 0–520–06722–3 (pbk. :
alk. paper)
   1. New York (N.Y.)—Description.   2. New York (N.Y.)—
—History—1775–1865.   3. New York (N.Y.)—Social life and customs.
I. Blumin, Stuart M.   II. Title.   III. Title: New York by gaslight
and other urban sketches.
F128.44.F758   1991
974.7'1—dc20   90–35290
                                                                          CIP

Printed in the United States of America

4 5 6 7 8 9

The paper used in this publication meets the minimum requirements of
American National Standard for Information Sciences—Permanence of
Paper for Printed Library Materials, ANSI Z39.48–1984.♾™

Contents

Introduction

George G. Foster and the Emerging Metropolis
by Stuart M. Blumin

"NEW YORK BY GAS-LIGHT! What a task have we undertaken! To penetrate beneath the thick veil of night and lay bare the fearful mysteries of darkness in the metropolis—the festivities of prostitution, the orgies of pauperism, the haunts of theft and murder, the scenes of drunkenness and beastly debauch, and all the sad realities that go to make up the lower stratum—the under-ground story—of life in New York!" With these words George G. Foster, city reporter and sometime litterateur, invites us to New York City at the mid-point of the nineteenth century, and to the new literary genre of nonfictional urban sensationalism. Both were particular specialties of Foster's. New York he knew as intimately as any man or woman living—although he shared the city with half a million other residents and additional hundreds of thousands who visited the city each year for business and for pleasure—and the genre was very nearly his own, however rooted it may have been in the urban sketches and *romans-feuilletons* of Pierce Egan, Eugène Sue, and their first American imitators. Let us try, before we accept Foster's invitation, to understand a little more about the city and the genre, and, while we're at it, one or two other aspects of Foster's world that form the context of his fascinating little book.

Foster begins by invoking the city itself, and so should we, and what must be emphasized at once is the novelty of New York's size in 1850, when *New York by Gas-Light* was published. To the twentieth-century reader there is nothing novel about the idea of New York as a very large city; indeed, what may be difficult to grasp is that there was a generation of New Yorkers who experienced the *emergence* of a metropolis on and around the site of what had been, for many previous generations, a substantial but by no means imposing town. As late as 1800 the United States census reported only 60,515 residents for New York City, a number slightly smaller than the 61,559 reported for Philadelphia and its adjacent "liberties." To be sure, Philadelphia and New York were the largest towns in the new nation and were a good deal more cosmopolitan than these population totals suggest. But many of the activities and institutions that we ordinarily associate with major urban centers existed only in rudimentary form. In New York, the eight-year-old stock exchange met at the Tontine Coffee House (and outdoors under a buttonwood tree on Wall Street), the four-story City Hotel went a step or two beyond the accommodations offered by traditional taverns, and the Park was the city's only theater. Several pleasure gardens were built on the outskirts of the city on the model of London's Vauxhall and Ranelagh Gardens, but most public entertainments were still found within the taverns, just as they were in smaller towns. There were no large factories, no large stores, and, for that matter, no large buildings of any kind—just a larger number of structures of ordinary size, alongside a few that were somewhat more imposing than those found in less populous places. Most tellingly, no public transportation system carried New Yorkers and their visitors around the city, for neither the size nor the extent of the population demanded it. At its farthest edge, the built-up portion of New York extended no more than a mile and three-quarters from the southern tip of thirteen-mile-long Manhattan Island before giving way to the marshes and farms that separated the city from Greenwich Village and Crown Point (Corlaer's Hook) to the north and east. More than half of the city's population lived within a mile of the Battery. In short, New York was still what urban historians are pleased to call a "walking city," accessible from end to end to any pedestrian possessing an hour and a good pair of boots.[1]

Foster's New York was a different place entirely; larger, spatially and institutionally more complex, and much more easily traversed by horsecar and omnibus than by foot. The city was growing rapidly even before the turn of the century, but its nineteenth-century growth burst the bounds of the walking city, and brought to the American landscape a type of urban environment never before seen on this side of the Atlantic. The city of 60,000 added 100,000 new residents during the first quarter of the new century, establishing New York as the largest city in the nation. And yet this remarkable growth was only a prelude to that of the next generation. By 1850 New York had grown by an additional 350,000, to a population of more than half a million. The built-up area of 1800 now contained some 90,000 residents, and a greatly increased number of businesses and public institutions, many of which were housed in new, larger buildings, giving New York the reputation of a place that was constantly and impatiently renewing itself in response to expanding opportunities and rising rents—and in the process losing touch with the townscapes of its own past. Most of the city's growth, however, was on new ground, and the most dramatic change in the cityscape was one of horizontal scale. More than 400,000 of the half-million New Yorkers found homes beyond the area that had defined the city in 1800, moving the boundary of dense habitation swiftly

1. This description is based on the manuscript population schedules of the United States census for 1800, a detailed map published in 1797 and reproduced in John A. Kouwenhoven, *The Columbia Historical Portrait of New York: An Essay in Graphic History* (New York, 1972), pp. 104–5, and Sidney I. Pomerantz, *New York: An American City, 1783–1803* (New York, 1938), esp. p. 228.

northward. By 1850 there was very little vacant land on Manhattan south of Twenty-third Street, which lies some three miles from the Battery. Along one or two avenues the city was densely built beyond Forty-second Street, four miles and nearly a third of the way up the island. Expansion was occurring to the east as well, even beyond Corlaer's Hook. Across the East River, Brooklyn and Williamsburg had grown from small villages into partly urban and partly suburban satellites of New York, linked to Manhattan by seven ferries, and adding nearly 130,000 residents and considerable new space to the metropolis as a whole.[2]

New York had quite suddenly become a big city, totally surrounding most of its residents with a busy and densely built environment of brick buildings, bluestone sidewalks, paved streets, and perpetual human traffic, a distinctly urban environment that was no longer within sight or easy reach of the retreating countryside. Some 200,000 New Yorkers squeezed into an increasingly unattractive, parkless East Side, where even the East River, when visible beyond the warehouses, docks, gashouses, and dockside factories, provided a view that consisted mainly of waterborne traffic and the built-up waterfront of Brooklyn. Many of those who established homes in less crowded uptown districts commuted by horsecar or omnibus each day to a crowded, busy, and rapidly expanding downtown business district. Hardly anyone escaped this urban environment, and since it had taken shape so quickly, virtually under the feet of those who were now experiencing it, there were many who were not fully prepared for its consequences. Nor were the changes only those of scale and pace. New York's population and social structure changed too, most visibly as a result of the massive immigration of destitute refugees from the Irish potato famine, a much smaller but consequential immigration

2. *The Seventh Census of the United States: 1850* (Washington, 1853), pp. 99–102; Kouwenhoven, *Columbia Historical Portrait*, p. 188; Robert Ernst, *Immigrant Life in New York City: 1825–1863* (New York, 1979), p. 21; city ward maps for 1850.

of aggressive businessmen from New England (possibly the ultimate source of that curious anomaly of institutional nomenclature, the New York Yankees), and the increasing size of the individual fortunes of those who profited most from New York's extraordinary physical and economic growth. Fueled by new demand at various levels of this attenuating social structure, the city's institutions multiplied and became more distinctively urban. By mid-century, New York had no fewer than forty-six hotels, several of which were large, ornate structures that rivalled the luxury hotels of Europe. The most fashionable of these hotels served well-to-do local residents as well as visitors, as did the new luxury restaurants and ice-cream saloons such as Delmonico's and Taylor's, and the new, elegantly designed retail shops that lined Broadway. Chief among the latter was A. T. Stewart's "Marble Palace," the largest and fanciest dry goods store in the country, and the precursor to the modern department store. Only a great city could support institutions such as these, or the large museum of curiosities that P. T. Barnum operated a little farther down Broadway from Stewart's, or the theaters that were now numerous enough to cater to specific tastes and social classes.[3] New Yorkers had to learn their way around these new institutions, the spaces that contained them, and the social forms and codes that defined their relation to the city's class structure. This was not necessarily a daunting task; indeed, it could be a very exciting one. But it was significantly more complex

3. *Doggett's New York City Directory, for 1850–1851* (New York, 1850), p. 23. These developments have been discussed in many places. Two very good discussions are in Edward K. Spann, *The New Metropolis: New York City, 1840–1857* (New York, 1981), and David Grimsted, *Melodrama Unveiled: American Theater and Culture, 1800–1850* (Chicago, 1968). Lawrence W. Levine, in *Highbrow/ Lowbrow: The Emergence of Cultural Hierarchy in America* (Cambridge, Mass., 1988), accepts the early class compartmentalization of metropolitan theater cultures described by Grimsted, even while arguing that cultural divergence as a more general American phenomenon would become manifest only later in the nineteenth century.

Broadway at mid-century: American Museum on left, Astor House on right.

than the adaptive process that had previously differentiated the city dweller from his country cousin. It required and produced those new skills that would become the hallmark of the metropolitan.

The consequences of New York's growth were by no means felt only by those who lived within its boundaries. Almost as quickly as New York became a big city it became a national center as well. In 1850 New York's port was by far the biggest and busiest in the nation, with respect both to freight and to the human cargo of foreign immigrants, Wall Street was the center of banking and finance, and the city's merchants were a dominant force in the organization of inland commerce. It is perhaps less well known that New York was the leading industrial center in the United States, and that it was already establishing itself as the arbiter of national taste in such things as theatrical production and fashionable clothing. There are also less visible indicators of New York's growing national importance. From the *Report of the Postmaster General* of 1852 geographer Allan Pred has discovered that more than 22 percent of the nation's letters passed through the New York post office (a figure that does not include letters that New Yorkers mailed to each other), at a time when the city represented only a little more than 2 percent of the national population. The New York post office also handled more than 60 percent of the letters and 75 percent of the newspapers mailed between the United States and foreign countries. According to Pred's analysis the newspapers of other important cities, from Boston to New Orleans to San Francisco, were two to three times more likely to mention New York than any other city, including nearby ones, when discussing economic matters.[4] George Foster was one of many who sensed how all of these lines of influence had made New York the node of an expanding network. "In civilization," he wrote in 1849, "every powerful nation

4. Allan Pred, *Urban Growth and City-Systems in the United States, 1840–1860* (Cambridge, Mass., 1980), tables A.43, A.45, A.50.

New York's City Hall, completed in 1812.

must have one intellectual centre, as every individual must have a brain, whose motions and conceptions govern the entire system. In the United States, New York is that centre and that brain."[5]

The external influence of the new metropolis was most keenly felt within its immediate vicinity, especially by those people who visited the city. It is impossible to measure the number of people who came to New York on temporary journeys of business or pleasure, but it was certainly very large. Small-town and country storekeepers did not order goods by mail in those days, but made semi-annual visits to New York wholesalers to select their stock. They were joined by businessmen of many other sorts, by increasing numbers of tourists, and by visitors to family members and friends who had migrated from surrounding farms and towns to the big city. These visitors availed themselves of, and quickened the demand for, hotels, restaurants, theaters, pleasure gardens, museums, dry goods palaces, specialty shops, and all the other institutions (including the illicit ones described in *New York by Gas-Light*) that made New York so exciting, and so different from smaller places. This difference needs to be emphasized, and understood in categorical rather than quantitative terms. The metropolis contained not merely more of everything, but many things that were simply unavailable elsewhere. Barnum's American Museum and Stewart's Marble Palace were on Broadway and nowhere else; theaters, fancy hotels, and backstairs saloons featuring *tableaux vivants* were not part of the general American landscape. The increasing presence of such institutions in New York contributed significantly to the changing character of the city, and to the nature of its influence.

That influence could be good, or at least harmless. Writing a few years later, James Dabney McCabe observed that visiting merchants, once stimulated by New York, could "go

5. George G. Foster, *New York in Slices: By an Experienced Carver* (New York, 1849), p. 63.

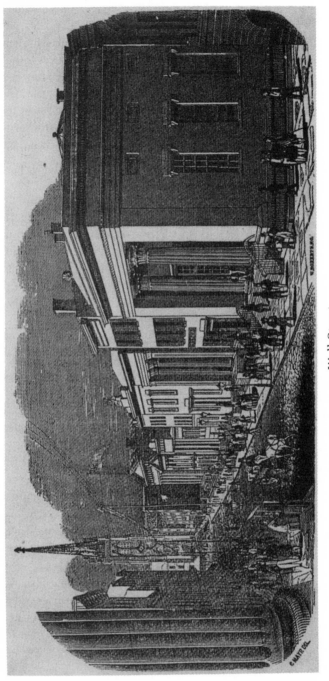

Wall Street.

back home braced up to their work, and filled with new and larger ideas," while Edward K. Spann recently has made the point that many Americans of this era were introduced to the comforts of gas lighting, steam heat, and indoor plumbing by staying in a New York hotel.[6] More often, however, the urban influence was seen as harmful to, and even destructive of, the most basic tenets of civilized society. We will take up the theme of the "wicked city" a few pages hence, and set the works of Foster and others in the context of the specific threats that the big city seemed to pose to the fabric of Victorian society. For the moment let us simply notice that, for good or for ill, the big city, and New York in particular, was an ever more prominent and consequential fact of American life. The walking city of the eighteenth century had metamorphosed into something greater, more powerful, and, at the same time, much less easily comprehended. Foster's *New York by Gas-Light*, indeed, ought to be seen first and foremost as one of a number of attempts to undertake the significant (and, let it be said, profitable) task of *explaining* the new metropolis to a society that was in so many ways affected by its development. Before we look at how Foster and other writers responded to the growing interest in urban affairs, however, we need to consider one other, closely related aspect of New York's role as the nation's new metropolis. We need to understand New York as the center of a revolution in publishing.

The printing of newspapers, magazines, and books was one of a number of industries that were utterly transformed during this era by accelerating developments in technology and industrial organization. As late as the first decade of the nineteenth century printing was carried out on small, flatbed, screw-type presses that hardly differed from those used hundreds of years earlier. These presses were slow and rela-

6. James Dabney McCabe, Jr., *Lights and Shadows of New York Life; or, the Sights and Sensations of the Great City* (Philadelphia, 1872), p. 442; Spann, *The New Metropolis*, p. 98.

tively inexpensive, which meant that printing, like most other artisanal trades, was performed almost entirely by small producers. And though these modest artisans were concentrated to a degree in the largest port cities (where news and European imprints were most easily obtained, and markets for printed matter were larger and more easily reached), they were found as well in smaller numbers in secondary towns throughout the country. In 1800 perhaps 150 to 200 newspapers were printed in the United States, many of them in quite small towns; in the decade 1810–1820, according to John Tebbel's estimate, approximately half of the books of fiction written by American authors were published outside of New York, Philadelphia, and Boston, the three major publishing centers. Especially in the smaller centers, but even in the big cities, printers often combined newspaper publishing, book publishing, job printing, and even bookselling and other forms of retailing, for none of these activities was conducted on a large scale. Most newspapers were four-page weeklies consisting mainly of advertisements, public notices, commercial information, and political news and discussion culled from a few major papers in England and the larger American towns, while most books were reprints of volumes already printed in Europe. Circulations were small. The two dozen city dailies existing at the turn of the century averaged only some 500 papers per day, while the dozen or so magazines achieved circulations that ranged from a few hundred to perhaps a thousand. Magazines, indeed, were rarely successful enough to sustain publication for more than a few years—the first to last as long as a decade was the *Port Folio*, which was first printed in 1801.[7]

7. On newspaper, magazine, and book publishing before the Jacksonian era see: Frank Luther Mott, *American Journalism: A History: 1690–1960* (New York, 1962), pp. 3–211; Alfred McClung Lee, *The Daily Newspaper in America: The Evolution of a Social Instrument* (New York, 1947), esp. pp. 1–61; Mott, *A History of American Magazines: 1741–1850* (Cambridge, Mass., 1939), pp. 13–335

Technological changes in printing (as well as in paper-making, typefounding, bookbinding, and other related trades) accelerated the publishing process and made possible much larger and cheaper press runs. Presses that used levers rather than screws were introduced to commercial production in 1816, and ten years later the importation of David Napier's cylinder press, which replaced the flat platen with a cylinder that could be rolled across the flat type bed, raised printing speeds from a few hundred to two thousand impressions per hour. Robert Hoe, whose New York firm would become the largest manufacturer of printing presses in the nation, introduced a two-cylinder press in 1832 that raised speeds to 4,000 sheets per hour. This was doubled in 1845 with Hoe's revolutionary type-revolving press, which mounted the type as well as the platen on a cylinder, and permitted the feeding of sheets, and later rolls, between a series of revolving cylinders. By 1855 Hoe's presses were printing up to 20,000 sheets per hour.[8] All of these improvements significantly increased the size of printing presses, and as the larger cylinder presses required the application of steam power, they further increased the cost of the capital equipment required of any publisher who sought to take advantage of these astonishing new speeds.

The few publishers who could afford the new presses revolutionized the printing industry; more accurately, they succeeded in superimposing a new industry over the traditional trade of printing, which, from countless small printshops in cities and smaller towns all over the country, continued to perform nearly all of the nation's job printing, publish most of the small-town weekly newspapers (there were more than two thousand weeklies in 1850), and even publish a few books. While this was once the entire trade, however, it was

---

(the reference to the *Port Folio* is on p. 120); John Tebbel, *A History of Book Publishing in the United States: Volume I: The Creation of an Industry, 1630–1865* (New York, 1972). Tebbel's estimate concerning the dispersal of fiction publishing in America is on p. 206.

    8. Lee, *Daily Newspaper*, pp. 116–17.

now only a localized niche within a nationalized industry. A relatively small number of mechanized publishing houses took over most book publishing, created an industry of successful, nationally circulating magazines, and introduced a new form of journalism, the mass-circulation "penny press." Without exception, these large-scale publishers were located in big cities, and among the big cities there was none so important as New York. A few figures drawn from Tebbel's comprehensive history of American book publishing suggest the direction and dimensions of change. Before 1842, the year of "the great leap forward" in the mass distribution of books, American publishers offered an average of approximately 100 books per year, which produced revenues of some $2.5 million. In 1855, no fewer than 1,092 books were published in the United States, yielding revenues of $16 million. Nearly $12 million, or three-quarters, of these revenues were generated by publishing houses in New York, Philadelphia, and Boston, and fully $6 million, or three-eighths, of the national total, belonged to New York alone. As early as 1840, only 8 percent of American fiction was being published outside the New York–Philadelphia–Boston axis. And in each city it was the large houses—Harper & Bros., D. Appleton & Co., J. B. Lippincott & Co., Ticknor & Fields, and a handful of others—that accounted for much of this business.[9] We might also note in passing that these same publishing giants were the source of many of the successful new magazines. *Harper's New Monthly Magazine*, for example, which survives today, was first published in 1850 by one of New York's biggest houses, and reached a national circulation of 200,000 before the Civil War.[10]

By that critical pre–Civil War decade the big cities, and New York in particular, had become what we would now call "media centers," sending out to a vast hinterland publications written and produced in the heart of metropolitan

9. Tebbel, *History of Book Publishing*, pp. 206, 221, 262 ff.
10. Frank Luther Mott, *A History of American Magazines: 1850–1865* (Cambridge, Mass., 1957), p. 391.

Literary New Yorker (N. P. Willis).

central business districts. Books such as Foster's *New York by Gas-Light*, according to *The Literary World* (a weekly review whose own editorial offices were at 157 Broadway), "horrify many a farmer by the perusal of [their] pages, as they are scattered over the country by the book pedlars who swarm its extent like busy bees—humming into every doorway, and leaving behind honied sweetness or stinging poison."[11] Many other less horrifying books, offering honied sweetness or plain porridge, circulated every bit as widely as those that instructed farmers in the poisons of city life. A few, such as Harriet Beecher Stowe's *Uncle Tom's Cabin* (which sold half a million copies within five years of its publication in 1852), went much further afield. But it is interesting to observe that increasing numbers of books *from* the city were *of* the city as well, and that these books formed a new genre that was clearly the product of forces transforming both the big city and the increasingly urbanized publishing industry. Adrienne Siegel has counted only 38 urban novels published in the United States between the years 1774 and 1839, and fully 340 published in the much shorter period of 1840–1860. More surprising, perhaps, is Siegel's discovery that during the three decades following 1840, a period of dramatic westward exploration and expansion, "more than three times as many books were written about life in the city as about conditions beyond the Appalachians."[12]

Some of these urban novels (along with Foster's nonfictional city books) were products of what Tebbel calls the first paperback revolution.[13] Almanacs, chapbooks, and pamphlets had for many decades been published in inexpensive paperbound form, but it was only in the 1830s and 1840s that other kinds of books that had traditionally been issued within more expensive covers began to appear as paper-

11. *The Literary World* 6:158 (February 9, 1850): 122.
12. Adrienne Siegel, *The Image of the American City in Popular Literature: 1820–1870* (Port Washington, N.Y., 1981), p. 6.
13. Tebbel, *History of Book Publishing*, pp. 240–51.

backs. The first of these new paperbacks, appearing in the early 1830s, were solid, edifying works intended to diffuse useful knowledge among literate masses who could not afford to buy expensive books. But the impact of these books, even at prices well below a dollar, was limited. Of far greater significance were the still cheaper sentimental novels and thrillers that resulted from a chain of events set in motion by several weekly literary magazines in the 1840s. Much fiction in this era, and even some nonfiction, appeared serially in magazines before being published in book form; indeed, a large number of magazines (a few were printed in the format of newspapers to avoid higher postage rates) had come into existence primarily to serve as vehicles for such work, which was often pirated from foreign publications appearing serially or in book form in England. One of the problems these magazines faced was the appearance of a book on the American market before it could be fully serialized. To counter the competition of the book publishers, therefore, the weeklies began to publish complete novels as "supplements" or "extras," bound in paper covers for sale by newsboys on city streets, and mailed without covers (at newspaper rates) to subscribers. The book publishers were forced to respond with cheap paperbacks of their own, and by 1843 some shorter books were being sold as cheaply as six cents per copy, with longer books ranging from eighteen to thirty-seven and a half cents.

These were ruinous prices, but the post office soon intervened by declaring that the supplements would be charged book rather than newspaper postage rates, a decision that drove the weeklies out of the book market and allowed the book publishers to stabilize prices. But the cheap paperback had become part of the industry. Books by prestigious European and American authors generally returned to clothbound form (technological improvements and the aftershock of the paperback revolution had driven their prices down too), but paperbacks found their niche with popular sentimental novels (those of Mrs. E. D. E. N. Southworth were the most successful), sensationalist accounts of the wicked city, and adventure stories of the frontier and the sea, the last two of these finding expression just before the war in the "dime novels" of the house of Irwin and Erastus Beadle.

Book publishers such as the Beadles had taken over the market for cheap paperbacks, but the connections between book and magazine publishing were by no means severed. Indeed, a number of new "story magazines" were founded to serialize sensationalist literature that would later appear in book form, and at least one new journal, the *National Police Gazette* (first published in 1845), specialized in true and fictional tales about crime and other horrors in the big city. We must note, moreover, one other connection, since it is directly pertinent to Foster's *New York by Gas-Light*. Hoe presses and the drive for mass circulation affected big-city newspaper publishing as much as or more than any other print medium. Daily papers that once sold 500 copies at prices ranging from six cents to twelve cents for individual issues (annual subscribers received much lower rates) could by mid-century sell tens of thousands of copies each day, hawking them on the streets at a price of one or two cents. Horace Greeley estimated in 1851 that five cheap New York dailies sold 100,000 newspapers each day, led by the first of the successful penny papers, the *New York Sun*, with 50,000, and followed by Greeley's own two-penny paper, the *New York Tribune*, with a daily circulation of 20,000.[14] A later historian counted fourteen dailies in New York in 1850, with a total circulation of over 150,000, a figure that contrasts strikingly with the 2,500 total circulation of the five New York dailies printed at the start of the nineteenth century.[15] The penny papers in particular had cultivated this larger market by changing their content and tone in the direction of what we now call tabloid journalism—reporting in lurid detail the murders, criminal trials, riots, and everyday mis-

14. Dan Schiller, *Objectivity and the News: The Public and the Rise of Commercial Journalism* (Philadelphia, 1981), p. 14.
15. Lee, *Daily Newspaper*, p. 730.

haps that earlier would have been limited to a few lines or excluded entirely. As these were big-city papers, operating in a pre-electronic era (that is, until the telegraph became available to them after 1844), many of their most exciting stories were set in the city itself, and it is in the penny press that we first find many of the wicked-city motifs that would later work their way into nationally circulating paperbound books. The *Sun*, again, was the leader in this role, but we can observe here that it was in Greeley's more high-toned *Tribune* that George Foster's initial foray into urban sensationalism first appeared, as a series of prominently featured sketches bearing the collective title "New York in Slices." Thirty "Slices" appeared in the *Tribune* between July and October of 1848 (twenty-one were on the front page of the newspaper, and three were at the head of column one of the front page), and by January of 1849 the book *New York in Slices: By an Experienced Carver* was available in a press run of 20,000 copies. *New York by Gas-Light* was the sequel to this successful transformation of the newspaper sketch into a nationally circulating paperbound book.

By the 1850s the new metropolis had found its voice in these various home-grown media, which provided a new genre of urban commentary, "a set of discursive practices" appropriate to "a new kind of city and city life. . . . Something new came into the world," Thomas Bender observes, "and it had to be endowed with meaningful representation."[16] How did George Foster and others arrive at this "meaningful representation"? How did urban writers of this era set out to explain the new metropolis?

Questions such as these must be understood on a much larger than local scale, for the emerging metropolis impinged upon people who still lived in the country and in small towns, and upon a culture that took shape in and re-

16. Thomas Bender, "The Culture of the Metropolis," *Journal of Urban History* 14 (1988): 494.

flected these pre-metropolitan milieux. Nor should we see the problem and its responses exclusively in American terms or, for that matter, entirely in terms of an unprecedented explosion of urban growth in the western world. Writers have been responding to big-city growth ever since Sodom and Gomorrah, and there are nearer precedents for the nineteenth-century genre, even as it appeared in the United States, in a variety of better or lesser known English texts of the eighteenth and early nineteenth centuries. These range from *Tom Jones* and other picaresque novels built around the country hero's adventures in the city to a number of now forgotten nonfictional or semi-fictional texts bearing such titles as *Tricks of the Town Laid Open* (1747), *The Devil upon Crutches in England: or, Night Scenes in London* (1755), *London Unmasked* (1787), and *The Midnight Spy: or, ... London from 10 in the Evening until 5 in the Morning, Exhibiting a Great Variety of Scenes in High Life and Low Life* (1766).[17] Suggestive as these latter titles may be of George Foster's New York books of the 1850s, however, there is no evidence that they were known to Foster or any other nineteenth-century American writer. A convincing line of influence can be drawn back only to the publication in 1821 of Pierce Egan's extension of the genre, *Life in London: or, the Day and Night Scenes of Jerry Hawthorn, Esq., and his Elegant Friend Corinthian Tom, Accompanied by Bob Logic, the Oxonian, in their Rambles and Sprees through the Metropolis.*

Egan, a journalist of the sporting life, had made something of a name for himself a few years earlier with his *Boxiana: or, Sketches of Modern Pugilism*, but *Life in London* would, as his biographer claims, "make Egan as well-known an author on the vulgar level as Scott was on the polite one."[18] Illustrated by Robert and George Cruikshank (and

17. These and a few other such titles are listed in J. C. Reid, *Bucks and Bruisers: Pierce Egan and Regency England* (London, 1971), p. 51. The following discussion of Egan draws heavily on Reid's biography.
18. Ibid., p. 50.

apparently based on Egan's own sprees through London with the brothers Cruikshank), the book sold furiously, was frequently reprinted, and, according to Egan's complaint, bred more than sixty imitations and derivations ranging from plays to painted tea trays. The idea and structure of the book were simple and traditional enough, and cannot alone explain its popularity. In it the savvy and well-to-do London idler, Corinthian Tom, repairs to the country for a health-restoring breather from city pleasures. At his uncle's estate he meets his cousin, Jerry Hawthorn, who is much like Tom in everything except his lack of city polish. Not surprisingly, Tom invites Jerry to join him on a tour of the metropolis, which the cousins, occasionally in the company of Tom's friend Bob Logic, bring off with great gusto, Tom instructing his appreciative student in the styles, mores, and even the language of London's high and low life—from fashionable ballrooms, the opera, Bond Street, and the Royal Exchange to East End gin shops, cock fights, street beggars, and Newgate prison. The book ends when the tour ends, Jerry having been sent back to the country to recover from a cold.

Perhaps it was Egan's jaunty prose style that made *Life in London* so popular, or the Cruikshanks' illustrations, which were part of what the young Thackeray loved about the book. But London itself must take part of the credit. Egan, a journalist, had rooted his saga in urban realities that seem not to have been portrayed before in books of this sort. His catalogue of London slang was itself a notable contribution to what people could learn about the city's various classes and sub-communities. And as Dickens and others would soon understand, it was just this kind of knowledge that readers were coming to appreciate, if not in the dry statistical accounts of reformers and sanitary inspectors, then certainly in the livelier form of the reality-grounded, fictional "urban sketch." Dickens's own *Sketches by Boz* (illustrated by George Cruikshank) were clearly influenced by Egan, and many of his later novels were built upon the growing demand for fiction, however fanciful and sentimental in plot and language, that evoked the realities of the nineteenth-century city.

Egan's sketches were influential in America, too, but by the time the growth of New York, Philadelphia, and a few other large cities made the urban theme compelling to American writers, there was a more immediate inspiration that gave their work a somewhat different shape. Eugène Sue's sprawling *Les Mystères de Paris* was serialized in the *Journal des Débats* in 1842 and 1843, and appeared in book form in Paris in the latter year. Perhaps the most popular of the serialized stories (or *romans-feuilletons*) of the era, it was quickly translated for English and American readers, who were just as avid as the French in their appreciation of Sue's various plots and sub-plots, and of his quite vivid evocation of the seamy side of life in the metropolis. American editions began to appear in book form even before serialization was complete in Paris—a second 1843 edition, put out as an "extra" by the *New World*, bore the title and sub-title *The Mysteries of Paris: Being the Last and Concluding Chapters of the Story Just Received from Paris and Wholly Omitted in Harpers Edition!* Sue, we are told, was himself heavily influenced by Pierce Egan,[19] but in form, focus, and political program *Les Mystères de Paris* is quite different from *Life in London*. Sue's tour of the metropolis centers on proletarian hardship and degradation (in particular the poverty-induced sin of prostitution), and is accomplished by means of elaborate and improbable Dickensian plots rather than the simple sequence of initiatory visits characteristic of the urban sketch. The most important of these plots (which bears a striking resemblance to that of *Oliver Twist*) concerns the tragic history of the young prostitute Fleur-de-Marie, turned up by Rodolphe, Grand Duke of Gerolstein, on one of the good nobleman's sympathetic visits to the Pa-

19. For example, by Louis James, in *Fiction for the Working Man: 1830–1850* (London, 1963), p. 140.

risian slums. Sensing her innate goodness, Rodolphe sends
Fleur-de-Marie off to a model farm (from which she is tem-
porarily abducted by former associates of the Île de la Cité),
eventually discovers her to be his own long-lost daughter, re-
stores her to her proper place in his household, and happily
assents when his friend Prince Henri proposes marriage to
her. Fleur-de-Marie loves Henri, but, alas, she cannot allow
herself to be married to him. Oliver Twist was an unwitting
accomplice to a pickpocket, but Fleur-de-Marie had sunk
much lower, and it seems that (even in France!) the emerging canons of sentimental fiction prevented her from ever
being fully redeemed from the sin of unchastity. Rodolphe
cannot convince his daughter of her innocence—her victimization by the evil city—and Fleur-de-Marie's very goodness
impels her to understand that, forever deflowered, she cannot assume the role of wife and mother in a respectable
home. Off she goes to a convent (we are in France after all),
where, denied even the consolation of cloistered purity, she
dies a Franco-Victorian death that is the only possible resolution of her victimization.[20] Oliver, by now a strapping
teenager, was no doubt on his way to his tailor.

Prostitutes (or "Cyprians") had flitted in and out of
Egan's *Life in London*, but in a mostly lighthearted and only
faintly condemnatory manner, as expressions of the wicked
gaiety of the metropolis. Sue made of the prostitute a much
grimmer symbol of modern urban life, and in so doing
struck a deep chord among at least some of his readers. For
in no other way did the city (the locale of the prostitute in
nearly every literary account) so clearly threaten the most
basic values of proper society. Countless studies have told us
how the middle-class family was reshaped during the early
decades of the nineteenth century, giving new meaning and
strength to gender distinctions on the basis of romantic conceptions of womanhood and childhood. On these and other,

20. This theme is discussed extremely well by Peter Brooks in
"The Mark of the Beast: Prostitution, Melodrama, and Narrative,"
New York Literary Forum 7 (1980): 125–40.

more practical grounds (such as the more frequent absence of the husband-father from the home during the work day), respectable Europeans and Americans reorganized gender roles so as to give greater responsibility to the wife-mother in the nurturance and socialization of children, and in the maintenance of the home as a place of peace and moral nourishment in what was perceived to be a more fast-paced and amoral world. In admonitory literature, and surely in day-to-day domestic life, a great deal of what came to be called Victorian morality was placed squarely on women's shoulders, by men as well as women authors, by husbands as well as wives. Hence, when women failed in the performance of their central role as domesticated guardians of virtue, society itself was threatened. And there was no more fundamental failure than the package of violations that was prostitution—the surrender of chastity, the commercialization of sex (taking this darkest of domestic secrets into the very marketplace that the home was supposed to exclude from its sacred premises), the implication of the husband-father in the sin most perilous to his own commitment to the hearth, and, perhaps most disturbingly of all, the apparent reversion to outmoded male assumptions of female lasciviousness and moral inferiority.[21]

It is by no means surprising, therefore, to find a concern bordering on hysteria in Victorian discussions and fictional accounts of prostitution. Nor is it surprising to find prostitution at the center of Victorian accounts of the wicked city. Prostitution, however, was not the only crime in Sue's Paris, merely the pivotal one. His many imitators would quickly expand upon a variety of urban "mysteries," or "miseries," in *The Mysteries of London*, *The Mysteries of Berlin*, *The Mys-*

21. Brooks points out that to middle-class readers prostitution was not necessarily the same kind of crime for the working classes as it was for the middle classes. He notes one of Sue's sub-plots, involving the redemption of the dark and fierce prostitute, La Louve, the She-Wolf, whose sordid past does not prevent her from becoming a working-class wife and mother. Ibid., pp. 133–34.

teries and Miseries of New York, and, on the American side
alone, similarly titled works set in Philadelphia, Cincinnati,
St. Louis, New Orleans, and San Francisco. Even smaller industrial cities, such as Lowell, Worcester, Springfield, and
Troy were mysterious enough, or contained enough human
misery, for such treatment. It was the largest cities, however, that gained the most attention. New York had a *Mysteries of*, and a *Miseries of*, in addition to the *Mysteries and
Miseries* noted above. There was also a *Mysteries of* and a
Mysteries and Miseries of Philadelphia. Moreover, the genre
was by no means restricted to books that appropriated Sue's
title. Popular writers such as George Lippard, E. Z. C. Judson (Ned Buntline), Joseph Holt Ingraham, Osgood Brad-
bury, and Timothy Shay Arthur churned out dozens of
variously titled urban romances that revolved around the
sins, deprivations, and personae of the big city. Lippard's
*The Quaker City; or The Monks of Monk Hall, A Romance of
Philadelphia Life, Mystery, and Crime*, was particularly popular, as was his sequel, *The Nazarene; Or, The Last of the Wash-
ingtons: A Revelation of Philadelphia, New York, and Washington, in the Year 1844*. Judson offered several explicit sequels
to his *Mysteries and Miseries of New York*, including *The
B'hoys of New York* and *The G'hals of New York*, while Ingraham joined his *Miseries of New York* to such titles as *Frank
Rivers; or, The Dangers of the Town*, *The Beautiful Cigar Girl;
or, The Mysteries of Broadway*, and *Ellen Hart; or the Forger's
Daughter*. George Foster tried his hand, though not very successfully, with *Celio: or New York Above-Ground and Under-
Ground*.[22]

Sue's narrative, as I have already noted, was more than a
set of individual tales of vice, virtue, and redemption. It was
also a reformist tract that laid bare the exploitation and

22. Urban sensationalism has been examined many times, most
recently and extensively by David S. Reynolds in *Beneath the American Renaissance: The Subversive Imagination in the Age of Emerson
and Melville* (New York, 1988). Reynolds makes numerous references to Foster's work.

misery of the Parisian working class, and the experience of writing it turned Sue into an active socialist. His American imitators, too, frequently announced their books as exposés of working-class exploitation and poverty, and of the hypocritical sinfulness of the commercial and industrial bourgeoisie. Their narratives were explicitly grounded in the theory that "the laborer is worthy of his hire," and that the determined assaults of lascivious merchants, stockbrokers, and lawyers on the frail virtues of the poor reflected a dangerous new structure of power in American cities. This radical program no doubt enlarged the market for the mysteries-and-miseries romances among urban workers. But, as later critics have observed, it did not impel such writers as Lippard or Judson to portray the neighborhoods of the urban poor, or the industrial workplace, or the city itself as the specific setting of capitalist exploitation, with anything approaching realistic detail. It may be too extreme to claim, as one critic has done, that for the city writers "the urban scene was simply an excuse for thrillmanship."[23] Their highly sensationalized romances did address certain anxieties about the direction of change in industrializing America, and did find a convincing setting in a kind of generalized, evil metropolis. As Michael Denning has observed with reference to Lippard's labyrinthine and darkly sinister Monk Hall, where most of the dreadful events of *The Quaker City* take place, even a single and quite improbable building could symbolize the big city without much loss of representational power.[24] And yet elliptical settings such as these, and sensationalist romances such as *The Quaker City*, did not constitute the "meaningful representation" that the first metropolitan generation sought. They did not *explain* the city or create a satisfying means of discourse about urban

23. Janis P. Stout, *Sodoms in Eden: The City in American Fiction Before 1860* (Westport, Conn., 1976), p. 42.

24. Michael ·Denning, *Mechanic Accents: Dime Novels and Working-Class Culture in America* (London and New York, 1987), pp. 91–93.

problems, even on a popular level. There was still a considerable audience, in short, for other forms and other styles.

George Foster supplied a closely related alternative that proved as popular as the sensationalist city novels, even while differing from them in crucial ways. Hearkening back to Egan, and responding as well to the day-to-day reportage that he and others were supplying to the big-city daily press, Foster developed in the (mostly) nonfictional urban sketch a new and much more satisfying method for addressing the concerns that made the sensationalist city romances popular. All the themes of the mysteries-and-miseries stories are in Foster's sketches, but so too is the city itself—the tangible city, in much of its particular and realistic detail. Foster manipulated and embellished this detail—sensationalized it, if you prefer—and it is not always easy to find in his work the line that separates description from illustrative fabrication. But even when he is caricaturing the treacherous parvenu or his snobbish and deceitful wife, or holding out a sympathetic hand to a fictional struggling seamstress on her way to seduction, prostitution, and death in a lonely room, Foster supplies a city that is far more real, and far more complete, than any found in the pages of Lippard, Judson, Ingraham, and the other romancers. It is a city one can enter, understand, and, making certain allowances, even believe. Foster, therefore, is at once representative of and unique within the striking new phenomenon of mass-produced (and mass-consumed) urban sensationalism, and has left us works that in most respects are considerably more valuable than those of his contemporaries.

It may reasonably be said that what made Foster's work distinctive was the way he drew upon his own experience. The addition of the sub-title *By an Experienced Carver* to his *New York in Slices* is significant. Foster was offering not meaningful fancy but well-seasoned expertise in city ways. Such expertise underlay the romances as well, but it was the very essence of the city sketch, the medium that Foster made his own. Before we turn to the sketches themselves, therefore, we ought to learn what we can of the man who made them, and in particular of those experiences that made him so skillful a carver of cities.

Of Foster's family, birth, and childhood we know virtually nothing, even his place of birth remaining obscure.[25] One of his obituaries describes him as a native of Vermont, another as having been born in Providence, Rhode Island. Foster himself claimed once to have been "born and educated on the banks of the Hudson," and added a few descriptive details that strongly suggest the village of Peekskill, New York, in the northwestern corner of Westchester County.[26] The year of his birth is also uncertain, although 1814 is probably correct and is certainly not far from the mark. In any case, Foster makes a less ambiguous appearance in Albany, New York (an easy trip up the river from Peekskill), in 1830, when he began to share living quarters and literary opinions with a rebellious fifteen-year-old lad named Rufus

25. There is no biography of Foster, and unless a good deal of fresh documentation is discovered it is unlikely that there will ever be one. The only extant summary of his life consists of a few pages in George Rogers Taylor, "Gaslight Foster: A New York 'Journeyman Journalist' at Mid-Century," *New York History* 58 (1974): 297–312. The following account differs at some points from Taylor's.

26. George G. Foster, "The Ideal: German Literature, and a Love Story," *Graham's Lady's and Gentleman's Magazine* 19:6 (December, 1841): 293–94. The context of Foster's autobiographical remarks— a defense of romantic literature—makes his claim to a Hudson Highlands boyhood somewhat suspect (the Highlands are just where a budding romantic *should* be from), as does his mention of the railroad depot that he found on the site of his old church when he visited his native village ten years before writing the essay. In fact, there was no railroad depot anywhere in the Hudson Valley in 1831, and none in any riverfront village in 1841. Local records are sparse, but the manuscript census of 1820 for the Town of Cortlandt, in which Peekskill is located, does list a household headed by one Robert Foster, in which there lived a boy classified as under ten years of age. This could have been George. I would guess that Foster was from Peekskill, and that he allowed himself a few small liberties when describing the unfortunate modernization of his sublime Hudson Valley boyhood home.

Griswold, who would later become a prominent literary editor and anthologist in New York and Philadelphia. Griswold recalled Foster in these days as a passionate and very good romantic poet, who had composed a 3000-line "Seventeenth Canto," now lost, that Griswold thought improved in some parts upon Byron's own concluding canto to *Don Juan*.[27] Their close companionship ended about a year later, when each young man took his Byronic quest to other places. Foster, though, was probably already evolving from "the dreamy poet of sixteen" (as he would describe himself years later) to "the patient worker at the laboring oar of every-day journalism."[28] We next find him in 1834, much farther upstate, as the exceptionally young editor of the *Oswego Democrat*.[29]

Foster appears to have done a good job as editor of this Whig paper. Eight years later William H. Seward himself wrote to Foster, recalling "with pleasure the newspaper you published in Oswego in 1834 and the spirit and ability with which it was conducted."[30] Yet Foster remained in Oswego no longer than a year. By February of 1835 he was in Utica, vainly urging Griswold to join him, and claiming to be making arrangements to transfer to Utica a satirical magazine Griswold was editing in Syracuse. It is not clear why Foster

27. *Passages from the Correspondence and Other Papers of Rufus W. Griswold* (Cambridge, Mass., 1898), pp. 7–8. Foster's and Griswold's relationship is also described, with slightly different dates, in Joy Bayless, *Rufus Wilmot Griswold: Poe's Literary Executor* (Nashville, 1943), pp. 8–11.

28. George G. Foster, *New York Naked* (New York, [1854]), p. 12.

29. Foster to Griswold, September 30, 1834, Boston Public Library; Foster to William H. Seward, August 26, 1842, University of Rochester Library.

30. Seward to Foster, August 29, 1842, University of Rochester Library. The real purpose of this letter was to brush off a solicitation by Foster to back a new Whig monthly magazine (see below). But Seward's compliment does seem sincere, and Foster's own letter points out to Seward that two of their mutual acquaintances "have frequently told me that you have spoken well of it [that is, Foster's earlier editorship]." Foster to Seward, August 26, 1842, University of Rochester Library.

left Oswego, or what he was doing in Utica. Two things that
are clear are that somewhere in his travels (which included
a stay in the village of Pulaski, north of Syracuse), Foster
had married and fathered a child, and that both domestic
bliss and worldly success were proving elusive. "For God's
sake, don't get married," he advised Griswold, and he was
soon again on the road, "wandering to and fro upon the
earth," stopping to write his obviously reticent friend once
more from Pittsburgh later the same year. In this letter Foster would express, among other things, a racial and ethnic
prejudice that would appear again in his journalism and his
urban sketches. The year 1835 was one of intense, often violent conflict between the opponents and defenders of southern slavery, and Foster left little doubt as to where he stood,
adding a dig at the Pope to his denunciation of blacks and
abolitionists: "[D]amn the negroes! I hate them and their
northern instigators as I do his Satanic majesty."[31] Not surprisingly in light of these sentiments, Foster's next migra-
tion was southward, to Alabama, where for a year or so he
edited a country paper at the respectable salary of $2,000
per annum. This paper soon failed, however, and Foster
moved to Mobile, where, failing to find work on a newspaper, he took a job as a flute player in a theater orchestra.
Probably in that capacity he then moved to St. Louis.[32]

Foster did not remain long in the orchestra pit, but he did
spend several years in St. Louis, where for a short time he
tasted the worldly success to which, "dreamy poet" or not,
he was clearly committed. After submitting a number of
anonymous articles to the *St. Louis Bulletin*, which according to Foster attracted much public attention, he was taken
on as a reporter and de facto assistant editor at a salary of
$600. Dissatisfied with "writing the editor into popularity
and consequence" on so small a salary, Foster demanded a
raise and acknowledgment as a junior editor. When these

31. Foster to Griswold, November 23, 1835, University of Virginia Library.
32. Foster to Griswold, May 12, 1841, University of Virginia Library.

were refused he left the *Bulletin*, and somehow found the backing to purchase the *Pennant*, "a little sickly evening paper, with scarce two hundred subscribers." Foster built this paper up, first with simple hard work, then by committing the paper to the increasingly popular anti-immigrant political program of Native Americanism, which attracted fresh capital to his enterprise. By May of 1841 Foster estimated the *Pennant* to be the second most popular newspaper west of the Alleghenies (after the *Louisville Journal*), and his own position to be worth at least $5,000 per year and on the increase. "I shall be," he wrote Griswold, "for some six months to come, somewhat straightened [*sic*] to meet some heavy demands becoming due," but after they are settled a fortune awaits. In two more years, Foster promised, he would come to New York to spend the summer, and the two old friends might even travel together to Europe, "and 'stand' in Venice, on the Bridge of Sighs. Eh! Don't that make your heart beat?"[33]

Of all the shrines of European tourism, Foster would have to choose the Bridge of Sighs to objectify his worldly dreams. The "heavy demands" he optimistically brushed aside in 1841 sent him to New York earlier than he predicted, but not in any condition to continue on to a European tour, with or without Griswold. The *Pennant* failed, and by the spring of 1842 Foster was in New Orleans, looking for passage to New York from "a captain who will take me a sailing all for love and no money. Penniless, hopeless, and almost broken-hearted," he wrote, "I go to commence my insignificant career anew."[34] Griswold, by contrast, had just established his own career with the publication of his first major anthology, *The Poets and Poetry of America* (Foster's work was not included), and by succeeding Edgar Allan Poe as the literary editor of *Graham's Lady's and Gentleman's Magazine*, perhaps the leading literary monthly of the

33. Ibid.
34. Foster to Griswold, May 21, 1842, Historical Society of Pennsylvania.

day.[35] This, indeed, is what provoked Foster's latest letter. During the previous twelve months Poe had published four of Foster's poems and one of his essays in *Graham's*, and had included him in his "Chapter on Autography," a collection and analysis of the signatures of what Poe called "the most noted among the living literati of the country."[36] Poe's comments in the "Autography" about Foster's poetry, essays, and editorial career were very favorable, and he touted a monthly magazine that Foster was proposing. Foster must have been very pleased by this attention, just as Poe was two years earlier when he wrote to a friend that the *St. Louis Bulletin*, whose editor he did not then know, had been giving him favorable reviews.[37] Poe soon discovered his western friend, and was pleased to reciprocate by advancing Foster's literary career. But now Poe was leaving *Graham's*, and Griswold, an older if not a better friend, was to replace him. Foster pointed out that he had just "sent a few trifles" to Poe, which he offered at two dollars a page (half of Poe's own rate). "If he should turn them over to you," wrote Foster, "do what your conscience will permit in my behalf—for verily, I know not by what means to procure bread for my poor family." Perhaps, too, Foster asked, Griswold could find work for him on Graham's other magazine, *The Saturday Evening Post* (which, Foster did not yet know, Griswold was also helping to edit).

When Foster arrived in New York during the summer of 1842 he called on Griswold dressed "in the grotesque cos-

35. Bayless, *Griswold*, pp. 44–50.
36. Foster's publications in *Graham's* can be found in 18:5 (May, 1841): 223; 19:1 (July, 1841): 39; 19:6 (December, 1841): 293–97; 20:2 (February, 1842): 84; 20:4 (April, 1842): 225. Poe's "A Chapter on Autography" was published in 19:5 (November, 1841): 224–34, and 19:6 (December, 1841): 273–86. It was continued the following month in "An Appendix on Autographs," 20:1 (January, 1842): 44–49. In all, 128 signatures were included.
37. Poe to Frederick W. Thomas, November 23, 1840, in John Ward Ostrom, ed., *The Letters of Edgar Allan Poe* (New York, 1966), p. 148.

tume of the South-West, but otherwise scarcely changed"
from what Griswold remembered him to be a decade
earlier.[38] Neither this reunion nor Foster's earlier letter,
however, procured much help from Griswold. During his
editorship only one of Foster's poems was published in
Graham's, and that took fully a year to appear.[39] Meanwhile,
Foster set out on various editorial ventures of his own. In
August he sent Seward the printed prospectus of a Whig political and literary magazine to be called the *United States
Monthly Review*, which Foster proposed to edit with one
J. W. Moore.[40] He also approached Poe with a proposal to
co-edit a literary magazine. Poe gave serious consideration
to Foster's invitation, but in the end nothing came of it.[41]
Neither was the *United States Monthly Review* ever published. Rebuffed in these efforts in magazine writing and
publishing, Foster fell back on his experience in newspapers,
and got a job "writing squibs and paragraphs," as he put it,
at the *New York Aurora*.[42] This was not an auspicious start to
a career in the New York publishing industry, but in one
respect the *Aurora* job may have helped Foster on to bigger
things. Foster would no doubt have met Horace Greeley no
matter where he happened to work in New York, but it is
worth noting that shortly after the newcomer began working in the *Aurora*'s offices at 162 Nassau Street, Greeley's
Tribune moved its headquarters from Ann Street to 160 Nassau, right next door.

It is impossible to say how long Foster remained at the
Aurora, but according to his own recollection he did not
move directly from 162 Nassau to 160. "Having been for
some months out of employment," he wrote, "I ... under-

38. Griswold, *Correspondence*, p. 8.
39. See *Graham's* 23:2 (August, 1843): 104.
40. Foster to Seward, August 26, 1842, University of Rochester
Library.
41. Poe to Frederick W. Thomas, September 12, 1842, in Ostrom,
ed., *Letters of Edgar Allan Poe*, p. 212.
42. Foster to Seward, September 13, 1842, University of Rochester Library.

took the task of local reporter, or gatherer of petty items of intelligence about the courts and the city generally, for one of the morning journals," clearly the *Tribune*.[43] Judging from the listings in the city directories, Foster's tenure as a city reporter at the *Tribune* began some time in 1844, and lasted until 1846 or 1847.[44] Foster is actually designated "editor" in these directory listings, but his responsibilities in the embryonic city news department were more reportorial than editorial, and Foster claims to have been paid "at a rate of compensation considerably less than that received by the compositors who set up the type for the paper."[45] Perhaps he was, but Foster could at least claim (and did claim) to have made significant contributions during these years to the evolution of the distinct role and style of the big-city newspaper reporter. Before he arrived, local news in the *Tribune* consisted mainly of straightforward descriptions of police court trials, coroner's inquests, meetings of the Board of Aldermen, and other official proceedings, gathered into columns headed "City Intelligence" and "City Affairs." Individual items in these columns were headed, simply, "Police Office," "Coroner's Inquests," or "Court of Sessions." In April of 1845, items of this sort were retitled "A Sad Story," "Police Doings," "Touch and Go," or "Drunken Fight and Probable Murder," and were written in a much livelier style. More importantly, a new "City Items" column, which soon replaced the other two, took both the reporter and the reader beyond the courts and official meeting rooms to fires,

43. Foster, *New York Naked*, p. 14.

44. Foster's work address is listed as 160 Nassau Street in Doggett's 1844–45 directory, and in Groot and Elston's 1845 directory, and as 158 Nassau Street in Doggett's 1845–46 and 1846–47 directories. On February 5, 1845, the *Tribune* office at 160 Nassau was destroyed by fire. When the new Tribune Buildings opened on May 29 of that year, the editorial offices were, officially, at 158 Nassau Street. See *Tribune*, May 29, 1845. Foster is not listed in Doggett's directories for three years beginning in 1847–48.

45. Foster, *New York Naked*, p. 14.

militia parades, concerts, arrivals of famous people, and any number of other events that could be found on the streets of the city. All this was clearly the work of Foster, partly as a kind of city editor, but primarily as a reporter, eagerly (or wearily) tracking down stories in every corner of the metropolis. Foster later recalled his daily trips to the police court ("that shrine of petty larceny, drunkenness, vagabondism, and vagrancy"); his coverage of innumerable fires, day and night, followed by his hunting up of "dismayed presidents of trembling insurance companies . . . to ascertain the exact amount of salt pork and mackerel" lost in the fire; and his attendance at "the Demosthenian debates" of the Board of Aldermen, "receptions of great men by our most hospitable city papas," "masonic funerals and odd-fellow processions which embellished the week," celebrations of the Fourth of July and other holidays, and parades of "every ragged regiment" of the city's volunteer firemen. In the color and spirit of the firemen's parade Foster found a metaphor for his own work: "My column [advanced] line by line with its column—and the grand parade of the 'City Item' department and the fire departments both astonished the public on the same occasion."[46]

Foster remembered this work as grueling and time-consuming, but it did not distract him from older literary ambitions. In May of 1845 (a month after the "City Items" column debuted in his paper), Greeley informed Griswold that "our friend Foster has got up Shelley's poems in the best style, with appropriate introductions," and asked him to recommend it to the Philadelphia publisher Carey and Hart. "There is no risk," Greeley observed, "and Foster don't stand on terms, unless they ask pay from *him*, and that you know is inadmissable."[47] Griswold again seems to have let Foster down, but the book, apparently the first

46. Ibid., pp. 14–15.
47. Greeley to Griswold, May 23, 1845, in Griswold, *Correspondence*, pp. 184–85.

American edition of Shelley's collected poetry, was brought
out later that year in New York.[48] *Graham's* gave it a
lengthy review (Griswold was no longer editor), lauding Foster for his editorial work and noting his reputedly "lofty and
generous nature," but also criticizing him for an introduction that too enthusiastically embraced Shelley's Fourieristic freethinking, while neglecting to condemn the poet for
having deserted his wife to marry another woman.[49] This
was not to be the last time Foster offended the sensibilities
of proper Victorians.

About a year after the appearance of his edition of Shelley, Foster helped found *Yankee Doodle*, a satirical magazine
published in New York. Cornelius Mathews was the editor,
Foster and Richard Grant White were assistant editors, and
Greeley was an occasional contributor, along with N. P. Willis. This magazine lasted a year, and when it folded in October of 1847 Foster seems to have left New York for
Philadelphia, where, according to one account, he took a job
at the *Philadelphia North American*, a newspaper published
at the same address as *Graham's Magazine*.[50] Simulta-
neously, Foster's poems and stories began to appear again
in *Graham's*, four of each being published between October
1847 and October 1848, a pretty impressive rate. Foster also
teamed up with Thomas Dunn English during these months
on two notable ventures backed by the Philadelphia
publisher G. B. Zieber. One was the quite detailed, richly
illustrated *French Revolution of 1848: Its Causes, Actors,
Events and Influences*, which gave an almost day-by-day account, and which was published in April, only days after the
last of the events it described. This was obviously the work
of men skilled in the journalist's trade. The other venture

48. The full title is *The Poetical Works of Percy Bysshe Shelley.
First Complete American Edition. With Some Remarks on the Poetical
Faculty and Its Influence on Human Destiny: Embracing a Biograph-
ical and Critical Notice*, by G. G. Foster (New York, 1845).

49. *Graham's* 28:2 (February, 1846): 96.

50. Taylor, "Gaslight Foster," p. 302.

was *John-Donkey*, a satirical weekly magazine that, in Frank Luther Mott's terms, "sprang into the arena, kicking right and left and braying fearsomely."[51] Hardly anyone in American politics or letters escaped the *Donkey*—not Foster's political idol Henry Clay, nor his sometime employer and backer Horace Greeley (with "New York in Slices" about to appear in the *Tribune*), nor his friend (but English's enemy) Edgar Allan Poe. Ned Buntline's *Mysteries and Miseries of New York* had just appeared, and in the third number of *John-Donkey*, under the title of the book, we find this brief note, surely written by Foster: "The greatest mystery of the city is, how Ned Buntline ever got a publisher—the misery is that his book has no purchasers."[52] Buntline might have responded that the mystery of *John-Donkey* was how its editors could imagine getting away without a string of libel suits (they reported seven by May)—the misery was that the magazine ceased publication after seven months, in July of 1848.

Still, these must have been heady times for Foster. Just as *John-Donkey* ceased to bray, "New York in Slices" began its three-month run in the *Tribune, to be followed* immediately by eleven "Slices" of Philadelphia, running into February of 1849. Foster's poems and stories were still appearing in *Graham's*, although they would abruptly cease after October 1848, possibly in response to the notoriety Foster was gaining from his *Tribune* columns. In the closing days of 1848, increasingly alert to topics of the day, Foster brought out a small volume of descriptive documents entitled *The Gold Regions of California*, not forgetting to include an introduction arguing that the wealth to be gained by California gold, and the impetus it would give to the westward march of the Anglo-Saxon race, would contribute to the eventual triumph of Fourieristic principles in the United States. And within weeks of the appearance of this little volume, *New York in*

51. Mott, *American Magazines, 1741–1850*, p. 780.
52. *John-Donkey* 1:3 (January 15, 1848): 48.

Slices: By an Experienced Carver would be announced, as we have already noted, in an edition of 20,000 copies.[53]

Curiously, just as Foster was gaining a much more prominent profile in American newspaper, magazine, and book publishing, we encounter a significant gap in our knowledge of his affairs. *New York by Gas-Light*, which appeared in January of 1850, could not have absorbed more than a few weeks of his time in 1849, and the two books that immediately followed, the romance *Celio* and an edited collection of items relating to Jenny Lind's tour of the United States (another of Foster's attempts to cash in on a fashionable topic), do not account for 1850. Perhaps there were editorial adventures or reportorial assignments that can no longer be traced. Or perhaps the brisk sales of *Slices* and *Gas-Light* freed him to pursue other interests that did not leave a paper trail. According to Foster's own (and possibly exaggerated) account, written in 1854, *New York in Slices* sold some thirty to forty thousand copies in its first year, and continued to sell a thousand copies a month thereafter.[54] *New York by Gas-Light* did even better, and went through at least three editions within a month of its initial publication. Newspaper ads for the book referred to "immense orders from the country," and an "unparalleled demand."[55] This was not simple puffery. Frank Luther Mott has classified *Gas-Light* as a "better seller," suggesting total sales upwards of 200,000 copies. On the other hand, both books were cheaply priced, and Foster might not have had favorable terms from William H. Graham or Dewitt & Davenport, his publishers. We can be sure that neither these nor any of his other efforts made him rich or even comfortably well-off. But 1849 and 1850 were surely Foster's most profitable years since his return east from St. Louis.

Did Foster use his fees from Greeley and his royalties from Graham and Dewitt & Davenport as a means of escape

53. *New York Tribune*, January 13, 1849.
54. Foster, *New York Naked*, p. 16.
55. Ibid., *New York Tribune*, January 17, 1850; January 25, 1850; January 28, 1850.

from his writing desk? In an obituary a few years later, the *New York Times* referred to Foster as "a genuine bohemian," and described (with imperfect accuracy) a career that included various undated connections with the theater as an actor, musician, and dramatist. Apparently, too, "he was, at one time, member of an Equestrian Company, and formed one of the band of a traveling menagerie."[56] Some of these activities are more likely to have occurred during lean rather than good times—in the year or two after Foster came to New York, for example—but it is also possible that Foster used newly found leisure after 1849 to indulge a taste for the urban *demi-monde*, in which he seems to have been as much player as spectator. The *Times*, moreover, was only one place where Foster was accused of being "hopelessly loose and uncertain," and incapable of being "constant to any employment." The *Philadelphia Sun*, which found Foster a warm-hearted fellow, regretted that "he had not the will nor the way for continuous application," and Poe's "Autography," referring perhaps to more than Foster's signature, observed "a *fatigability* of temper" and "vacillation of purpose."[57] If any of these characterizations is at all accurate, we might well expect to have a little trouble finding Foster at work during his most prosperous years.

We do, however, find him there occasionally in subsequent years, and increasingly at tasks that do not suggest independence of means. Foster had returned to New York some time in 1850, and is listed in the 1850–51 city directory as a "publisher" at 122½ Fulton Street. However, what Foster was publishing there remains a mystery, and the designation was probably a hope or boast rather than a reality. The next two directories list him as an "editor" at the same address, but now we can at least point to tangible editorial efforts and products. In October of 1851, the *New York Times* observed the appearance of a new magazine called *The Verdict*, edited by G. G. Foster, Esq., and Julie de Marguerittes.

56. *New York Times*, April 17, 1856.
57. *Philadelphia Sun*, April 17, 1856; Poe, "Chapter on Autography," p. 283.

"Its first numbers," wrote the *Times*, "do not speak very well for its ability, popularity or success," a judgment shared widely enough to sink the magazine fairly quickly.[58] In August of 1852 Foster sought backing of $3,000 from Thurlow Weed and, once again, William H. Seward to buy the *Day Book*, a Democratic paper, and convert it to Whiggery in time for the fall election.[59] Backing was not to be found in high political circles, however, for the author of *New York by Gas-Light*. Meanwhile, Foster was contributing frequently, along with his old collaborator, Thomas Dunn English, to *Diogenes hys Lanterne*, a new satirical magazine edited by the actor John Brougham.[60] And around this time, probably early in 1853, Foster returned again to the urban sketch. *Fifteen Minutes Around New York* was intended in part as a kind of guide book to the city for visitors attracted by the New York Crystal Palace Exhibition of 1853.

When the *Lanterne* ceased publication late in 1853, Foster returned once more to Philadelphia, where he apparently helped edit a nativist paper called the *Sachem*. He also wrote a final book of urban sketches, *New York Naked*, which he presented in his introductory remarks as a more mature reflection upon city life—a kind of middle-aged revisit to the scenes of *Slices* and *Gas-Light*—but which turned out to focus more on literary and journalistic personalities than on the streets and institutions of the metropolis. Ominously, it is Foster's darkest book, containing more than one bitter reference to the hardships of life in the trenches of urban journalism. Still more ominously, neither *Fifteen Minutes Around New York* nor *New York Naked* sold particularly well, or attracted much attention.

Foster may have returned to city reporting by this time, as he was no longer enjoying even the illusion of prosperity.

58. *New York Times*, October 2, 1851.
59. Foster to Thurlow Weed, August 27, 1852; Foster to Seward, August 27, 1852, University of Rochester Library.
60. Mott, *American Magazines, 1850–1865*, p. 181.

We may be sure of the latter point, for the next time his name is found on the printed page it is as the subject, not the reporter, of a newsworthy scandal. All the papers carried it, but this item from the *Tribune* of January 9, 1855, will do for the others: "G. G. Foster was committed, yesterday, on a charge of forging Wm. E. Burton's name to a note for over $100. The note was given in exchange for clothing, the balance being given back in cash. Bail was fixed at $2,000."[61] The bogus note (actually in the amount of $140) had been drawn to the order of G. G. Foster, and was passed by Foster to the firm of Peters, Kelley, & Co., whose store was on fashionable Chestnut Street in Philadelphia.[62] Foster had frequently satirized in print both the fashionable dandy and the dishonest manipulator of negotiable instruments (usually the crooked "stockjobber," but also occasionally the forger). A brief item in *John-Donkey* had observed that "Dandy M —— , . . . excels in sculpture—having recently chiseled his tailor—out of a new suit of clothes."[63] And now Foster, who does seem to have been a bit of a dandy himself, was caught forging a note to his own tailor. The signature he chose to forge is itself worthy of comment. William E. Burton was an actor and theater owner in New York, and was known by Foster, who might even have played in or written for Burton's theater. Perhaps he had Burton's signature on a letter or some other document; perhaps he simply signed his name and hoped for the best. And yet there is another, rather more poignant possibility—Poe's "Autography"! Poe, surely, did not intend his curious little essays on literary signatures to be used this way, but as his own M. Dupin could have told him, here, in the very public pages of *Graham's Magazine*, was a ready-made catalogue of opportunities for the would-be forger. Many of these signatures were of men not so prominent as to draw suspicious attention. Foster's

61. *New York Tribune*, January 9, 1855.
62. *Philadelphia Sun*, January 9, 1855.
63. *John-Donkey* 1:3 (January 15, 1848): 48.

own signature was there, above two paragraphs intended to boost the young poet-journalist's literary career. Burton's was on the facing page.[64]

Foster was sent to Moyamensing Prison on the southern edge of the city to await trial. Within a week he was charged again for forging Burton's signature, this time on a note for $350.[65] There may have been other forgeries as well. Having read of the imprisonment, one of Griswold's correspondents (who claims to have detected a "latent rascality" in Foster's expression) observed that Foster had tried to buy out a magazine publisher using "Burton's paper."[66] Burton himself, in a letter emphatically refusing to help Foster in response to Griswold's appeal, claimed that Foster had forged his name no fewer than four times on notes totalling $1,300, and that there were three other forgeries he knew of adding up to another $2,000.[67] None of these other notes materialized, but the two charges were enough to keep Foster in jail, searching for ways to raise the money to settle the complaints against him before he came to trial.

Learning of Griswold's unsolicited efforts on his behalf, Foster wrote to encourage him further. In this letter we encounter a surprise almost as great as the forgery itself: "My wife—my only real, legal wife, and noblest and most devoted of God's creatures—has come to New York, to see what can be done."[68] What could Foster have meant by this phrase, "my only real, legal wife"? The woman to whom he referred was Julie de Marguerittes (or Marguerites), whom

64. Poe, "Chapter on Autography," pp. 282–83.
65. *New York Times*, January 16, 1855.
66. Charles G. Leland to Griswold, January 26, 1855, Boston Public Library.
67. William E. Burton to Griswold, January 12, 1855, in Griswold, *Correspondence*, p. 292. The printed version of this letter is incorrectly dated 1854. The date and month could be incorrect as well.
68. Foster to Griswold, February 20, 1855, in Griswold, *Correspondence*, p. 294. Again, this letter is incorrectly dated 1854 in the printed version.

Foster had just married, apparently in the prison. (The *Philadelphia Sun*, when Foster died, sympathetically offered "to condole with her, who, with the true devotedness of woman, 'ran out into a storm' and linked her fate with his, when the sky was darkest and clouds lowered portentously over the prospects of poor Foster.")[69] Madame de Marguerittes seems the perfect wife for Foster. The daughter of a successful Italian Jewish doctor who lived and practiced in London, she had moved to America with her first husband, the Baron de Marguerittes, and attempted a career in opera singing in Philadelphia and other cities. Not succeeding in the opera, she moved to New York and began to write for newspapers, serializing in the *Sunday Times* and then bringing out in book form an obviously timely *Ins and Outs of Paris*. She collaborated with Foster at least once in magazine publishing, as we have seen, and may have done so again after both had moved to Philadelphia. By this time Madame de Marguerittes was a widow, and supported herself in Philadelphia by writing for the *Morning Times*.[70] A likely couple, to be sure, but did not Foster already have a wife? Foster's curious phrase suggests that the first Mrs. Foster was still alive, and that no divorce had occurred. To this I would add that a search of the well-indexed court records of New York and Philadelphia pertaining to all the years Foster lived in these cities reveals no divorce to which George G. Foster was a party. It is indeed more than possible that Foster added bigamy to his crimes in 1855.

The new Mrs. Foster's efforts to see Griswold were not immediately successful, prompting two anguished letters from Moyamensing in March. The first of these reveals that Foster was pursuing other avenues with more success. The larger note had been settled, according to Foster, by assignment of the copyright to the *Ins and Outs of Paris*. The smaller one was covered with the copyright to *Philadelphia by Gas-Light*,

69. *Philadelphia Sun*, April 17, 1856.
70. *New York Times*, June 24, 1866. This is Madame de Marguerittes's obituary.

a book that Foster must have promised but was never published. Foster now claimed to need only $200 bail to get out of prison.[71] The editor of Griswold's published correspondence notes that Griswold did raise the money for Foster, but it is not clear what role, if any, he played in Foster's release. Court records show that Foster was granted a continuance on May 8, and that on September 3, when no one appeared to prosecute the case, he was ordered discharged. Foster was released from Moyamensing Prison on September 5, 1855.[72]

On leaving prison Foster obtained a job as a reporter on the *Morning Times*, the paper for which his wife already worked. He and his wife moved into a house on Ninth Street below Catherine, in a modest neighborhood not far from the prison.[73] He did not live there long. On the morning of April 16, 1856, Foster died of what the newspapers labelled "congestion" or "fever" of the brain. The *Philadelphia Sun* added that Foster's illness had begun with a cold he had caught while covering a fire, which tells us that the old "City Items" man was still on the beat.[74] Perhaps appropriately, the *New York Tribune* printed the death notice itself as a "City Item," just below an announcement of the commencement of spring lectures at the New York Medical College, and just above a report describing how a young woman threw vitriol on her neighbor's drying laundry.[75] Foster would have appreciated that, although he probably would have bristled that the *Tribune* printed no obituary for its former associate.

71. Foster to Griswold, March 12, 1855, Boston Public Library; Foster to Griswold, March 14, 1855, in Griswold, *Correspondence*, p. 298.
72. Appearance Docket, Court of Quarter Sessions, vol. 44, p. 365, no. 474; Prisoners for Trial, from March 16, 1854, to January 16, 1855, pp. 601, 609.
73. *Philadelphia Daily Morning Times*, April 19, 1856.
74. *Philadelphia Sun*, April 17, 1856.
75. *New York Tribune*, April 17, 1856.

Foster was only about forty-two when he died, and there is no evidence that he even set foot in New York or Philadelphia before his late twenties. Yet in the nearly fourteen years he lived in the nation's two largest cities he became a highly expert participant in and observer of most aspects of big-city life. It was Foster's job, as well as his avocation and temperament, to observe, record, and interpret the emerging metropolis. The *Tribune*, and other papers that did print more extensive obituaries, remembered Foster primarily in this role, and it was agreed that he possessed an unmatched talent for portraying the realities of the big city, including those that some commentators would have preferred to remain unrecorded. Foster himself, in the introduction to his last book, pointed to his urban sketches, not his poetry or literary and political satire, as his most important contribution.[76] To be sure, Foster was an outsider (like so many others), raised in and shaped by smaller and more typical communities, and he retained to some extent the outsider's perspective. This, I will argue shortly, was crucial to his exposures of and solutions for various forms of urban wickedness. But there can be no doubt that Foster relished the city, from the Bowery to the Opera House, and that once having experienced it he could not have lived anywhere else, certainly not in one of the Fourieristic communities he sometimes dreamed of. More importantly, he *learned* the city, and conveyed his learning, with the skill and wit of the journalist and the satirist. If he took a little too much delight in violating Victorian sensibilities, what matters most is that Foster showed his readers truly enough the city he truly knew.

"The book before us," wrote the *Tribune*'s reviewer of *New York by Gas-Light*, "is designed to exhibit the Night-side of our City, and is replete with descriptions of Night resorts,

76. Foster, *New York Naked*, pp. 11–17.

night gatherings, night orgies, &c. with here and there a strong flavor of night soil."[77] We have the same book before us now (along with selections from two of Foster's other New York books, collected in a section I have called "New York by Daylight"). What shall we make of these urban sketches, written so long ago? Our relation to them is necessarily different from that of Foster's original readers, if only because the source of our ignorance about the emerging metropolis is different from theirs. For them—particularly those who remained outside the big city—it was physical distance, the newness of the metropolis, and the increasing divergence of metropolitan from village norms and modes of living. For us it is historical time, and the difficulty of stripping from our minds further developments of metropolitan scale and structure. We are, perhaps, equally in need of expert guidance of the sort Foster provides; hence, we have the chance to recapture the feeling of Foster's original readers as they turned the pages of his city books. But to do so more effectively we must remind ourselves of their predominantly rural and small-town world—the experiences and the values that differentiate their ignorance from ours.

Understanding this difference illuminates the very structure of Foster's most successful production, and the meaning of his night-time rambles through the city's gas-lit streets. Foster's essential purpose was to explain the unique character of the big city in terms that his contemporaries would find engaging and convincing. This was accomplished in *New York by Gas-Light* through a variety of recognizable details, and also by means of a basic structure—the tour of the city at night. In our own age of night shifts, all-night radio and television, and various other around-the-clock services, the meaning of the night differs from that of an age when, except during the occasional crises of birth, death, sickness, and fire, *all* of rural and small-town America used the hours of darkness only for sleep. How alien, and how suspicious,

77. *New York Tribune*, January 17, 1850.

must have been the idea of routine late-night activity. How easy it was for Foster, as the *Tribune* reviewer understood, to heighten the big city's sins by surrounding them with darkness, and revealing them in the artificial light (sometimes dim, sometimes harsh) of the gas lamp. This, clearly, was Foster's strategy, although he does not sustain the structure or the color of his narrative throughout. His book begins, logically, in the evening, and on the recognizable and presumably safe sidewalks of Broadway. But within a page, with the night barely begun, we encounter the first of the many prostitutes that populate Foster's nocturnal city. Oyster cellars, which might seem innocent enough by day, quickly establish the dominant color of the urban night, "their bright lamps casting broad gleams of red light across the street," their barkeepers' faces emitting a satanic, "fiery glow." The pace quickens into a "turbid tide of life" despite the warning of church bells that it is now ten o'clock, time for decent people to be asleep. Somewhat later, well after the concert halls and theaters have emptied their patrons onto the street, the pace does slacken, and Broadway nearly empties of people. Nearly, but not quite. Some remain for a "midnight revel" in an underground coffee house or brothel, a few prostitutes continue to solicit on the streets. Drunkards clinging to lamp-posts or roaming in gangs, billstickers, drivers of cabs and night-carts (the *Tribune* reviewer did warn of the "flavor of night soil"), policemen, and sub-editors of the morning papers creeping "wearily homeward" populate the night until a new day begins.

The first chapter establishes the scheme for much of what follows. On subsequent nights the reader is taken to various quarters of the city to visit gambling dens, whorehouses, seedy saloons, underground dance halls, and "model artist" exhibitions, where naked women form *tableaux vivants* under the thin pretext of art. A few somewhat less unseemly places are also visited, such as the theaters, but even these are discussed in part as hunting grounds of the ubiquitous prostitutes. Foster is not entirely consistent in his form, and there are a few "streaks of sunshine" that brighten the book. A chapter on the ice-creameries is one (although Foster points out at least one assignation and an assortment of other hypocrisies in a fashionable Broadway ice-cream parlor). A delightful chapter on the b'hoys and g'hals of the Bowery is surely another. So too, metaphorically at least, is an affectionate visit to Butter Cake Dick's, night-time eatery of the city newsboys. In this chapter the doings of the city at night are not evil, but the implied contrast between city and country is every bit as clear as it is elsewhere in the book.

Thus, the night-time ramble serves as more than a mode for presenting the various sins of the big city. On a simpler level, it establishes a fundamental contrast between the country, where all is still in the small hours of the night, and the city, which never sleeps. This powerful distinction is underscored by another that is more subtle, and that also grows at least in part out of the depiction of the city by gaslight. The emerging metropolis was an increasingly complex array of structures, spaces, institutions, and social types, many of which, Foster warns, presented to the unknowing viewer a deceptive surface appearance, as poor Zerubbabel Green, the archetypical rustic victim whose tale is told in chapter 13, discovers only the morning after his systematic fleecing.[78] This theme of deceptive appearances and hidden realities is central to *New York by Gas-Light*, where darkness is both a method and a metaphor of the evil city, but it is reiterated throughout Foster's other city books.[79] Much of

78. Much of the analysis contained in this and the following paragraphs, and even some of the phrasing, appeared earlier in my article, "Explaining the New Metropolis: Perception, Depiction, and Analysis in Mid-Nineteenth-Century New York City," *Journal of Urban History* 11 (1984): 9–38. I would like to thank the editors of this journal for their permission to reprint small portions of that article here.

79. Reynolds, *Beneath the American Renaissance*, alludes briefly (p. 86) to the unmasking of hidden corruption as a theme common to city writers of this era, and quotes a passage from Foster's *New York Naked* to illustrate the point.

Five Points oyster cellar.

the immorality of the city occurs underground, in oyster cellars and in basement-level gambling dens and dance halls, reached only through well-guarded and labyrinthine passageways. Above-ground debauchery occurs upstairs, behind deceptive facades, in brothels and gambling houses that look exactly like the respectable homes that surround them. In *Celio*, for example, a gang of thieves assembles to divide its loot in "a small decent-looking house . . . which to a stranger presented no appearance to indicate its real character."[80] Even innocent-looking ice cream parlors disguise illicit meetings of upper-class lovers, who consummate their affairs in buildings that appear to house dressmakers' shops and dentists' offices. "How conveniently civilization arranges every thing!" Foster concludes. The convenience, of course, is for those who know how to "decode" the city's surface appearances. Those who do not—who cannot see beneath these surfaces either by gas-light or by daylight—become the victims of deceit.

Evil lurks behind personal facades as well as physical ones, as the unfortunate Zerubbabel learns after placing too much trust in the "real gentleman" who politely leads him to ruin. But Foster finds deception beyond the city's con men in a much wider range of social types, and links it to another of his fundamental complaints about the city, the attenuation of community in the urban population. Foster observes, in ways that were already becoming typical, that the city was becoming a collection of diverging groups—ordinary people who were growing rich, rich people who were growing richer, and poor people in large numbers and from a variety of ethnic and racial backgrounds who had little prospect of reaching even a decent standard of living. There is more here than increasing socioeconomic distance of the sort that was not ordinarily found in rural and small-town communities. And there is more to Foster's complaint than

80. George G. Foster, *Celio: or New York Above-Ground and Under-Ground* (New York, 1850), p. 17.

the increasing improbability of communal relations between the richest and the poorest residents of the city. Degrading poverty and the race for riches were destroying community even within the city's socioeconomic strata. Consider first Foster's indictment of the urban rich. Exempting only a small, "true, well-bred, and unpretending aristocracy" of old Knickerbocker families, Foster relentlessly attacks the "shopkeeping aristocracy of the new world," unequaled "in all that is pompous without dignity, gaudy without magnificence, lavish without taste, and aristocratic without good manners."[81] The "Snobbish Ten Thousand" consists mainly of socially ambitious parvenus who build mansions on fashionable streets "above Bleecker," attend the opera in order to be seen there, promenade conspicuously on the fashionable side of Broadway, and, in general, "do every thing exactly as the French waiting-maid and upholsterer prescribe."[82] Their social climbing is not only ridiculous but is also destructive of any genuine community among the wealthy, partly because of the ferocity of their competition for status, and partly because the whole enterprise is fundamentally deceptive. Foster's books are populated with respected businessmen who steal and swindle, with loving brides who marry for money and meet secret lovers, with upright citizens who go whoring, drinking, and gambling "by gas-light," and by former soap boilers and shoemakers who conceal their humble origins as carefully as they cheat their customers and cultivate their manners. The parvenu "shop-keeping aristocracy," in short, lives in an artificial world, a society that is not a community because the individuals within it never present their true selves to one another.

Nor do the poor, in Foster's view, reconstruct genuine, village-like communities within their squalid neighborhoods. Foster occasionally expresses considerable sympathy

81. Foster, *New York Naked*, p. 75; Foster, *Fifteen Minutes Around New York* (New York, [1853]), p. 19.
82. Foster, *New York Naked*, p. 71.

At the opera.

toward the urban poor (in, for example, "The Needle-women," included in the "New York by Daylight" section of this book). But in the main he distances himself from the predominantly Irish and black urban underclass, and places many of the most vicious "underground" institutions in their neighborhoods, where it would seem that virtually every house is a poor man's bar or brothel. Nor is there a Fleur-de-Marie among Foster's prostitutes. The two "Cyprians" we meet in chapter 4 of *New York by Gas-Light* are granted several pages of self-explanation, which turn on conventional motifs of sexual ruin (in the country, by both the innocent young lover and the cynical local pastor!) and overwhelming urban poverty. But explanation is not expiation. Foster's Cyprians have become hardened by their profession and express no remorse: "I know I am a demon—a she-devil—as are all women who have lost their virtue; and I mean to make the most of it." This is from the once-innocent country girl, who in other accounts might have retained enough sweetness and sad regret to remind us that she is a victim rather than a villain.

By explaining the realities that lie beneath the deceptive appearances of the city and its people, Foster offers the reader the solution of expertise. *Gas-Light* is a virtue- and life-protecting tour offered by a street-wise expert in city ways. Or, more cynically, it is a tour for those who would spend their virtue without overspending their resources of life, limb, or wallet. Foster would develop the theme of expertise in a different way in Captain Earnest, the hero of his novel *Celio*, who executes an elaborate (and initially deceptive) plan of urban redemption by mastering all the mysteries of the metropolis, and by skillfully guiding all of the novel's characters through and around various urban pitfalls to a happy resolution. Captain Earnest in *Celio* and Foster himself in *New York by Gas-Light* might in this important sense be placed alongside Poe's C. Auguste Dupin as predecessors of more recent fictional detective heroes of the city—where Dupin excels in reason, Foster and Earnest excel in the experience that would later lead a Sam Spade or a Mike Hammer to the right informant in the back room of the right waterfront bar. But street wisdom is a solution of an individual sort—a crime solved rather than criminality stamped out—and Foster would offer no plan for eradicating the wickedness of the metropolis. Captain Earnest does have a more or less collective solution, which, not surprisingly, is to remove all of the characters of the novel, good and evil alike, to a Fourieristic community on the banks of the Connecticut River. This idea pops up in strange ways in a variety of Foster's works, but it is difficult to take it seriously, except as a suggestion that Foster, an outsider by birth and breeding, could not help referring metropolitan mores and social patterns to those of an idealized rural community.

Foster himself stayed put in the city, where he did manage to find more than one "streak of sunshine" to offset the harsh glare of gas-light. The city, for one thing, provided him with the characters, incidents, and settings for a form of writing that obviously gave him a great deal of pleasure—sketches such as "A General Dash at the Ferries," "The Eating-Houses," "A Plunge in the Swimming-Bath," and "A Quarter of an Hour Under an Awning" (all collected in the final section of this book). These are not exposures of urban wickedness, but comic essays about the petty trials of day-to-day life in the big city. City dwellers are not evil or beset by evil in these essays, but are caught in those comic predicaments that would reappear in somewhat different form in the twentieth-century sketches of James Thurber, Robert Benchley, and Russell Baker: they are pushed around by waiters and fellow commuters, outwitted by wise-guys, and exasperated by rush-hour rainstorms and the futility of devising a strategy for getting a seat on the uptown omnibus. Foster thrived on this material, no less than on the model artists, the prostitutes, and the underground dance halls, and no doubt realized that he could find both types only in the metropolis.

A more focused ray of sunshine illuminated the lives of Mose and Lize, the Bowery b'hoy and g'hal, characters that Foster (along with E. Z. C. Judson and a number of other writers) plucked from the New York stage after their highly successful first appearance in Benjamin Baker's comic melodrama, *A Glance at New York in 1848.* In the play and its sequels, these characters represented the young, single, native-born white workers of the city; or, rather, a particular sub-community of such workers who were evolving distinctively high-spirited styles of life and dress.[83] Like most good comic characterizations, Mose and Lize were at once funny and serious, and we see in Foster's treatment of them a combination of comedy and social criticism that reveals the expert sketcher's unsettled relation to the metropolis. The b'hoy and g'hal were, first of all, very much of the city. Working as butchers' boys in the city markets or as pressmen on the big-city dailies, fighting fires and other b'hoys as members of volunteer fire companies, joining in the raucous fun of a Bowery theater audience, or simply promenading or swaggering through the streets of the East Side, Mose and Lize (but particularly Mose, the male worker) were defining a life and a physical environment that were as new as the metropolis itself. Their social identities, moreover, were formed in conscious contrast to both the bourgeois and underclass spheres of the city, rejecting the first as snobbish and effete, rejecting the second as ethnically and racially alien. To Foster, this localized "negative reference" was an important aspect of the emergence of the Bowery b'hoy and g'hal. One could not understand them except in relation to metropolitan society as a whole and in particular to the evils associated with the big city's highest and lowest classes.

And yet if Mose and Lize are distinctly new and metropolitan types, what Foster finds to celebrate in them are tradi-

83. See Sean Wilentz's discussion of the "Republic of the Bowery," in *Chants Democratic: New York City and the Rise of the American Working Class, 1788–1850* (New York, 1983), pp. 257–71.

Chatham Square.

tional virtues suggestive of the village or small town—
independence, spirit, honesty and directness of speech,
simplicity in feelings and taste, loyalty and generosity to
friends and neighbors. The b'hoy and the g'hal recreate the
traditional community within the non-traditional spaces of
the Bowery. And in doing so they carry into this alien and
unpromising world of tenements, factories, gashouses, and
endless city streets a reassuringly American presence, so
that Foster can equate the "b'hoy of the Bowery" and the
"rowdy of Philadelphia" with "the Hoosier of the Mississippi, the trapper of the Rocky Mountains, and the gold-
hunter of California." Lize, for her part, is "absolutely
identical" to the "belle of a Wisconsin ball-room," and the
two "might change places without any body being the
wiser." In this bit of nonsense Foster finds his most satisfying antidote to both the hypocrisies of the "upper ten thousand" and the dissipations of the immigrant poor.

But do Mose, Lize, and other true Americans a little
higher on the social scale, "the substantial tradesmen, mechanics and artizans of the city," who "eat well, sleep well,
digest well and have easy consciences and no envy," provide
a convincing blueprint for a reintegrated metropolis of the
future? Foster, to the end, was more genuinely an "experienced carver" than he was a reformer, and we must be careful not to turn his lively sketches into a treatise on urban
reform. He surely did not expect Mose and Lize, or his own
celebration of their values and spirit, to influence the behav-
ior of the rich or the alien poor. Occasionally, though, Foster
did long explicitly for a more genuine metropolitan community in which the rich, the poor, and the "broad middle
stripe" would recognize how their lives were linked, as residents of the same city, through their common occupation of
urban space. In his introduction to *New York in Slices*, for
example, Foster writes of the "boundless horizon of sympathies and affections" that ought to be found in the "great
city." "What a world of thought and wisdom and imagination and benevolence and friendship and love ought we not

to expect from this mighty concentration of so many immortalities, so many heavenly faculties!''[84] Intended mainly to give greater force to the exposures that immediately follow, statements such as these are far from being a program or a prognosis, but they do reveal—along with Foster's occasional fits of Fourierism—the shape of his more or less sincerely felt longing for communal sympathies in the big city.

The same longing may be sensed by collating Foster's various rambles through New York into an overall image or mental map of the city. As he moves through the city, locating his observations in specific places, Foster develops an easily understood and surprisingly small-scale map of the city's social and moral life. With very little variation, Broadway/Wall Street, Chatham Street/the Bowery, and Five Points are the loci of upper-class, native-born working-class, and immigrant lower-class life in New York, and together constitute the essential structure of the city as a whole. In nearly all of his sketches, Broadway represents the opulence and grandeur and Wall Street the power of the city's "upper ten thousand," while Five Points represents the squalor and misery of its very poor. Even more insistently, Chatham Street and the Bowery are the beat of the native-born b'hoy and g'hal. These districts were widely known. However, it seems significant that Foster does not describe new ones that had come into being as the city grew, to convey more forcefully the growth and increasing complexity of the metropolis. On the contrary, Foster is careful to stress the proximity of the symbolic zones to one another—that the intersection that gave Five Points its name is only three blocks from Broadway—even though by doing so he ignores the massive spread of the wealthy to the north and the poor to the east of the point where they become near neighbors. Perhaps he did not do so deliberately, but by clinging in this way to the older and more proximate zones of a smaller city Foster both heightens the tragedy of the attenuated urban

84. Foster, *New York in Slices*, p. 3.

Liquor grocery.

community and resists the conclusion that the attenuation is permanent. Foster's New York is not yet incomprehensible or unmanageably large, and has not lost touch with its past. In this there is at least the hope that a more tightly bound community can be restored.

Foster's city books add up to a curious mixture of indictment and celebration, and running through even the latter is a longing for the restoration in the city of simpler and more genuine country ways. Later writers working in and extending the genre would differ from Foster in this respect. Authors such as Matthew Hale Smith, James Dabney Mc-Cabe, and Junius Henri Browne, writing after the Civil War, accepted the diversity of the metropolis without mourning the loss of an integrated community. "If New York is a city of contrasts," explains Browne, "it is because it is a little world in itself, and must necessarily be made up of all the elements of good and evil."[85] Comfortable with the city as "a little world" of irreducible extremes of wealth and poverty, virtue and vice, these authors argue that New York "is steadily though slowly getting better,"[86] and unreservedly admire those new and quite modern institutions that have introduced systems for ordering, rather than reducing, the complex affairs of the metropolis. At the American Telegraph Company, observes Smith, "everything is systematized, and order and quiet rule." "Order, system, and despatch reign" at the Adams Express Company. Newspaper offices, publishing houses, department stores, and the police department are all admired in the same way—as special-

85. Junius Henri Browne, *The Great Metropolis: A Mirror of New York* (Hartford, 1869), p. 697. For analogous works by the other two authors, see Matthew Hale Smith, *Sunshine and Shadow in New York* (Hartford, 1868); McCabe, *Lights and Shadows of New York Life*. The latter work was originally published under the pseudonym Edward Winslow Martin as *The Secrets of the Great City: A Work Descriptive of the Virtues and the Vices, the Mysteries, Miseries and Crimes of New York City* (Philadelphia, 1868).

86. Browne, *The Great Metropolis*, p. 697.

ized institutions that coordinate the flow of messages, goods, and authority throughout the disparate metropolis.[87] During the 1880s and 1890s *Harper's Monthly* would run a series of articles on the banks, exchanges, and other coordinating institutions of the city, written in the same spirit. To be sure, Boss Tweed had shown that the systems of the metropolis could malfunction,[88] and Jacob Riis, Stephen Crane, George Bellows, and other realists in journalism, fiction, and painting would return to the Lower East Side to depict the continuing miseries of the city's squalid neighborhoods. Prostitution and the other specific evils of the wicked city had by no means disappeared. But what *had* disappeared, at least among native-born Americans who were no longer aliens in the metropolis, were the concerns that inform Foster's texts. Or, at the very least, these concerns were greatly modified, or displaced into other forms and terms, so that they are no longer recognizable, just as Mose the Bowery b'hoy is no longer recognizable as the archetype of the young urban working man. "Mose," wrote Browne, was "a provincial product, the growth of a period."[89] And so was George Foster. His was a voice that echoes, sometimes in rather strange tones, from the first metropolitan generation, a generation positioned in a unique way between the rural past and the urban future. We learn much, therefore, of the *initial* force and meaning of metropolitan development by listening to that curiously articulate voice.

87. Smith, *Sunshine and Shadow,* pp. 42–51, 101–8, 257–63, 412–20, 423, 469–71, 511–25, 605–30, 635, 658, 666. The quotations are on pp. 417, 259.

88. Seymour J. Mandelbaum, *Boss Tweed's New York* (New York, 1965), is written from this point of view.

89. Browne, *The Great Metropolis,* p. 137.

A Note on the Texts

Foster's urban sketches were cheaply printed to reach a mass market. Not surprisingly, in each book there are several uncorrected typographical errors and broken letters, and surviving copies have been damaged slightly over the years. To reconstitute each text it was necessary to work from more than one copy (four in the case of *New York by Gas-Light*), but in each case the copies used were printed, or appear to have been printed, in the initial year of publication, and it is clear that there were no authorial or editorial changes between imprints. I have made only a few editorial corrections and have added footnotes only where it seemed necessary to clarify a reference or phrase.

I have incorporated several of the illustrations from Foster's *New York in Slices* into my introductory essay and into the final section of this book. I have not placed any within the pages of *New York by Gas-Light*, in order to preserve as much as possible its original character. Except for its paper cover (reproduced here as a frontispiece), *New York by Gas-Light* was not illustrated.

—Editor

New York by Gas-Light

With Here and There a Streak of Sunshine

by George G. Foster

(The unabridged text)

Contents

No. I

Broadway at Evening

*The Sidewalkers—Hooking a Victim—Balcony
Music and Drummond Lights—Scene at the
Cosmorama—The Oyster Cellars—Midnight
Orgies—Broadway Asleep*

NEW YORK BY GAS-LIGHT! What a task have we under-taken! To penetrate beneath the thick veil of night and lay bare the fearful mysteries of darkness in the metropolis—the festivities of prostitution, the orgies of pauperism, the haunts of theft and murder, the scenes of drunkenness and beastly debauch, and all the sad realities that go to make up the lower stratum—the under-ground story—of life in New York! What may have been our motive for invading these dismal realms and thus wrenching from them their terrible secrets? Go on with us, and see. The duty of the present age is to discover the real facts of the actual condition of the wicked and wretched classes—so that Philanthropy and Justice may plant their blows aright. In our own humble way we profess to seek for and depict the truth. Let it speak for itself.

But let us begin moderately and go on gradually, instead of diving at once into the depths of our subject. Let us start fair with the young night and take our first walk in Broadway. Fashionable, aristocratic Broadway! Certainly we shall find nothing *here* to shock our senses and make our very nerves thrill with horror. Broadway, with its gay throng and flashing lights beaming from a thousand palace-like shop-fronts, where fortunes are spread out to tempt the eye of the unwary or the extravagant, surely will not afford us material for much of the horrible, nor draw largely upon our pity or our sympathies. On the contrary, we shall rather be in danger of envying the fortunate position of those we see and hear upon the great fashionable promenade. Well, well—let us look and listen.

Here are two ladies approaching us, magnificently attired, with their large arms and voluptuous bosoms half naked, and their bright eyes looking invitation at every passer by. Their complexions are pure white and red, and their dresses are of the most expensive material, and an ultra fashionable make. Diamonds and bracelets flash from their bosoms and bare arms, and heavily-wrought India shawls, of that gorgeous scarlet whose beamy hue intoxicates the eye, hang carelessly from their superb shoulders, almost trailing on the walk. But for their large feet and vulgar hands, they would be taken for queens or princesses, if such things were ever seen among us. They walk with a free and sweeping gait, and shuffle their feet upon the flag-stones with a noise that sets your teeth sharply on edge. As they pass, they look hard at you, and exclaim familiarly,

"How do you do, my dear? Come, won't you go home with me?"

We of course take no notice of this address, and the fine ladies pass on, stopping for a moment to exchange oaths and the most disgusting obscenity, in a loud and mocking voice, with those flashily-rigged young men who stand at the entrance of an oyster-cellar. They are on the look-out for victims, and will rendezvous an hour later at one of the aristocratic gambling-houses just down the side-street from where they stand. The ladies pass on; and as they reach the next corner a young man stops and stares wistfully at them—hesitates, goes on, returns upon his steps and walks slowly down the side-street. The two "fishers of men," seeing that there is some game afoot, have now separated, and the youngest and handsomest keeps on, while her companion, casting a leering glance at the young man, and giving a leering scrape of the feet, tosses her head, and follows down the side-street—but on *the other side*. The victim knows not exactly what to make of it; wonders if he was not mistaken; and at length makes up his mind that it is some timid creature making her first essay in vice. His vanity, and even some better and more chivalric feeling is appealed to. He will make her acquaintance, at least—there can be no harm in that—and if she is yet pure and virtuous, he will save her. Full of these fine delusions he crosses the street—that street is to him the Rubicon—and accosts the painted demon who has lured him on. From that moment his doom is sealed. Need we follow him to the filthy street, the squalid chamber where Prostitution performs her horrid rites and ends by robbing her devotees?—Where drunkenness is brought in to aid the harlot in her infamous work—and where, if all else fail, the sleeping potion mingled in the foaming goblet does its inevitable work, and delivers the victim helpless into the hands of the despoiler. No—at least not now.

Here we are at the American Museum, crowned with its Drummond Light, sending a livid, ghastly glare for a mile up the street, and pushing the shadows of the omnibuses well-nigh to Niblo's. From the balcony of the third-story windows a cascade of horrent harmony, issuing from an E flat bugle and three mismatched trombones, is tumbling down upon the up-turned faces of the boys and negro-women on the opposite walk—while that untiring chromatic wheel goes ever round and round, twining and untwining its blue, red and yellow wreaths of light in unvarying variety. Although it cannot strictly be said of it that it is without change, yet the shadow of its turning is painfully perceptible. Let us go up stairs and listen to the negro and Yankee abominations on the little stage in the garret, see the big anaconda, and watch the innocent wonder of those who come here principally and chiefly to be amused. It will be a fine study.

But there are plenty of others who come for entirely different purposes. Not only here, but at the ice-cream saloons and Christy's Minstrels, and the Art-Unions and picture-galleries, are assignations made for almost every hour of the day and night, between cautious libertines and women whose licentiousness has not yet been discovered and who pass for virtuous and respectable wives, mothers and daughters. Let us make use of our Asmodean privilege[1] and listen to this beautiful creature closely veiled, and her gallant companion, who seem to be admiring the mysterious beauties of "Naples by Moonlight," as seen through a round piece of glass with a penny engraving and a lamp behind it.

"Dearest Louise," he whispers passionately, "I can live in this manner no longer. Do we not love each other better than everything else in the world? And what care we for the place that holds us, only if we are together?"

"Oh, Edward, don't talk so—you quite frighten me; and then somebody will be sure to overhear us. But let it be just as you will: my fate is in your hands. Have I not given you everything?" and she leans her veiled head lovingly against his stooped shoulder. He presses her lightly, yet oh, how tenderly, to his breast, beneath the convenient shadow of the half-darkened room, and they hurry down stairs and into a carriage. A whisper to the driver, who replies with a wink and a chuckling "I know, sir!" and they whirl through the throng to a fashionable assignation-house, to accomplish a husband's dishonor and a wife's infamy.

1. Asmodeus is a demon who, among other traits, possesses the ability to lift off the roofs of houses to discover the secret evils of those within. Not surprisingly, he was frequently invoked during this era by city writers.

The oyster-cellars, with their bright lamps casting broad gleams of red light across the street, are now in full tide, and every instant sees them swallow up at one entrance a party of rowdy and half-drunken young men, on their way to the theater, the gambling-house, the bowling-saloon, or the brothel—or most likely to all in turn—while another is vomited up the other stairway, having already swilled their fill of oysters and bad brandy, and garnished their reeking mouths each with an atrocious cigar, which the bar-keeper recommended as "full-flavored." If we step down one of these wide entrances we shall see a long counter gorgeously decked with crystal decanters and glasses, richly carved and gilt, and the wall ornamented with a voluptuous picture of a naked Venus—perhaps the more seductive from being exquisitely painted. Before the long marble bar are arranged some dozen or score of individuals, waiting their turns for liquor—while on the other side a man with his shirt-sleeves rolled up and his face in a fiery glow, seems to be pulling long ribbons of julep out of a tin cup. At the other end of the room is a row of little stalls, each fitted up with its gas-burner, its red curtain, its little table and voluptuous picture, and all occupied with busy eaters. In the rear of these boxes is a range of larger apartments called "private rooms," where men and women enter promiscuously, eat, drink and make merry, and disturb the whole neighborhood with their obscene and disgusting revels, prolonged far beyond midnight. The women of course are all of one kind—but among the men, you would find, if you looked curiously, reverend judges and juvenile delinquents, pious and devout hypocrites, and undisguised libertines and debauchees. Gamblers and fancy men, high-flyers and spoonies, genteel pick-pockets and burglars, even, sometimes mingle in the detestable orgies of these detestable caverns; and the shivering policeman who crawls sleepily by at the dead of night, and mechanically raps his bludgeon upon the pavement as he hears the boisterous mirth below, may be reminding a grave functionary of the city that it is time to go home to his wife and children after the discharge of his "arduous public duties."

St. Paul's tolls ten o'clock, but the crowd begins to show no signs of decrease, but pours along its turbid tide of life with a sullen roar and rushing, like the sound of the surf trampling upon the rocky beach. Before the theatres, the Tabernacle, and the concert-rooms the omnibuses are drawn up in solid phalanx, and at *the* place where the popular entertainment of the night is given, a row of carriages extends for a quarter of a mile either way. It is the night of Strakosch's farewell concert at the Tabernacle and the fashionable world, and all especially who would be thought to belong to it, are out in full force. Dainty perfumes and delicate-toned bravos float out through the dark door-way and under the gloomy, prison-like entrance. Suddenly the doors are thrown open and the audience rush out tumultuously—the ladies seeming, for such delicate creatures, to stand the squeeze and scramble remarkably well. "Carriage, sir—take you home for a dollar!" "Broadway and Bleecker street—right up!" "South Ferry—all aboard!" and so amid a clatter and confusion that would have done honor to the farewell appearance of the Babel-workers, the immense and gloomy recess discharges its thousands, who at length have all departed, and everything is left to night and silence. In another hour the Broadway, the Olympic and Burton's will be over—the omnibuses will go over the same exciting ground again, and Broadway will prepare

> to wrap the drapery of his couch
> About him, and lie down to pleasant dreams.

It is growing late, and the crowd has somewhat thinned— although there are still many hundreds in the street—some hurrying home to their wives, after an evening out, prolonged beyond the allotted conjugal hour; some creeping reluctantly to their cold, narrow, grave-like bedrooms in private boarding-houses where they receive "the comforts of a home" for five dollars a week, with breakfast and tea. Others, held all day indoors by their employments, are just escaping to the club, the gambling-house, the brothel or the midnight revel in some underground coffee-house, such as we have described. Here and there a flashily-dressed woman shuffles—or sometimes reels—by, while groups may occasionally be seen on the corners, waiting for a last and desperate chance of game. Most of the sisterhood, however, have been more fortunate, and each has succeeded in ensnaring her victim and dragging him to her den. One by one the late shops close their shutters, and at length the oyster-cellars extinguish their gigantic painted lamps, and shut their inside windows. With the exception of the dim and distant public lamps the street is now dark. Once in a while a belated omnibus rattles furiously homeward, and the side walk sends along a hollow echo beneath the feet of the lonely passenger. Here and there a lamp-post is embellished with a human swine who leans, a statue of drunkenness, against it for support, and consigns his undigested supper to his fellow pigs who rise early o'mornings. A company of happy rowdies, reeling and hiccuping as they go, pass arm in arm and shouting at the top of their voices,

> Oh carry me—hic—to—hic—Virginny,
> T—ic ole Virginny's ic—shore!

Close at their heels follows the bill-sticker with his hieroglyphic paper bed-blankets over one arm and his paste-bucket hanging upon the other. With nice discrimination he selects the fresh bills put up by outsiders and carefully and neatly plasters them over with his own—while those put up by the regular members of the bill-posting profession receive the honors of a pasty passover. Anon the night-carts thump heavily over the pavements, perfuming the cool "cisterns of the midnight air" with a most unsmellable infusion of sulphureted hydrogen—the sub-editors of the morning papers creep wearily homeward—the thief comes out to take the air and hold up his head like an honest man—the policeman settles himself for his grand central nap—the solitary cab drives swiftly away from Sanderson's club—and Broadway shuts its eyes and prepares to go to sleep, just as the stirring noises of the new day begin to murmur in the dawn's gray distance.

No. II

The Model Artist Exhibitions

The "Walhalla"—Susannah in the
Bath—History of Model Artists—Frimbley and
the Living Statues—Dr. Collyer—The Goddesses
and the Police—Reflections

Having taken our preliminary stroll through the great thoroughfare, and observed its bearings and aspects by gaslight, we will diverge a little and use our eyes in a more limited sphere—where still there is much, very much, to be seen. Beaconed by yonder tongue of flame forever leaping up and sinking back again in that tall black monumental chimney, which scatters such clouds of uncrystalized otto of roses over the city, we stop before a dirty hack-stable thatched with straw manure and reeking knee-deep in filth. Beside the main entrances for the horses to stagger through at night, is a small door opening upon a dark passage, at the end of which we stumble up a narrow staircase and find ourselves in a dimly lighted room—the famous "Walhalla," residence of gods and goddesses, and evidently directly over the stable. The front is occupied by a rough counter furnished with certain bottles of variously-colored raw whisky, which passes under the various names of brandy, gin, Jamaica or cherry bounce, according to the taste of the customer. A few fetid camphene lamps, hung at dreary intervals along the walls, exhale a gentle lamp-black shower upon the air, and the aromal peculiarities of the place are completed by a delicate mingling of odors from the stable and the smoke of American cigars. The floor is slippery with mud and tobacco-juice, and about half filled with a pretty hard-looking set. A green rag runs across the lower end of the room, and at one corner sit two men, one scraping a villainous fiddle, and the other punishing a rheumatic piano. The music changes to a slow and plaintive air, a little bell jingles, and up goes the rag. We refer to our programme and ascertain that the tableau in order is "Susannah in the Bath." The same brawny female, who has already appeared as Venus, Psyche, and the Greek Slave, is now seated as Susannah in the bath, with her face and frontage to the audience. A light gauze drapery is held in her right hand and falls in a kind of demi-curtain before her knees—otherwise she is *in puribus naturalibus.* Behind her are the "elders," stooping and leaning over each other, trying to get a good sight. Susannah, seated upon the "revolving pedestal of Canova," commences her circumgyrations; and when she has got nearly once round, one of the elders begins speaking to his neighbor in his excitement—or we believe he drops his plug of tobacco on the ground—which startles the fair Susannah, who raises her hand, still holding the little curtain, to her head. The consequence may be imagined. And in this condition she completes her revolution before the audience, who fairly yell with delight as the curtain goes down, continuing their furious applause until the very old horses in the stable below wake up and whinnow out their delight. Overcome by these unexpected demonstrations of popularity, the obliging *artiste* comes out again and goes through the same performance three or four times more, without stopping to take breath.

Such is an unexaggerated description of a specimen of the exhibitions known in the handbills as "tableaux vivants," and which are now openly advertised, posted, countenanced and common-councilled in this virtuous and reputable metropolis. We have by no means selected the worst of these tableaux to pass our pen over. "Venus rising from the Sea," "the Lady Godiva, or Peeping Tom of Coventry," &c. &c. are quite as bad, and others, whose titles we have forgotten, absolutely worse.

The history of these exhibitions, their commencement, rise and progress, may be instructive, as throwing light on the public taste for amusement in this country; and, as we have taken some pains to gather the facts, we will devote a page to the recording of them.

The earliest representative of the "Living Statues" (now called "Model Artists") in this country, was a little Englishman named Frimbley. He was a knotty, knurly, well-formed manikin of a fellow, and used to dress himself neatly in skin-tight cotton fleshings, which he then plastered all over with flour, until, at the distance of stage from audience, he really looked very like a statue in plaster-of-paris, by Garbeille—very well modeled, but rather overcharged in outline and exaggerated in position. Thus accoutred, and furnished with pasteboard shield and helmet, Frimbley would throw himself into all sorts of shapes and attitudes, however, well-chosen, and sometimes really beautiful—of which we recollect a favorite picture, of "Ajax defying the Lightning," "The Dying Gladiator," and two or three others, equally classic and effective. These representations were very popular all over the country, and were really well worth seeing: for Frimbley was a good artist and studied his attitudes carefully. He had been originally a dancing and fencing master, comic pantomimist and stage dancer, and might have made a fortune by his "Living Statues." But he was strongly given to drink; and we heard, a few years ago, that he had died miserably, in some obscure place, without friends or money to bury him. Now and then, imitators of Frimbley have appeared, singly or in groups; but they never made any sensation—simply, we suppose, because they were not artists, and their exhibitions were merely ridiculous. For an undisciplined naked man, as the article is turned out in these latter days, is the most uncouth and ludicrous thing in existence—always excepting an untutored naked woman.

A couple of years ago, however, a man named Collyer, formerly known as a traveling animal magnetizer, returned from a visit to England, his native land, with what he called a troupe of "model artists." Up to this time, these exhibitions had been composed exclusively of men, and we never heard of their being considered immodest; but the moment the ladies made their appearance, an outcry of outraged public decency rose on all sides. The doctor was familiar with the science of humbugging the public, and proceeded very adroitly. At first, vague and mysterious paragraphs appeared here and there,—smuggled into respectable papers, wherever that was possible—to the effect that "the celebrated Dr. Collyer" had organized, in Rome or London, a company of the model men and women who stand or sit to the painters of the academies, and who are of course selected expressly on account of their symmetry and beauty of form—some for voluptuousness, some for strength, some for grace and delicacy, &c. &c. It was announced that they would give representations of scriptural and classic pictures, being draped and grouped in strict accordance with the works of the great masters. When the exhibition opened, however, it was found that this was only a part, and an insignificant part, of the entertainments—the principal portion consisting of groups of living statuary, such as we have described.[2]

2. Robert H. Collyer, who does seem to have been the humbug Foster claims he was, made an early but slight contribution to the genre of urban sensationalism with a small book entitled *Lights and Shadows of American Life*, published in Boston in 1843.

The fact in respect to these exhibitions was, that they were neither immodest nor exciting, to decent people,—simply obscene and disgusting. The women, so far from being the models from the European academies, were lank-sided, flabby-breasted, in-toed concerns, whose attitudes were about as lascivious as those of a new milch cow; and who shrunk and scrambled about in such fashion as to set one's stomach, for the time being, against all womankind. And then the fleshings, being baggy and unfitted to the form, drew across the bosom, until it looked like a bag of bran, rather than an exquisitely-proportioned female bust. So that lasciviousness and excitement were out of the question. But the doctor's exhibitions were constantly crowded, at first, and, in a few weeks, Yankee enterprise and emulation had established "model artist" exhibitions all over town, provided with abandoned women of the lowest grade, who thus managed to earn a *bare* subsistence, by a new disposition of charms which had ceased to be marketable in another way. In many of these establishments things were carried to the most filthy and incredible extent—dances being sometimes performed by men and women in a state of complete nudity, (without even the tights,) and every device resorted to in order increase the "richness" of these abominable orgies. At length even the municipal modesty was shocked, and the isle fairly "frighted from its propriety." Our readers, we suppose, have not yet forgotten the laughable accounts of the descent of the police upon a squad of naked Olympians, last October, at a hole in Twenty-first street, wherein Venus was trundled off to the Tombs[3] in a wheelbarrow, minus her chemise, and Bacchus had a narrow escape through a back window, leaving his trowsers to the vigilant guardians of the public morals—while the Three Graces—as naked as they were born—made an unsuccessful attempt to scramble, most ungracefully, out at a back basement. However, noth-

3. New York's Halls of Justice and municipal prison, a forbidding Egyptian-styled building on Centre Street, was popularly known as the Tombs.

ing very serious ever came of it—and notwithstanding the "majesty of the law," the model artist exhibitions, if not as numerous and popular as ever, are carried on with perfect immunity from municipal inspection or opposition.

But perhaps, after all, the most interesting and instructive portions of these degrading exhibitions are the audiences who attend them, and who furnish a fertile field for philosophical speculation upon the perverted operation of the sexual appetite—an appetite intended by Nature as the language of the purest and holiest passion implanted in the heart of man and woman. Until one has seen the worn-out rakes and sensualists, the ambitious young libertines and hypocritical old lechers, who sneak into these exhibitions, spy-glass in hand, to gloat over the salacious developments of the poor models who are thus forced by necessity or a beastly shamelessness, to expose themselves to public gaze for a few dollars a week, he can scarcely form an adequate idea of the shifts to which dissipation and conventional restraint have driven the audience, or the want of shifts to which other causes, no less apparent, have forced the performers. Many a man whose daily walk and conversation is held up to the admiration of the community as a "model" of virtue and propriety, may here be seen nightly devouring, with sparkling eyes and panting breath, the flabby figures of these other "models"—while the records of the cases which have now and then come before the courts will show that the models themselves have either stepped from the brothel to the public stage, or are young women from the country, destitute of home, friends and work, and compelled to adopt this repulsive and abhorrent profession, merely for the purpose of procuring bread. As to the first class, nothing is to be said—they are past hope. But who can forbear a sentiment of keenest pity for those innocent and ignorant girls whom the hard fate and ill reward of woman's labor have driven to such dire straits? Their future is scarcely doubtful. The associations into which they thus enter, both before and behind the curtain, speedily and infallibly do their work. From seduction they go rapidly through the various stages of depravity, until disease, dissipation and the exaggerated appetites engendered by their new mode of life, conduct them in turn to the brothel, the hospital, the penitentiary and the grave. Yes—the life of a "model artist" is easily written. After a brief season of hollow pleasure and unnatural excitement, she sinks willingly to the lowest type of human degradation—the public prostitute; and the pure and gentle woman, capable of all high and holy duties and affections, as wife and mother—endowed by her Creator with faculties fitting her, if properly directed, for the guardian angel and the consoler of man—goes, in utter recklessness of herself and all the world, to add one more to that frightful phalanx of female depravity which is the terror and the curse of an enfeebled and depraved civilization. Let us forget, in sleep, these dreadful sights and gloomy reflections.

No. III

Bowling and Billiard Saloons

*"Rooms" versus "Saloons"—Contrasts of
Character—Plucking a Pigeon—The Tall Son of
York and His Chums—Horn and His Last*

It is only within a few years that bowling and billiard saloons have been introduced among us. We used to have
bowling "alleys" and billiard "rooms," in abundance; but
the grandiloquent cockneyism which dignifies the commonest and most trivial affairs with the language of poetry and
sublimity, had not then broken out among us to so fatal an
extent as to deserve the name of an epidemic. Now, however,
it has become as pervading as the cholera. Every steamboat
is a "floating palace," every muddy Daguerreotype is a
"magnificent specimen of the fine arts"—and every grog-
shop harangue is pronounced by the "intelligent and independent press" to have been a "thrilling and masterly effort
of genuine eloquence." This ridiculous and annoying disease
has spread, cholera-like, upward and downward, beyond the
reach of camphor or veratrum. Our billiard-"rooms" and

ten-pin-"alleys" have been transformed into "saloons"—our oyster "cellars" and drinking-shops have emulated their example; and as to a good old-fashioned barber's shop, there is not such a thing to be found within the circumference of the city. To what extent this saloon-mania will spread, it is impossible to calculate; but we expect every day to see the oyster-stand in front of the Tribune Office disport a gilded sign inscribed "Pat Rafferty's Central Saloon;" while the penny ice-cream man at its side will give a blow-out to the editors, and be chronicled in all the daily and Sunday papers as one of the greatest benefactors of the age.

But whether we treat of them as saloons, alleys, or simply rooms, the billiard and bowling establishments with which the city abounds are well worth a night's attention, as being frequented by a greater diversity of strongly-marked characters than almost any other class of public places of resort. Here the gay and reckless southerner, the half-frightened and half-fuddled country merchant, the watch-stuffer, the green-horn, the blackleg and the clerk, the editor and the genteel pick-pocket, meet and mingle on equal and familiar terms. The polite keepers of these establishments, ever on the watch for customers, take the new-comer by the arm, ask him if he "feels inclined for a game," and introduce him to some regular hanger-on of the concern, who is charged nothing for the games he loses, and whose business it is to troll in strangers, and make them pay as dearly as possible for their whistles. With one or two exceptions, every billiard-room and bowling-saloon in the city supports in liquor and lunch a regular detachment of these stool-pigeons, who, by incessant practice, can play just about such a game as they please, and know how adroitly to "throw off," in such a manner as to escape the suspicion of the stranger, who comes so very near winning every game that he is perfectly certain of the next. Something, however, happens invariably to turn up, just at the close of the next, and the next,—either an unexpected ten-strike, or a tremendous scratch,—which again throws the game into the hands of the decoy, and only serves to stimulate the baffled visitor to renewed and still more hopeless exertions.

Or it may be that he is the object of a deeper conspiracy. If so, he is permitted, after being considerably excited by his "infernal run of luck," and several well-timed glasses of brandy and water, to win three or four games in succession—the poor decoy at length throwing down his cue in violent indignation, and declaring with an oath that he never had such a run of bad luck in his life, and that he "cannot play for shucks." Now is the stranger's turn for triumph. He chuckles a little, looks at the clock, takes another "stiffener," and suggests that they play one more game for "drinks all round." But the stool-pigeon is tired—he has played enough—he can't see a ball. "I will tell you, though," he says at last, "what I'll do. If you will give me twenty in a hundred, I'll play you for half a dollar a game." The stranger hesitates, and finally consents—"for," (he says to himself,) "if the fellow was a blackleg, he wouldn't ask *odds* of me; and, besides, he don't play well enough for a blackleg." The result, we suppose, we need not trouble ourselves to record. Of course the pigeon is neatly and thoroughly plucked, and sent home somewhere about daylight, with his head ready to split with the compound pressure of bad brandy, excitement and tobacco-smoke, and his purse as light as a feather.

Let us, however, do the billiard-rooms justice. As a general thing, the better class of them prohibit gambling, at least openly, and endeavor to conduct their establishments quietly and respectably; and, although gambling will of course now and then creep in, and be winked at, or altogether ignored by the proprietor, yet the billiard-rooms are by no means the worst places into which a stranger is likely to stumble. The game of billiards itself is one of the most elegant and fascinating amusements in the world, and requires some quietness and refinement of taste for its enjoyment. For an hour of leisure, refreshing recreation or healthy exercise, we know of nothing better than a game of billiards; and if the stranger will remember never to bet a penny, never to drink, and never to smoke while at play, he may safely indulge himself with an evening at billiards, with no greater expense than the cost of seven-eighths of the games—and that is buying a very delightful amusement at quite a reasonable price. Perhaps, in this connection, the reader will be obliged to us for telling him, that altogether the best tables in New York, and the places where the visitor is safe from disgusting associations or stool-pigeon impositions, are at Bassford's in Ann street, under the American Museum, (now kept by Parsons,) and at Otis Field's Irving Rooms, in Broadway, opposite Florence's. At either of these places you may play at all times with perfect safety.

Bowling is an amusement of a much more generally popular character than billiards, as everybody can appreciate it. The accommodations for it in New York are of almost fabulous extent and splendor. Some of the finest halls and saloons on the continent, luxuriously fitted up with costly furniture, ceiled with immense French plate-glass mirrors and lighted with magnificent chandeliers, are devoted to the business of rolling ten-pins. Some of them contain as many as eight alleys, which are kept in the most careful order, and almost incessantly in use, from noon till midnight. The mornings are usually occupied by your ten-pin bowler in trying to get a little sleep.

The company of the bowling-saloon is of a decidedly lower grade than at the billiard-rooms. Of course there are great varieties of both kinds; but generally speaking, the descent from the billiard-room to the ten-pin alley is very marked. The players are more boisterous, more flashily dressed, swear more, drink more, chew more tobacco, are more apt to quarrel, and not less intent upon winning, than the billiard-players. They are likewise much more indiscriminate, and it is an easy thing to pick up a loafer, a pickpocket, a burner or a Bowery blackleg at even the most dashing bowling-saloon. In the lower varieties, located in cellars and back premises, out of Broadway, it would be difficult to find "anything else."

Bowling is an amusement especially affected by a rather tall class of our metropolitan journalists and literary athletes. They are very chary, however, in the distribution of their patronage, and never make their appearance except at certain rather exclusive and *recherché* establishments, where the liquors are unimpeachable, the cigars delicately flavored, and the company generally select. Among the most conspicuous of this gay and strikingly characteristic type of literary life—conspicuous as well for the eminence of his talent and the goodness of his heart as for the immense distance from the ground he wears his hat—is William T. Porter, the world-renowned editor of the "Spirit of the Times," and altogether so good-natured and excellent a fellow that he will overlook the liberty we have taken with his name, and the next time we meet in Barclay street will hold out his hand to us like a regular brick, and most likely ask us to step into Frank's and imbibe a private smile. It is ten to one that he has a book of rich and rare MS. caricatures in his hat, just sent on from Bob Clarke—or if not, he is "safe" for half-a-dozen new anecdotes, full of roaring fun. If the weather and season are not too tempting for sport among the bushes, it is more than probable that Frank Forrester— not only our best novelist, but our best writer upon the sports of the field and angle, and the most expert practitioner at both—is somewhere in these latitudes: in fact, here he comes, just in time to "join" in our solemnities. If Clarke himself, (the "O.K." whose inimitable sketches of the b'hoys of New York, have preserved to posterity a character whose parallel the world has never yet seen, and who, but for Clarke's graphic pencil, would have passed away unchronicled,) were not in Philadelphia fiddling away at a "blasted" panorama, "or some such wagon," he would be sure to make up a quartette in this agreeable little party. But as it is, we will remember him in our dreams.[4]

4. Clarke provided several of the illustrations for Foster's *New York in Slices*. Two are reproduced in the "New York by Daylight" section of this book.

It would be an unpardonable omission, in an account of the bowling-saloons of New York, were we to neglect mentioning the "Horn," whose "last" has been traveling over the country as if impelled by boot and spur, any time during the past five years. The truth is, in respect to Horn, he has been made the victim of a conspiracy—all the stupidities of the press (our own among the number) having combined together to saddle our bad puns and pointless jokes upon poor Horn. Any one who has the faintest conception of the boundless resources in this direction of which Horn has been made the victim, will easily understand the pitch of desperation to which he must necessarily have been driven. Finally, the poor man having become insane from the effects of our combined attacks, actually started a newspaper himself! Having thus become a living spectacle and specimen of the horrible consequences of vicarious punning, he grows more and more "Inveterate" every week—price two dollars a year in advance.

Somebody,—we think it was Elia,—once wrote an essay on bowling, and the way it was or probably would have been done by various great men of the day. It was an ingenious speculation—and by stepping in at Graves's or Frank's, almost any pleasant evening, you may see it in practical operation. Porter rolls a free and easy ball, yet with a great deal of elegance and suavity, neither too hurried nor too deliberate—just comfortable and natural, and taking time as it goes down by the first quarter-pin to brush the center, as much as to say, "I could easily have taken you, old fellow, if I had been so disposed—but look out for next time!" He usually makes nine pins with three balls, but if hard pushed, can easily get a spare every time, and often two of them. He is very much like a high-spirited horse on the road,—jogging on quietly enough so long as every thing else is *behind*: but the moment anything attempts to *pass* him—whew! get out! there's trouble in the camp directly!

Herbert lobs slightly, though not enough to come within the "rules and regulations." He is rather fiery and impatient, and makes you hold your breath as he rushes down the alley and launches his ball, as if it were a big marble, smack at the center-pin. He usually hits it, too—for he is a devil of a shot—but his aim has been so true and sportsmanlike that it very often "guts" and breaks up his entire frame, where a much poorer player would have been sure of at least seven, and probably eight or nine.

Clarke takes the ball daintily between his thumb and fingers and contemplating it in silence, for a moment, as if he were about to take its likeness, launches it with a graceful glide at the pins, making it describe the true Hogarthian line of beauty as it slips along. Sometimes he makes three ten-strikes in succession—sometimes doesn't hit a pin at all. But it is all the same to him. The fun of seeing the balls travel down the alley so smoothly is all he cares about. His ambition (if he has any) is somewhere else. Briggs, of Holden's Magazine and the Custom-House, rolls fairly and easily down the center of one alley, while you think he is watching the game of his antagonist on the other. He generally makes his full ten, and now and then has a spare laid up against a rainy day. But even if you should beat him a dozen pins he would be very apt to convince you, before he had done with you, that you had absolutely lost the game. His mania is logic; and he regards every pin in the light of a proposition, against which he is to roll either the heavy ordnance of the lignum vitae number ones, the medium sized blunderbuss of number two, or the keen and cutting rifle-ball poney, until they are all down. After he has tumbled them all over he will go to work and convince you that they are still standing—that the moon is made of green cheese—that H——
——— is a humbug, or any thing else equally reasonable and preposterous.[5]

5. The disguised reference is probably to Horace Greeley, who is the subject of the next paragraph. The other men Foster describes in this sketch were prominent personalities on the sporting side of New York journalism. Here and elsewhere, Foster takes obvious delight in sketching his friends and acquaintances from the little world of Nassau Street.

We never saw the editor of the Tribune bowl down any-thing but politicians; but if he makes as much havoc among the pins as among his antagonists, he is sure of a ten-strike every time. He has great advantages in bowling, from the fact that he wears no straps to his pantaloons; and if ever he should get fairly warmed up at it, we expect that it will keep at least one small boy busy enough to "set 'em up."

There are all sorts of bowling-saloons in town, frequented by all sorts of people—any one collection of them furnishing material enough for a rich night's reflection. At present, we will hold a brief consultation with our pillows. We have made a good game and the string is out. So home and to bed.

No. IV

The Golden Gate of Hell

*Prostitution in General—The Fashionable
Brothel—A Description That Thousands Will
Recognize—Personal Histories of Two Cyprians*

Let no prudish moralist condemn us because we go boldly
and thoroughly through the haunts of vice and dissipation
in our overgrown metropolis, and describe things exactly as
we find them. Such facts, accumulated in no wanton spirit
of levity, but carefully gathered and with a faithful desire to
do good, amount in the end to great truths, abounding in
deepest uses. It is such facts that society most needs—facts
which show the actual consistence, color and dimensions of
the cancer that lies eating at its very vitals. For how else
shall we know by what means to extirpate it and give the
system health? No investigation of this kind at all squea-
mish in telling the actual truth about prostitution, in all its
phases, can do any good—for prostitution, in one form or
another, is a mother and nurse of every vice that afflicts and
degrades humanity; and when we have found what prostitution is, and how to prevent it, we have accomplished the
great task of reform. Everything else is comparatively easy.

We have glanced at this monstrous iniquity in some of its less inviting aspects—to-night we devote to an examination of its more prosperous periods, and visit prostitution in its temple and court, surrounded by its devotees, still young and fresh and fair, with the bloom of womanly innocence still lingering here and there upon their cheeks, and the outward form of the inner wickedness as yet almost wholly undepraved. Here passes in idleness and luxury, amid sumptuous entertainments and surrounded by flattering and obedient admirers, the brief period of transition between the purity and peace of virtue and the swinish hell of filth and abomination into which the victim hastens to plunge and wallow forever. Yes—truth bids us say that, to all appearance, there is no repentance for the past nor terror for the future, here. The gay and joyous inmates of this place, betrayed by the men their young hearts loved, and then abandoned by the world which should have protected them, have made full use of this double lesson, and have fairly convinced themselves that the gratification of the present moment is really and truly the only good of life, and that all the talk about virtue and reputation and crime and punishment, is mere deception. And in fact, why should they not think so? Were they not virtuous, and did not the being to whom they had yielded up the very love and worship of the soul, basely betray and abandon them? And then, even worse than that, did not their own sisterhood spit and trample upon them and drive them forth with taunts and revilings, when they so sorely needed kindness and protection? Pooh! Talk not to *them* of female purity, and human sympathy, and such fine nonsense. They know better! So let us describe the fashionable assignation-house.

A green Venitian door is closed before the entrance, while the main door is thrown open, and a woman stands watching us through the blinds as we go up the steps. She seems to recognize our good-natured friend who has volunteered the task of guiding us, and saves us the trouble of ringing, by at once opening the little green door and admitting us to the splendidly lighted hall, richly carpeted and furnished. Without ceremony we enter the front parlor and are met by the lady of the house, an elderly, discreet and very respectable-looking person, dressed with great simplicity and modesty, with a neat mob-cap on her head. She receives us with extreme affability, and motions us to be seated till the young lady at the piano has concluded the piece she is playing. The piano is a superb one, and the touch and execution of the performer would do honor to Strakosch himself. She sings, but her voice is husky and seems to have lost its freshness and transparency, although it exhibits a thorough training and greater powers of execution than are usually possessed by amateurs. There is, however, no feeling nor expression in what she sings. All is cold as ice. Around the room are seated six or seven very conspicuously-dressed women, relieved by here and there a man, and all decorously listening to the music. With the exception of the somewhat bizarre and startling latitudes and longitudes of costume observed by the ladies, there is nothing to indicate that we are not assisting at the incipient crystallization of a regular evening party.

But the music is over—the young lady has risen from the piano and expressed the somewhat eccentric wish for a drop of brandy and water! The folding-doors are thrown open, and the other room is found to be filled exclusively by women. It is a fine *coup d'oeil*. The rooms are unusually large and lofty, and from the center of each apartment a large and magnificent chandelier depends, brilliantly lighted with gas, and throwing a soft flood of light through its ground-glass shades upon the objects and persons in the room. The floors are covered with white Wilton carpet, strewn with a rich crimson rose interspersed with a series of lovely bouquets, in which the harmonizing hue of green predominates. The hangings of the windows are of the costliest damask, of tints to respond to the carpets, and between the windows and above the Egyptian marble mantels rise to the ceiling walls of Parisian plate-glass mirrors of an intense and indescribable luster, like the deep sky of midnight moonlight. The furniture consists of an almost infinite variety of luxurious ottomans, sofas, divans and lounges, into whose recesses you sink with a feeling of voluptuous repose that takes your breath away. The walls are ornamented with four or five really excellent pictures, not freer in design nor richer in coloring and outline than many which stare from the panels and challenge admiration at our public institutions.

The presiding divinities of this modern temple to Aphrodite are some of them quite beautiful, and all tolerably good-looking—a decidedly ugly woman not being able even to sell herself to much advantage in this refined and fastidious age. Some are arrayed in the latest Parisian style, according to the cuts in Sartain's Magazine—while others emulate, in their style of costume, the Undine lately appearing in its pages, or the young lady combing her hair on the margin of the Fountain of Vaucleuse—her only garment having discovered the laws of gravity and slipped ———. On the sofa opposite the piano is a Miss in short frock and pantalettes, who passes for fifteen. But the regular frequenters of the house have seen her in the same costume for some years, and they merely put their tongues in their cheeks as they pass.

Perhaps the most conspicuous object in the rooms is a large and gaudy-looking arm-chair standing under the chandelier in the back parlor, facing the folding doors. It is about the size of Queen Victoria's throne, and is plentifully stuccoed with gilt ornaments upon a white ground in the ultra Louis Quatorze manner. The mystery of this chair is that whoever sits in it for the first time is fined champagne all round; and as ladies are always dry and always full of fun, it is amusing enough to witness the efforts of the fascinating creatures to get the victims into this gorgeous but expensive seat. At length a greenhorn from the West,—a country merchant come to replenish his dry goods and refresh his morals in the great metropolis,—is tempted into the fatal chair, and the fine is immediately claimed, with loud laughter and any quantity of no very dainty congratulation. The wine is forthcoming; and after duly honoring the foaming draught, the company begins to get excited and to drop off, two by two, until we look round upon our polite and attentive land-lady, who stands alone in the middle of the room, smiling upon our perplexity.

"Well, well," says she, smiling more and more, "they have all gone off and left you this time; but never mind! better luck next."

We explain to her that we are by no means disappointed, and are "mere lookers-on here in Vienna;" and after thanking her for her politeness, take our departure.

The house we have just left is one of the most expensive and "aristocratic" homes of vice in the city, and probably in the United States. Its regular occupants are about twenty women, who pay each ten dollars a week for board and two dollars a night for ———— but you must imagine that. So that the poor creatures, even in this best and briefest phase of their miserable existence, have hard work to pay their daily expenses: and when they get sick—which, alas! is very often—they have generally no resource but the Hospital, whence they emerge several steps lower down the steep-descending ladder of infamy, up which they can never again ascend. With a very few fortunate exceptions, in from five to ten years, on the average, all the gay and thoughtless crea-tures we have seen luxuriously reclining upon the velvet so-fas or pressing with elastic step the voluptuous carpets of this splendid mansion, will be drunkards in the kennels of the Five Points, full of loathsome diseases, tramping the streets at all hours and weathers, in search of sailors, loaf-ers, green-horns, negroes, anything or anybody, to decoy into their filthy dens, running the lucky chance of picking a pocket meanwhile. The more shrewd and business-like among them may form partnership with some panel-thief,[6]

6. Another villain peculiar to the city, the panel thief hid behind a false, moveable panel in the wall of the prostitute's room, emerg-ing at an appropriate moment to rob her customer.

and in this way make occasionally lucky hauls from country merchants and strangers uninitiated in the ways of the city. But the end of all is the same—welcome death, and a translation to the world of spirits in a condition fitting them to assume the form, habits and manner of life of swine, which they will retain forevermore. For in that world every one appears precisely as he is; neither the odor of sanctimonious hypocrisy, nor outward clothing, fine silks nor pungent perfumery, is there to conceal the outward swinish aspect of those whose licentious wills and loves have made them beasts in this life.

This is the place in which to introduce some facts relative to the causes of prostitution, and the history of public women, which we have collected from various sources, during a professional life of many years in the metropolis, as a daily reporter and journalist. So far as we have the means of judging, we believe them to be authentic; and as such they cannot be otherwise than interesting. Among the inmates of a fashionable boarding-house for public women, such as we have just described, the following personal narratives were taken down from the lips and in nearly the very words of those who enacted them.

A young woman, known in the establishment and to its inmates as "Princess Anna"—they all affect grandiloquent soubriquets of this description, which they have printed on their cards, and always carry about with them for distribution—related her story as follows:

"I am the daughter of a farmer in Cortlandt county. When I was about fifteen, my cousin Tom, who was the scholar of my uncle's family, and had just graduated, came to Homer, where we lived, to spend some weeks. He was a handsome young man, and seemed to me a perfect angel. He was so superior to the country boys I had been in the habit of seeing—so deferential and soft in his manner, that he completely won my child's-heart, before I knew what I was about. I really don't believe he meant any harm—poor fellow—and if he did, I freely forgive him. But, one day, we were rambling in the woods, all alone, and had walked very far, and got very tired, and sat down on a bank to rest. There—you smile, and shrug your shoulders—I see you know all about it—so I needn't go on. But I vow I didn't dream of any thing wrong. It was so delicious to be caressed and pressed to his bosom, that I completely forgot myself, and so did he. We were both children, and I think, now, that I was quite as much to blame as he. But so it was; and when all was over, we were a couple of the most frightened and foolish creatures that ever were seen. To tell the truth, however, I couldn't so well see the harm; but poor Tom went on at a dreadful rate, accusing himself of being my destroyer, and I don't know what. I remember very well replying, in my childish simplicity, 'Why, dear Tom, I don't think you've destroyed me—I don't believe but what I'm as good as ever I was.' But this only seemed to make him worse; so I began crying too, and we had a grand blubbering time of it. But at last we dried our eyes; and, after kissing each other, and swearing eternal fidelity, we washed our faces in the brook, and went home as gaily as if nothing had happened.

"Well—let me get on as fast as possible. In a few months after this I found out what I had been about, and was almost insane with terror and despair. My cousin had gone to the city to attend the lectures, and I saw no other chance than to break the hearts of my poor parents by telling them of my disgrace. But this I couldn't bear. At last I bethought me of going to the minister and making a confidant of him. He was a very godly man, and had always seemed to take a peculiar fancy to me, even from childhood. Therefore, after much ado, to him I went and made a clean breast of it. The old fellow seemed to be horror-struck; thought awhile, and then bidding me be comforted, told me he had hit upon a plan for getting me out of the scrape. But the preliminary condition insisted on by the old scamp was, that I should grant him the same favors I had done to cousin Tom! I seemed to have no alternative and so I yielded. The hypocritical old sinner, it seems, not only understood these things theoretically but practically; and beside enabling me to come off without any serious difficulty, but gave me an infallible prescription to prevent my getting into any more trouble. Thus, by my instinctive trust in love and my natural veneration for religion and its minister, was I, while yet a child, perverted to shame. Is it strange that I have grown hard-hearted and reckless and learned to look on life as a game of cards, at which he who wins most is the best fellow? What are men to me, but as victims to pluck, or food for my insane and fierce appetites? I have no position and no future. I live but for the present."

"True," we replied at this point of her narrative; "but pray go on."

"All the rest of my experience is commonplace enough. Cousin Tom, who I believe really loved me, soon finding from the levity and hollowness of my conduct that I was not what I had been, deserted me. I do not blame him—and I'm sure that can't be a tear!—but still I never should have given myself to him in the woods, only he said he should die without me, and I was willing to die to make him happy. But I forgive him. Of course it wouldn't do for a man's honor that he marry a poor girl after he had ruined her! Father and mother—ah, that was the cruelest blow!—at last found out all about it; and father, calling me one dreary, rainy evening into their bed-room, made me confess every thing. Mother took it to heart dreadfully, got sick and died; but father went to drinking, and soon had to sell his farm. His credit was gone, and he couldn't work—so he went to the county poor-house; while I, with madness in my heart and its determination and coolness in my brain, came on foot and alone to New York to seek and execute revenge upon mankind, and at the same time to indulge my perverted appetites to the full. I know I am a demon—a she-devil—as are all women who have lost their virtue; and I mean to make the most of it."

Another of these brief but instructive autobiographies is as follows:

"I haven't any fine romance and innocent babyhood, and all that sort of thing, to amuse you with, like Anna there, and all I know of myself is stupid enough. The first thing I can remember is being cold and hungry, and half naked and ragged, and sent out in the rainy mornings into the streets barefooted, to sweep the crossings and beg for pennies.[7] I have a sort of dim remembrance of suffering and misery before that—but nothing distinct. I was so young and used to plead so hard that I did a very good business, and often used to carry home half a dollar at night—which seemed to me quite a fortune. We lived in a little back cellar down in an alley in Orange street, where I don't remember at this moment ever to have seen the sun enter. The floor was only loose boards, and the black mud and slime used to ooze up through the cracks all about, until it was sometimes quite slippery. The fire-place wasn't made for drawing, and there was but one little bit of a window in the whole room, and that wasn't more than half above ground: half the glass at least being broken out and its place supplied with old rags. So the room was dark enough, and generally pretty well filled with smoke. The damp used to come out on the walls, and stand there year after year, in big, gummy drops. There was a little closet in one corner of the room—a pine table against the wall, three or four wooden chairs that had been gradually broken down to stools, and a large collection of rags, shavings, straw and other rubbish in the corner opposite the closet. I remember all these details very vividly, because they constituted the home of my childhood, and I knew no other place of shelter in the world where I could set my foot. Whether I remember it with pleasure or hatred you may judge for yourselves.

"At any rate, in this one cellar my father and mother, my two brothers and sisters and myself all lived together—ate,

7. The crossing sweeper was a common sight on the streets of New York. Poor girls begged for coins by stationing themselves next to the cobblestone pedestrian crossings of major streets, and by sweeping away the mud and manure at the approach of a prosperous-looking pedestrian.

slept, cooked, washed and ironed, did everything in this one dank and noisome hole. Of my relatives let me say nothing. Whatever they are or wherever they are, *I* have nothing to boast over them, except the possession of a little more energy and recklessness. But I will say one thing—they were mostly kind to me and to each other. They never beat me when I had been unlucky in my day's work; but oftener when I came home crying bitterly, with my little frozen fingers almost empty, and dragging my old broom wearily over my shoulder, my mother's face has beamed with an expression of genuine sympathy and affection—I know it must have been, for it was so different from all I have seen since. Both my father and mother drank whisky whenever they could get a chance, and I early imbibed a passionate fondness for it. Yet I remember perfectly well that I loathed the smell and taste of it. But after I had drank it I felt like another being; it seemed as if I was handsome and delicate, and wore fine clothes, and had on pretty shoes and stockings, showing my white bare legs, like the fine little ladies I saw walking in Broadway with their mamas. It appeared to transform all the world into the pleasantest, happiest place that could be conceived. At other times I pined and longed for I knew not what; and a vague but fierce feeling of despair and revenge filled my little heart almost to bursting. But when I had had a lucky day, and father used to give me a good drink of raw whisky out of his bottle—Oh, I felt perfectly glorious, and forgave and loved every body! I was right—I am right still. Drunkenness, of one kind or another, is the only thing left to a poor woman in this world.

"When I got older they wanted me to leave off street-sweeping and take to thieving. But I had not been on the crossing four or five years for nothing, and I had formed designs of a different character. In a word, I was ambitious; and finding that I was going to be handsome, I determined to make my own way through the world. I had already reflected a good deal, and had come to the conclusion that I couldn't be worse off, any how. And beside, I had formed a sort of acquaintance with a dashing, splendidly-dressed lady, who used occasionally to stop and give me a sixpence and talk to me. I of course almost worshiped her—she looked so fine, her cheeks were so red and her teeth so white; and she always wore brighter-colored dresses and longer feathers than the other ladies. I supposed she was the Mayor's wife, at least—or perhaps the Queen come over on a visit.

"I was now somewhat more than ten years of age, and had already made considerable progress in my grand but very indefinite schemes. I had gradually and cautiously secreted money enough to buy some second-hand clothes, which struck me as being overwhelmingly grand and splendid, as I used to contemplate them in the "fence" window, on my way to my daily station in Broadway. One day, as I was thrashing about with my broom, and holding out my hand mechanically to every one who passed, and wondering what had become of the great lady who used to stop and speak to me—when I heard some one say:

" 'There, little girl, that will do. Here's a sixpence, but don't spatter me.'

"It was she—and that hour decided my fate. From the victim of a cruel world I became at once one of its victimizers, its self-created scourges. I see I need not tell you my friend's character. Enough that she treated *me* honorably, and found me not backward in adopting her views. In a short time I was regularly established as a partner and assistant, wore clothes as gorgeous and fantastic as her own, and commenced my grand part of interesting and tender child—in which I was sold over and over again, during several years, to rich old lechers, blind with debauchery and palsied with age. After that game couldn't be carried on any longer, I passed for an interesting young widow, and inveigled in succession innumerable young sparks to squander their money upon me, imagining that they were recalling to life and affection the heart that lay buried in the coffin of my husband, and all that nonsense. Thank my stars, I have fleeced a pretty good number of the villains, and mean to do so to a great many more. I don't feel that I have done wrong.

On the contrary, when I remember the squalid, loathsome, suffocating home of my childhood, and contrast my condition then with what it is now, I feel as if I ought to be pretty well satisfied with the way I have managed to get on in the world. I live freely and generously, dress like a princess, drink, eat and sleep like a king's mistress, and care for nobody on earth. I sometimes, to be sure, feel a kind of heartsickness, when I am all alone, or it is a rainy, dismal day, such as when I used to stand barefooted and shivering on the crossings, begging pennies; and at such times something seems to whisper to me that I am a horrible creature. But I don't stand such hysterical spells very long. A good stiff glass of brandy and water soon sets me all right again, and I don't care *that* for society, its good opinion, nor any thing else."

We might easily prolong, from the materials in our notebook, these recitals to the end of our volume; but these are sufficient for our purposes—and beside, the stories soon degenerate to the merest commonplace of want, starvation, seduction and abandonment, the disgusting details of which have been of late years made sufficiently familiar to the public. One and all teach the same fearful and unvarying lesson—female prostitution is invariably the result of man's individual villainy in seducing and betraying the pure being who trusts her destiny to his keeping—or of the monstrous crime of society which dooms its daughters to degradation, want and misery, from which no virtuous effort of theirs can ever rescue them. Let society heed this one simple truth, and apply a thorough and efficient remedy, by furnishing the means of comfortable and happy existence to women who would be virtuous, and exclude from its presence all men who are guilty of seduction or libertinism, or who have trifled with the sacred affection of woman, in any form. Then nine-tenths of all crime and suffering will be at once abolished from the face of the earth. But this is something to be prayed for rather than hoped for.

No. V

A Night Ramble

The Upstairs Drinking-Saloons—"The Widow's"—Fashionable Oyster Palaces—Private Gambling—The Bowery Raffle—Contrasts and Contemplations

We will be a little desultory to-night, and make a kind of flying excursion through various and somewhat opposite scenes. The first pieces at the theaters are just out; and as we pass up Broadway the smack of billiard-balls and the sharp crack of the pistols from the Irving Rooms remind us that we are in the neighborhood of another establishment of which very little is generally known, but which is very well worth a passing look. Many similar ones exist in the city, and they are all so nearly alike that one will serve as a type of the whole.

Ascending a very unsumptuous staircase, we enter a large room which, at first view, appears to be the reading-room of some third-rate club, whose subscription is seventy-five cents a week, tobacco and pipes included. A round wooden center-table, covered with dog-eared newspaper files, and surrounded by common-looking arm-chairs, is embellished

by the presence of some half-a-dozen men in mouse-skin
moustaches and Chatham-street bernous, the sleeves of
which have the exact shape, grace and curvature of Yankee
boiled-pudding-bags. Every man is furnished with his glass
of hot toddy or whisky punch, and carries a cigar desperately clipped between his teeth and elevated at an angle of
forty-five degrees,—like the telescope on the side-walk
pointed at the full moon. The walls of the room are hung
with those not very elevated specimens of the fine arts
known as colored lithographs, exhibiting the female bust
and form in every possible and impossible attitude. On the
mantel is a string of those inevitable caricatures of Garbeille, representing Mr. Bennett in the act of writing a revolutionary leader for the Herald; Mr. La Forest clapping a
prima donna, forgetful of his beautiful wife; Signor Bene-
detti opening his mouth and shutting his eyes, as he appears
in his "tremendous and unparalleled act" (see the circus
bills) of *Madre mia!*; Mr. White, with a pen almost as long as
himself, and a pair of the most exquisitely conceited
epaulette-puckers on the shoulders of his *comme il faut*
opera-coat; and a few more of the same sort. In one corner
is a counter over which leans a piratical-looking fellow with
a big moustache, talking earnestly with a buxom, rather
good-looking woman on the other side. That is "The
Widow"—these are her upper-ten customers, bucks of the
blunt, lads of spirit, young men about town, fancy coves,
who spend hundreds nightly at the oyster-cellars, the
gambling-houses, and other worse places of the town, which
their prudent papas have laboriously earned and scraped together by wielding the goose and press-board, or by carefully watching the fluctuations in the pork-market. These
young bloods think it just the thing—in fact, dem foine—to
stop and patronise "the widow" on their way from the theater to their other nightly haunts: and although their pretty
sisters sit pensively at home in their gorgeously-upholstered
barn-parlors in Fishmonger Place, and would give their little fingers for somebody to speak to, yet these "nice young

men" would consider it altogether too "slow" for their use
to spend an evening decently at home among virtuous and
accomplished women, when there are such places as "the
widow's" and "Cinderella's" to go to.

These up-stairs drinking-saloons are a peculiar feature in
New York dissipation, and seem to be used mainly as semi-
naries of dissipation, and primary schools of debauchery.
The coarse-featured, badly-painted woman who tends the
bar is of course a prostitute, and has set up this as a sort of
decoy-house. The little door at the end of the bar leads to a
bed-chamber, and she will show you the way there for five
dollars; while the rooms up stairs are occupied with roulette and cards, kept by her "fancy man," who appropriates
one night in the week to himself, and divides the remainder
of the time between swearing at her and farming her out as
"a delicious tit-bit" to his credulous and gaping customers.
Many a young man, who could not possibly be persuaded
into a gambling-house or a brothel, is easily induced to call
with his more profligate companions on "the widow,"
merely to take a drink and have a little chat. A few visits
wear off the edge of his compunction, and he generally ends
by becoming a regular customer not only of the widow's but
many a worse place. There is not in town a more dangerous
ground for a young man to travel over than these up-stairs
drinking-shops.

But the guests are departing, one after another, seeming
in very bad humor, and each casting ferocious glances at the
man with the big black moustache leaning over the counter.
The addle-pated young "aristocrats" think this fellow is at
least the attaché of the Russian legation and has been cutting them all out with the widow. The fact, however, is that
he is simply an under-crust blackleg, and is the veritable
"man" to whom the widow and her whole establishment belong. It is his night; and scowling an unuttered curse at his
lady's customers, as they creak down stairs, he gruffly orders the widow to shut up shop directly, and disappears.
She listens a moment, pulls from her pocket a handful of
money of all sizes, and saying to herself slowly and with an

indescribable sort of chuck, "no yer don't, Frank!" conceals it in a back part of the drawer that has just been emptied of its contents. That is her portion of the day's earnings; and having read in the "Slices" that women are very badly paid for their work, she is determined that it shall not be so in her case. The widow is one of 'em—she can travel *she* can!

It is not yet late, and we will look in at some other public houses on our way to the Bowery, where we propose—if you have no objection—to spend the night. The spacious and really elegant establishment we are now entering may be termed the citadel of slang, the strong-hold of genteel rowdyism, the university of dissipation. It is called a hotel, but it has no table d'hôte, no public parlor, and its inmates and visitors eat either in their own rooms or in the public stalls of the restaurant below stairs. No "references" are required for a gentleman and lady entering there, so that they pay for what they order and behave themselves correctly in passing in and out. A spark of rowdyism or impropriety calculated to create observation would be promptly put down. But so long as you conduct yourself quietly and don't dispute the bill, you may do any and everything you please—stay as long as you like, go when it suits you, at any hour of the night or day, and no questions asked nor observations made. To be detected looking under a lady's bonnet or winking at his companions would be considered cause of discharge to a waiter, and all the attachés of the establishment are well trained in their duties. The ladies' entrance is not in Broadway, and the little room into which a lady and her companion are shown has the key inside. The moment your order for broiled oysters and champagne is filled the servant bolts through the door and leaves you to bolt it after him or not, as you please. He will return no more, unless you ring the bell. But no sooner does that go than the "29" from the office and the "answered, sir!" of the drowsy waiter immediately warn you of his approach.

The whole house is cut up into small private apartments, with the exception of a handsome suite on the second floor, always kept for the accommodation of "private families," but never rented. It is called a hotel, but ought rather to be styled a house of convenience for those who do not find themselves comfortable at a real first-class hotel, and who yet wish to live well and are willing and able to pay well. If the truth must plainly be told, the house is inhabited mostly by the aristocratic blacklegs—we beg pardon, sporting-men—of the city, with their friends, victims and mistresses. In the restaurant and drinking-shop down cellar the common public regales itself on good things—oysters, steak, game, and everything the market affords, but all cooked plain. The liquors and wines are of that negative quality which often deceives even good judges, and it is the habit of the bar-keeper to send, after the second bottle to the same party, counterfeit brands of the article they call for. Thus, within this gilded and gorgeously-lighted cavern, in the course of the year incredible quantities of adroitly fermented turnip-juice, charged with carbonic acid gas, are consumed to the delight of maudlin greenhorns striving to assume the blood, and who guzzle down the nefarious stuff under the firm impression that they are imbibing the genuine Mumm or Heidsick. Up stairs the ground floor is occupied by the sitting and reading-room, the office, another bar, and half-a-dozen small private rooms for customers. The walls of the sitting-room are hung with some very striking pictures, mostly of sporting and mythological subjects, and over the mantel rises a wall of French plate-glass mirror, richly set in gilt and reaching the ceiling. The wide windows are composed each of a single plate of glass, and the arm-chairs, lounges, &c. scattered about the room would almost answer for the deck of one of those "floating-palaces" of which we often read such glowing accounts in the daily papers.

Above the ground floor, with the exception of the "family-rooms" we have mentioned, the chambers are pretty much given up to the one great business, end and aim of the lives of those who form the majority of the inhabitants—gambling. Resident sporting-men from the clubs, outsiders of regular gambling-houses, rich young rakes and spendthrifts, sporting-men, (turfmen) from the south, with here and there a pigeon in the process of being plucked, fill almost every room. In every one it is the same. The hour is propitious, and the establishment is in the height of its operations. Room after room, story after story, from the second to the sixth, we see nothing but knots of three or four—sometimes only two—bending closely over a little table and watching the turn of the cards. There is no faro here; nothing but euchre, brag and poker. The latter, under the name of bluff, has been and will probably be for all time the favorite game with the southerners, who never feel so happy as when they can succeed in "bluffing" somebody off. The sums staked here are not generally large, and the gambling is mostly among fellow craftsmen, merely for necessary excitement and to keep their hands in. Once in a while, however, they get hold of a green one and show him the elephant, to the very last whisk of his tail.

You would very naturally take it for granted that these men were all avaricious and that money was their sole object in life. This, however, is far from being true. Take them anywhere away from the gambling-table or the race-course and they are free-handed and free-hearted fellows—always ready to assist a friend—or a stranger—and, with the exception of the vices of gambling and Bayaderism, altogether preferable characters to many who stand far above them on the social ladder. It is for the *excitement* that they play—excitement, without which they are as completely unnerved and prostrated as the drunkard deprived of his dram or the opium-eater of his pill. In the course of the year a man in this profession wins and loses many thousands—but he generally comes out in the end pretty much as if he had not played at all: while the poor dupes who only occasionally play, are stripped as completely as the traveler who fell among thieves, and seldom are so fortunate as to have any good Samaritan pass that way.

But we are not philosophizing to-night; and leaving our friends to their bluff and brag, we will cross over through this dark and dismal-looking street, toward the Bowery. The lights have just been extinguished in the theater and most of the glaring shops, cellars and coffee-houses in that region have closed their shutters—although through the half-open door streams a brandy-colored light, mingled with the sound of loud talking, laughter and blasphemy, showing that some knot of the Bowery aristocracy still remains to be untied. Here is an establishment, however, a little more *recherché,* and better worth the costly hours between the noon and dusk of night. It is a noted raffling shop, where the pretense is poultry and the real business gambling for money. It is true that there is a lot of poultry hanging about the dark and unfurnished room, and lying heaped up at the far end of the long deal table that runs through the apartment like a tailor's shop-board. But the real business of the players, who crowd around this table, is the betting on numbers and buying chances, which is carried on pretty extensively, considering the means of those principally engaged in it. We know an intellectual and gifted man who night after night neglects his wife and children to visit this miserable hole and lose his earnings among these coarse and ruffianly fellows. He naturally detests liquor; but whenever he has had an unusually bad night of it—and he sometimes loses an entire week's salary before going home after receiving it—he grows desperately remorseful, and to forget the stings of conscience gets beastly drunk and is a maniac for three or four days. Attempts have been made to break up this and other establishments somewhat similar—but it is "only for a little poultry"—"just by way of passing the evening"—and thus ends the investigation, while the game goes on brisker than ever. As to the poultry, we seldom hear of any body bringing much of it away with him—while every one who goes there is very likely to turn out a "gone goose."

If you would know what Mike Walsh means by his "underground democracy," you must visit the raffling and gambling establishments a little lower down.[8] These where we are must be considered the aristocracy, the "upper ten" of Bowerydom. Their shirts are brighter red, their panties wider round the bottom and their cigars cocked more sharply toward their noses, than the slier, sulkier and more desperate characters who compose the rank and file of the fierce democracie. Hereafter we will pay our respects to them in their pleasant midnight haunts. Now the night grows old and gray and we are weary.

8. Mike Walsh was one of New York's most radical and colorful politicians. Founder of the Spartan Association as an institutional base for Bowery workingmen within the Democratic party, and editor of a radical newspaper entitled the *Subterranean* (hence the reference to "underground democracy"), Walsh maintained for more than a decade a highly visible and unrelentingly vituperative assault on capitalism and "wage slavery." He was elected in 1846 to the New York State Assembly, and in 1852 to the United States Congress, where he served one term.

No. VI

Butter-Cake Dick's

*The Press—The Newsboys—Mark
Maguire—Mike Madden—Pat Lyons—Tommy
Ryan—Sunday Night with the Newsboys—The
Trade in Newspapers*

To-night we shall introduce you to some very distinguished company, dear reader, and we expect you to comport yourself accordingly. Hitherto we have had to do with classes of obscure individuals, important only from their extent and the illegal, subversive character of their lives and actions. But now we go into more distinguished and pretentious circles—now we penetrate to the aristocratic regions of intellect and trench upon the haunts of those awful personages whose movements move the hearts of millions and whose voices agitate communities by the slightest syllables.

All know and understand the power of the Press in this country, and, more and more, throughout the world. But few, except those actually engaged in the business of journalism, know much about the most important and active agent in supplying the world with intelligence—the Newsboy. Much has been written, by green paragraphists in want of a subject, about the newsboy, at which he himself has been the first to laugh—but few who buy his ephemeral wares, or are awakened from their Sunday morning nap by his voice crying the "Sunday Atlas, Mercury and Times— Sunday 'Erld, Dispatch and Cooryer!" have ever given themselves the trouble to inquire into his history—to follow him to his nightly haunts and sit with him in his "hour of secure ease." This is the labor of love that the writer of these sketches has taken delight in performing; and he feels some pride in presenting the present sketch as an authentic record of a class of incipient humans quite characteristic of the present age, and who are already beginning to disappear. In the natural course of events, the News *boy* will grow up into the News *man*, and the race of merry juvenile rogues whose voices now echo through the pit of the Olympic—who are always first at a fire or a fight, and are "some pumkins" at a horse-race—who "holler" on regattas and know the points and speed of every yacht and row-boat in the river better than its owner or the man at the helm—who are as brave as they are mischievous, and always "go in," even when they know they will be "squeezed"—will become extinct.

Perhaps it will be the best way to accomplish our purpose to go at once into the midst of things, and sketch individuals and groups from nature. An hour at "Butter-cake Dick's," near midnight, will tell us more about the Newsboy than we could learn in a month elsewhere. "Where and what is Butter-cake Dick's?" do you ask? Follow us and you shall learn. Do you see that bright camphene-drummond light stuck against the wall over the entrance to a cellar in Spruce street just below the Tribune office? That is an underground newsboy's eating-house, kept by a good-natured, shrewd, retired member of the craft, whose only present name is Dick, for he has superadded the epithet "Butter-cake" to his Christian, now become surname, by reason of dispensing to his customers a peculiar sort of heavy biscuit with a lump of butter in its belly, and which is technically

termed a "butter-cake." The price of this nutritious and unc-
tuous commodity is three cents, including a cup of coffee;
pies being held at four cents the biggest kind of a slice, and
dough-nuts, of the size and hardness of ebony walking-
sticks, being consumed in any quantities at a cent a piece.
The great staple of the establishment, however,—as its name
indicates,—is butter-cakes. These are always hot and always
ready, with the butter dripping at the edges where the severed halves have been put together, and the outside surfaces
crisp and blackened, as if they had been lying for a long
time on a hot tin for the purpose of being kept warm.

The great merit of this establishment is that it is kept
open all night; and when less enterprising caterers to the
demands of the human stomach are abed and asleep, probably dreaming of gigantic puddings and impossible pies,
Buttercake Dick stands all night long behind his little plebe-
ian counter, dispensing cups of steaming coffee and plates of
the inevitable buttercakes to his hungry and impatient customers. At the cherry tables which line both sides of the
room are seated the aristocratic boys, who, having already
done a sufficient business for the day at sundown, cease
their lung-distending occupation and start for the theater.
Some go to the Olympic, some to the Chatham, and others
do the grand and visit the Bowery to see "Jim Wallack in
Warwick." Some time about midnight they all meet here,
and after indulging in the conventional luxury of butter-
cakes and coffee, compare notes of their evening's employments and exchange criticisms upon the performances they
have witnessed.

But a party grouped round a table in the corner nearest
the bar deserves a more particular notice than we have time
to bestow on the οἱ πολλοί[9] of the room, who, settling for
their cakes and coffee with a truly lordly air of ostentation,
mingling their conversation with innumerable and superflu-
ous oaths, and sticking the largest and rankest kind of

9. Hoi polloi, or the masses.

American cigars into their mouths, issue up into the street for the purpose of "setting the town to rights." The party we have mentioned is composed of the great notabilities of the News-boy profession—once boys in fact, now men, and stout ones too—heads of families and altogether persons of note and respectability, but who still go by their old newsboy names, and on rare occasions, as at present, grace the scene of their former pleasures with their presence. It is seldom, however, that you are as lucky as we, and can catch them all together.

At the head of the table, his face resting contemplatively on his hand, sits Mark Maguire, long known and celebrated as the "King of the Newsboys." He commenced a poor, friendless and ragged little urchin, buying his two or three copies of the old *Sun*, and when he had sold them, going back and investing both capital and profit in another purchase. Wind and sunshine, rain and hail, winter and summer, found the little Mark urgently pursuing his occupation—always ready for a frolic or a row, but always in moderation, and never losing his eye from the main chance. A few years of this kind of thing of course wrought their inevitable result. From a newsboy he became a speculator; and, having credit with all the publishers, bought up large numbers of papers at a trifle below the rate when they were doled out by dozens, and soon surrounded himself with his hundreds of ragged little satellites—supplying them at the usual rates, and at the same time making a handsome profit for himself. Step after step rose the shrewd and patient speculator; until now that white-faced, impassive young man, not yet twenty-five, commands thousands whenever he wishes, owns house and lot, wife and children,—drives his "fast nag" on the avenue, and is considered good authority in matters of dispute among his neighbors. His ward have strong thoughts of running him for alderman; and we sincerely trust they will. Not half nor a quarter of those sent to the City Hall are half so deserving of the confidence of their fellow-citizens, nor half so able to legislate for the benefit of the city, as Mark Maguire the King of the Newsboys.

At the right hand of royalty sits his great rival and emulator, "Mike Madden," from whose garret-chamber in Ann street is disseminated to the two or three hundred newsboys of the metropolis that immense mass of nonsense, wit, originality, trash and obscenity circulating through all classes of the community under the generic title of the "weekly press." Mike's history is very much the same as that of King Mark, although the intellectual and moral calibre of the man is not so great. Like Mark, he is a son of the "gem of the say," and like him he has worked his way gradually up from ragged poverty to competence and respectability. For many years Mike supported his mother, brothers and sisters, from the profits of his business; but recently he has cut the maternal mansion and got married. The old lady, however, drives a good business by sub-letting nearly all the bill-posting of the weekly papers, and is in reality no longer in need of Mike's friendly aid.

In person Mike is the antithesis of Mark. Mike is long and slender—Mark is short and chubby; Mike is eager and restless—Mark is immovable and steady as marble; Mike swears a little, smokes a good deal and drinks some—Mark swears only when a good deal "put upon," drinks very sparingly and smokes only for company. Both, however, are right down good fellows, as the world goes, and deserve all the success that has attended their efforts to elbow their way through this cold, dreary and inhospitable life. With all the roughness and sometimes cruelty of their somewhat savage natures, we yield them our respect—for, without those advantages of guardianship, education and exemption from over-labor, which so many thousands abuse and throw away, they have made themselves an honest name and the certainty of a respectable and comfortable existence to their wives and families. How many, with every chance in their favor, have done infinitely worse!

Below Mike Madden is another tight Irish lad, possessing in a far greater degree the characteristics which most strongly mark his countrymen than either of the others. He is a rollicking, aisy-going boy, is Pat Lyons, and a universal favorite. He is very short and very stout—almost dwarfish in point of altitude, but the "divil for breadth and bottom"—while the lady rejoicing in the name of Mrs. Patrick Lyons, is very tall, and of a most majestic carriage. It is the general practice of Pat's associates, whenever they see him, to inquire,

"Well, Pat, how's your wife?"

"Sound as a drum, be J——!"

Patrick has not been quite so successful in laying up and investing his earnings as his two friends and patrons just described—but then his expenses have been much heavier, and a great allowance is to be made on that account. Mrs. Lyons has already presented him with half-a-dozen or more young lions and lionesses, and we believe there are strong hopes that she will still farther contribute to the native population of her adopted country ere that period so much dreaded by women and old bachelors—the grand climacteric, which renders them both past bearing—shall have arrived.

Opposite is another familiar face in Newsboydom—the jovial and modest-looking Tommy Ryan. He is a sort of assistant of Mike's, his indomitable good nature preventing him from laying a straw in any body's way by competition. He is a more amiable and finer-strung character than either of the others, and therefore by no means calculated to succeed so well in the world. He has, however, lots of friends and good ones; and with the boys he is emphatically "cock of the walk." He is a good-looking lad, too, and we will lay a handsome wager that all his sons (for he too has a wife) will be Whigs.

It is fortunately Saturday night, and we shall have an admirable opportunity for seeing the newsboys in all their glory. In half an hour the steam-presses will begin to work off the sixty or seventy thousand Sunday papers which will be distributed through every quarter of the city before breakfast. The party at Butter-cake Dick's has just broken up, and King Mark takes his departure homeward—his business being confined exclusively to the daily papers, and he never on any pretense interfering with the weekly and Sunday press, which belong legitimately and entirely to Mike Madden, Pat Lyons and Tommy Ryan. The method of transacting these newspaper sales is well worth describing, and will be perhaps interesting to those who sleep soundly and dream sweetly while it is going on, and wake only to find the welcome newspaper, still damp with the perspiration of its speed, ready to their hands.

Every paper of anything like a respectable circulation has its own list of regular carriers,—generally respectable men, engaged during the week in other occupations. They settle weekly or monthly with the publishers, and absolutely own the routes they serve, having purchased them at a rate of from one to three hundred dollars, or gotten them up gradually by their own exertions. These of course are entitled to their papers first; and as fast as the press can throw them off the carriers take them to the folding-boards and prepare for an early serving of their routes. During this time the newsboys are dozing in the corner of the press-room, in dry-goods boxes or under entries, or perhaps in the cellar where their parents "stay." But the busy yet sleepy clink-clank of the press at length brings the time to one o'clock, and the newsboys begin to show signs of life. In a few minutes Nassau street swarms with the rough and ready little philosophers, somewhat out of humor with their interrupted nap, and every one determined to be served first or die. Mike and his fellow wholesale dealers have provided themselves with the various papers by the thousands—paying one dollar and seventy-five cents per hundred and receiving two dollars from the newsboys. The trade, however, between themselves and the boys whom you hear crying the papers through the streets, is not direct. The spirit of mercantile exploitation and multiplied profit-makers pervades in full force the business of selling newspapers. The principal speculators sell to about twenty sub-speculators, who pay two dollars a hundred and sell them again to the street-boys for two shillings a dozen, "full change," as they call it—that is, exacting full two pennies instead of two cents for each paper, thus making four per cent on their capital. In this way—small as their profit appears—some of these sub-speculators do a very good business—of course taking good care not to take a five-cent piece and a cent for six-pence, nor a dime and two cents for a shilling, as that would melt the little speculator's profits directly. They have an understanding with Madden by which he takes back all the papers they cannot sell—so that they never get "stuck," as is sometimes the case with the street-boys, and even with the principal speculators themselves.

Butter-cake Dick, of course, has not been idle nor extravagant during the years that he has been the sole proprietor of this newspaper head-quarters—where, late at night may be seen, beside the newsboys, the editors, subs and reporters of the neighboring morning paper offices; and the consequence is that while they remain for the most part as poor and pauperous as when they set out, Buttercake Dick, once beyond the precincts of his dingy cellar, takes the cognomen of Richard Marshall, Esq., cocks his hat on one side and points his cigar toward his nose, like a regular b'hoy; and if he sees any body whom he thinks is looking sharp at him, inquires of him, in a voice as gentle as a sucking bear's, whether he wishes to kick up a muss, and whether he is not of the opinion that Richard Marshall, Esq., is some pumpkins.

No. VII

The Points At Midnight

Irish immigs

*The Core of Civilization—The "Old
Brewery"—Regent's Park—Cow Bay—The
Fences—Wholesale and Retail
Warehouse—Facts Respecting the Reform
of Courtezans*

Thomas Carlyle, the great Scotchman, looked up to the
starry midnight and exclaimed with a groan, "'Tis a sad
sight!" What would have been his exclamation had he stood,
reader, where you and I now stand—in the very center of
the "Five Points,"—knowing the moral geography of the
place,—and with that same midnight streaming its glories
down upon his head! *This* is, indeed, a sad, an awful sight—
a sight to make the blood slowly congeal and the heart to
grow fearful and cease its beatings. Here, whence these
streets diverge in dark and endless paths, whose steps take
hold on hell—here is the very type and physical semblance,
in fact, of hell itself. Moralists no longer entertain a doubt
that the monster vice of humanity is licentiousness—the
vice teeming with destruction and annihilation to the race
itself—pervading all classes,—inextinguishable either by re-
pressive laws or by considerations of personal safety.

The question how to recombine the elements of society so as to do away with this frightful evil, and thus at one blow abolish half the crime and horror of life, is not to be discussed in these pages—nor perhaps has the time yet arrived for discussing it at all. At any rate, before it is or can be profitably debated, we must be fully in possession of all the *facts* evolved from the present social relations, and must be enabled to view licentiousness and prostitution in all their aspects. It is mainly for this purpose that the present book is written: and to avoid the dryness of mere statistic or the tedious pomposity of a parliamentary report, we have chosen to throw the result of our observations into a series of pen and ink pictures, which will interest while they instruct.

So, then, we are standing at midnight in the center of the Five Points. Over our heads is a large gas-lamp, which throws a strong light for some distance around, over the scene where once complete darkness furnished almost absolute security and escape to the pursued thief and felon, familiar with every step and knowing the exits and entrances to every house. In those days an officer, even with the best intentions, was often baffled at the very moment when he thought he had his victim most secure. Some unexpected cellar-door, or some silent-sliding panel, would suddenly receive the fugitive and thwart the keenest pursuit. Now, however, the large lamp is kept constantly lighted, and a policeman stands ever sentinel to see that it is not extinguished. The existence of this single lamp has greatly improved the character of the whole location and increased the safety of going through the Points at night. Those, however, whose purposes are honest, had better walk a mile round the spot, on their way home, than cross through.

Opposite the lamp, eastwardly, is the "Old Brewery"—a building so often described that it has become as familiar as the Points themselves—in print. We will not, therefore, attempt another description of that which has already been so well depicted. The building was originally, previous to the city being built up so far, used as a brewery. But when the population increased and buildings, streets and squares grew up and spread out all around it, the owner—shrewd man, and very respectable church deacon—found that he might make a much larger income from his brewery than by retaining it for the manufacture of malt liquor. It was accordingly floored and partitioned off into small apartments, and rented to persons of disreputable character and vile habits, who had found their inevitable way gradually from the "Golden Gate of Hell," through all the intermediate haunts of prostitution and drunkenness, down to this hell-like den—little less dark, gloomy and terrible than the grave itself, to which it is the prelude. Every room in every story has its separate family or occupant, renting by the week or month and paying in advance. In this one room, the cooking, eating and sleeping of the whole family, and their visitors, are performed. Yes—*and their visitors*: for it is no unusual thing for a mother and her two or three daughters—all of course prostitutes—to receive their "men" at the same time and in the same room—passing in and out and going through all the transactions of their hellish intercourse, with a sang froid at which devils would stand aghast and struck with horror.

All the houses in this vicinity, and for some considerable distance round—yes, every one—are of the same character, and are filled in precisely the same manner. The lower stories are usually occupied as drinking and dancing rooms; and here, soon as evening sets in, the inmates of the house, dressed in most shocking immodesty, gather. The bar sends forth its poisonous steam—the door is flung wide open, if the weather will permit it; and the women, bare-headed, bare-armed and bare-bosomed, stand in the doorway or on the side-walk, inviting passers-by, indiscriminately, to enter, or exchanging oaths and obscenity with the inmates of the next house, similarly employed. The walkers in these haunts are mostly sailors, negroes and the worst of loafers and vagabonds, who are enticed and perhaps even dragged in by the painted Jezebels, made to "treat," and then invited to the dance—every room being provided with its fiddler, ready to tune up his villainous squeaking for sixpence a piece and a treat at the end of the figure. The liquor is of course of the most abominable description, poison and fire; and by the time the first dance is concluded, the visitor feels his blood on fire—all his brutal appetites are aroused, and he is ready for any thing. The first object is to produce stupifying intoxication. More drinking is proposed—then more dancing—then drink, and so on, until the poor victim loses what little human sense and precaution he is endowed withal, and hurries his partner off in a paroxysm of drunken lust. Of course if he has any money or valuables on his person he is completely robbed. If his clothes are decent they are stripped off him and a pair of tattered trowsers put on, when he is kicked into the street by a back door, and found by the policemen just in time for the loafer's reveillé at the Tombs, at day-light. Sometimes the victim is not quite so drunk as is supposed, and doesn't submit quietly to the touching operation. Another glass—or if he refuses, a good "punch" on the head—settles the question for him, with speediest logic, and the problem is solved at once.

In the cellars of these houses are the "oyster saloons," &c. &c. for the accommodation of thieves, burglars, low gamblers and vagabonds in general, who haunt these quarters, and whose "pals" are up-stairs carrying on the game of prostitution. They are usually kept open nearly all night, because the population forming the principal class of their customers burrow in their secret holes and dens all day, and only venture out at night. Indeed, this is mostly true of all the inhabitants in this region. They are the obscene nightbirds who flit and howl and hoot by night, and whose crimes and abominations make them shun the light of day—nor merely because they fear detection, but because day is hateful to them. Dropping in from their expeditions of the night—some from picking pockets at the theaters, some from general prowling after what they can pick up about town, and others from more important and regularly-ordered expeditions of robbery or burglary or arson,—they recognize each other with a sullen nod or gather in noisy riot, as the humor takes them. If a stranger enter, they immediately reconnoiter, and if they conclude that he is worth picking, they immediately commence their game. The most usual one is to get up a pretended dispute and call upon the stranger to decide. Often card-tricks or thimbles are introduced, and the conspirators bet carelessly and largely against each other—pulling out and showing pocket-books well crammed with counterfeit or worthless bills. If the stranger is not fully aware of the character of those among whom he has fallen, he is a "goner." If none of the ordinary tricks will answer, as a last resource they get up a sham row and fight, in the course of which general scramble the pigeon is pretty sure of being plucked to the last feather, and most likely left bleeding and senseless in the street.

Leading off easterly from the big gas-lamp we have mentioned, is a little three-cornered piece of ground about the size of a village potato-patch, enclosed in whitewashed palings, containing half-a-dozen stunted trees. This is the "Regent's Park" of that neighborhood, and the walk by which it is surrounded is continually crowded in pleasant evenings by couples chaffering and carrying on their infamous bargains—reminding one of the reverse of rural life with all its innocent blandishments and moonlight love-walks beneath the whispering trees. Indeed throughout the entire realm of metropolitan degradation one is incessantly struck with the ghastly resemblances to the forms of virtue and purity, everywhere starting out before him. There is no virtue nor innocence of a beauteous life which is not reflected in the dark sea of licentiousness and dissipation—though in an inverted position, like the images of green shores and pleasant trees in the turbid waters of the wild-rolling river.

A few steps from the Points is a little alley terminating in a blind court or *cul-de-sac*, into which is constantly pouring a stream of mephitic air which never finds an outlet nor an escape, save into the lungs of those who inhale it. This alley is called "Cow Bay," and is chiefly celebrated in profane history as being the battle-field of the negroes and police. Of course the negroes form a large and rather controlling portion of the population of the Points, as they bear brutalization better than the whites, (probably from having been so long used to it!) and retain more consistency and force of character, amid all their filth and degradation. They manage, many of them, to become house-keepers and landlords, and in one way and another scrape together a good deal of money. They associate upon at least equal terms with the men and women of the parish, and many of them are regarded as desirable companions and lovers by the "girls." They most of them have either white wives or white mistresses, and sometimes both; and their influence in the community is commanding. But they are savage, sullen, reckless dogs, and are continually promoting some "muss" or other, which not unfrequently leads to absolute riot. Two memorable occasions, at least, have recently occurred in which "Cow Bay" was rendered classic ground by the set fights which took place within its purlieus between the police and the fighting-men among the Ethiopian tribes. Both commenced at dusk and lasted for over an hour,—giving occasion for the display of individual prowess and feats of arms before which the Chronicles of the veracious Froissart sink into insignificance. But as we do not aspire to the historian's bays, we must leave the details to the imagination of our readers, in the good old-fashioned way of those who attempt a description to which their powers are unequal. It is related, however, that the police were for a long time unable to make headway against the furious onslaught of the blacks, who received the official clubs so liberally rattled about their heads, without flinching, and returned the charge with stones and brickbats, so gallantly that several of the protectors of the city had already knocked under, and the whole body began actually to give way—when the renowned Captain Smith bethought him that Cuffee's tender point was not the head, but the SHIN. Passing the word in a whisper to his men to strike low, he himself aimed a settler at the understandings of a gigantic negro who led the assault upon his wing, and brought him instantly, with a terrific yell of agony, to the ground. A shout of triumph, and a simultaneous movement of the police, as if they were mowing, soon decided the contest, and covered the shores and gutters of "Cow Bay" with the sprawling forms of the tender-shinned Africans. Once afterward the very same thing happened, with precisely similar results: and since, the woolly-heads are kept in tolerable subjection. If they ever become troublesome let but a policeman grasp his club tightly and take aim at the shins, and the ground is cleared in a twinkling.

Another peculiar and description-worthy feature of the Five Points are the "fences," or shops for the reception and purchase of stolen goods. These shops are of course kept entirely by Jews, and are situated in a row, in Orange street, near the Points. One who has never seen the squalid undercrust of a fine city would be at a loss to derive any adequate idea, even from the most graphic description, of the sort of building in which the great business of living and trafficking *can* be carried on. If the reader is a farmer, however, we shall succeed tolerably well in conveying some notion of what we mean. Let him imagine forty or fifty cow-sheds got together in line, furnished with dismal-looking little windows, half broken in and patched up with old newspapers— let him imagine half a hundred of these establishments, we say, standing in a row, with a dark paved street and an uneven narrow brick sidewalk in front, and he will not be far behind the reality of the place where we now stand.

These beggarly little shanties all have pretensions to being considered shops, and in each the front window is heaped up with an indiscriminate indescribableness of wares. Here is a drug-store, with a big bottle of scarlet water in the window, throwing a lurid glare out into the dark. The next is a clothing-store, another hardware, another gentlemen's furnishing, &c. &c. They are all, however, devoted to the one branch of trade, in all its varieties—the purchase of stolen goods. Whatever may be the sign in the window, the thief who has grabbed a watch, prigged a handkerchief or robbed a store, brings his booty confidently in and receives his money for it. Perhaps not at a very high figure— but then, you know "de peoplesh ish very poor in dis neighborhood, and we can't kif much—and besides we don't really want 'em at all." The felon, of course, anxious to have them off his hands, sells them at any price. Whatever may be the article purchased, the first care is naturally to destroy its identity, rub out its ear-marks, and thus prepare it against being claimed by the owner and the purchase of stolen goods fastened upon the "fence." If it is a coat or garment of any kind, the seams are carefully ripped open, the facings, linings, &c. &c. changed, and the whole hastily stitched together again and disposed to the best advantage on the shelves or in the window. If the article purchased is jewelry, it is immediately melted, and converted into bullion,—the precious stones, if there be any, carefully put aside. The most troublesome and dangerous articles are watches—and these the "fence" generally hesitates to have anything to do with, recommending his customer to the pawn-broker, who usually is not much less a rascal than himself. From particular customers, however, whose delicate organizations and long experience render them peculiarly successful in the watch business, the "fence" is willing to receive these dainty wares—although at a terrible sacrifice, and even then never keeping them on hand longer than is necessary to get safely to the pawn-broker's.

In the rear of each of these squalid shops is a wretched apartment or two, combining the various uses of sleeping, eating, cooking and living, with the other performances necessary for carrying on the operations of the front shop. They are generally densely inhabited—the descendants of Israel being as celebrated for fecundity as cats or Irish women. And here it is proper to state one of the most remarkable facts we have encountered in the course of our metropolitan investigations. However low the grade or wretched the habitation—and the latter are generally filthy to abomination—of the Jew, the race always retains the peculiar physical conformation constituting that peculiar style of beauty for which his tribe has been celebrated from remotest antiquity. The roundness and suppleness of limb, the elasticity of flesh, the glittering eye-sparkle—are as inevitable in Jew or Jewess, in whatever rank of existence, as the hook of the nose which betrays the Israelite as the human kite, formed to be feared, hated and despised, yet to prey upon mankind.

We could not expect to convey any tolerable idea of the Five Points were we to omit all attempt at describing one of their most remarkable and characteristic features—the great wholesale and retail establishment of Mr. Crown, situated on the corner opposite "Cow Bay." A visit of exploration through this place we regard as one of our most noteworthy experiences in life. The building itself is low and mean in appearance, although covering a good deal of ground. It contains three low stories—the upper one being devoted to the same species of life and traffic as all the other houses in the neighborhood. It is with the two lower stories, however, that we have at present to do—these being occupied as the store. The entrance is on both streets; and, although entirely unobstructed by any thing but the posts that sustain the walls above, it is not without difficulty that we effect an entrance, through the baskets, barrels, boxes, Irish women and sluttish house-keepers, white, black, yellow and brown, thickly crowding the walk, up to the very threshold—as if the store were too full of its commodities and customers, and some of them had tumbled and rolled out-doors. On either hand piles of cabbages, potatoes, squashes, egg-plants, tomatoes, turnips, eggs, dried apples, chesnuts and beans rise like miniature mountains round you. At the left hand as you enter is a row of little boxes, containing anthracite and charcoal, nails, plug-tobacco, &c. &c. which are dealt out in any quantity, from a bushel or a dollar to a cent's-worth. On a shelf near by is a pile of firewood, seven sticks for sixpence, or a cent apiece, and kindling-wood three sticks for two cents. Along the walls are ranged upright casks containing lamp-oil, molasses, rum, whisky, brandy, and all sorts of cordials, (carefully manufactured in the back room, where a kettle and furnace, with all the necessary instruments of spiritual devilment, are provided for the purpose.) The cross-beams that support the ceiling are thickly hung with hams, tongues, sausages, strings of onions, and other light and airy articles, and at every step you tumble over a butter-firkin or a meal-bin. Across one end of the room runs a "long, low, black" counter, armed at either end with bottles of poisoned firewater, doled out at three cents a glass to the loafers and bloated women who frequent the place—while the shelves behind are filled with an uncatalogueable jumble of candles, allspice, crackers, sugar and tea, pickles, ginger, mustard, and other kitchen necessaries. In the opposite corner is a shorter counter filled with three-cent pies, mince, apple, pumpkin and custard—all kept smoking hot—where you can get a cup of coffee with plenty of milk and sugar, for the same price, and buy a hat-full of "Americans with Spanish wrappers" for a penny.

Groping our way through the back room where the furnace and other machineries are kept—and which may be appropriately termed the laboratory of the concern—we mount a short ladder, and squeeze our way amid piles of drying tobacco, cigar-boxes, tubs, buckets, bales and bundles, of all imaginable shapes and uses, into a little room, similarly filled, but in a corner of which room has been dug for a single cot, upon which lie a heap of rags that evidently have never been washed nor disturbed since they were first slept under, save by the nightly crawlings in and out of the clerk of the premises, and the other inhabitants. Here too is a diminutive iron safe, containing the archives and valuables of the establishment—perhaps silver spoons, rings, watches, and other similar properties—who knows?

One thing is at least certain—the proprietor of this store has amassed a large fortune in a few years, by the immense per centage of profit realized on his minute sales. His customers, living literally from hand to mouth, buy the food they eat and even the fire and whisky that warms them, not only from day to day, but literally from hour to hour. Of many commodities a large proportion sticks to the measure, and on others the profit is incredible—often reaching as high as five or six hundred per cent. No credit—not for a moment—is given to any one, and everything is bought for cash and at the cheapest rates and commonest places.

Well—it is nearly dawn, and we might still prolong our stay upon the Points, there being no lack of subjects well worth our investigation and study. But this is enough for once. To-morrow night—should the fancy take us, for we bind ourselves to nothing—we will return and look in at some of the regular dance-houses and public places in this neighborhood—especially the well known "Dickens' Place," kept by Pete Williams, which, like other more aristocratic establishments, was shut up during the summer, "on account of the cholera." Before we leave this dreadful place—at once the nucleus and consummation of prostitution—we will state a fact or two and make a few reflections bearing generally on the subject. The great source whence the ranks of prostitution are replenished is young women from the country, who, seduced and in the way of becoming mothers, fly from home to escape infamy, and rush to the city with anguish and desperation in their hearts. Either murdering their infants as soon as born, or abandoning them upon a doorstep, they are thenceforth ready for any course of crime that will procure them a living,—or, if they still have struggling scruples, necessity soon overcomes them. As an instance of this we were recently informed of a case where thirteen unmarried mothers came from Canada to New York a few weeks before their confinement, and were all sent to the Asylum. Of these thirteen poor, deserted, heart-broken creatures, eleven are now inhabitants of the Five Points or the immediate neighborhood. How has society punished the respectable seducers and destroyers of these women?

Another fact is that those who once enter into this diabolical traffic are seldom saved. The poison is active as lightning, and produces a kind of moral insanity, during which the victim is pleased with ruin and rejects the hand outstretched to save her. We have avoided no pains nor labor in our researches on this subject, and we wish all virtuous and benevolent men and women to mark well our words:—After a woman once enters a house of prostitution and leads the life of all who dwell there, *it is too late*. The woman is transformed to a devil and there is no hope for her. There may be, and doubtless are, exceptions to this rule, but we are convinced they must be rare. When a woman has once nerved herself to make the fatal plunge, a change comes over her whole character; and sustained by outraged love transmuted to hate, by miscalculating yet indomitable pride, by revenge, and by a reckless abandonment to the unnatural stimulus and excitement of her new profession, her fate is fixed. Take heed, then, philanthropists, and fathers and mothers, and husbands, whose wives and daughters have drank deeply of that damning draught of ambition for dress and display, that makes so many prostitutes! Expend all your watchfulness and tenderness and care upon your charges *before* they fall. Lay open to them with a bold and faithful hand the horrors of the career which lies before them, unless they learn to unlearn vanity and to learn content. For one whose hair is gray, and whose heart has often and often bled for grief at sight of so many beautiful creatures wrecked and cast away forever, in the wild pursuit after admiration, tells you that vanity and a love for social distinction are the rocks upon which these noble vessels, freighted with the wealth of immortal souls, have foundered. Strive, oh young woman! whose heart pants with envy at the gay equipages and fine dresses of the more fortunate or more guilty sisters who glitter by you—strive to win to your bosoms the sweet and gentle goddess Content. So shall memory and hope embalm your life and time shall crown you alone with blessings.

No. VIII

The Ice-Creameries

*A Streak of Sunshine—The Fashionable Lunch
for Upper Tendom—Well-Known
Characters—The Steam
Ice-Creamery—Contoit's*

A fit of sunshine is upon the earth, and the city lies bathed
in a sea of flashing light, whose sparkling foam penetrates
to the innermost chambers of life. Let us also escape for a
time from darkness and the lurid glare of gas-light. The
darkest pictures (excepting one particularly dark one by
Mr. ———) require here and there a "spark" of light to set
them off and bring out their gloomy beauties to advantage.
Pen and ink, too, need this relief, as well as pencil and pal-
ette; and we paper-stainers have this advantage—that we
can keep on good terms with our audience by letting them
into the secret of all our little tricks as we go along. Sometimes, it is true, our foolscap grows dim and dingy in the
light of the gas-burner at our head, and the midnight traces
of our pen go wide and weary, like the footsteps of an over-
traveled pilgrim. Yet after all, these inky pictures, if but

truly drawn, go to many a heart untouched by picture, music-burst or dramatic heart-history enacted before the eyes. Though sometimes we may sigh for the brilliancy and softness of colors, or the grace of form and outline—for the panting tones of music or the terrifying energy of the drama, yet after all we would not exchange this little, golden-pointed wand, (they used to be of goosequill,) with fitting skill to wield it and command the genii who are its slaves, for the highest gift of art.

We will step aside from the gay and motley procession in Broadway, and enter this fashionable ice-creamery, where we shall find some dainty amusement to embellish this glorious October day withal. We pass between two long counters laden with fruits, cakes, confectionery and all sorts of knick-knackery—behind one of which stand three or four grisette-looking girls, jauntily dressed and evidently as jauntily disposed. Mounting a couple of steps, we enter a long room, filled with little tables, at almost every one of which people are seated, and nearly all of them are ladies. The room is darkened—ladies love such subdued atmospheres, unless they are very young and handsome—and our eyes are not yet enough accustomed to it to take in the details of the scene. We will order a *meringue à la crème* while our pupils are contracting. You see we have an extensive bill of fare here—ice cream—oysters, stewed, fried and broiled;—broiled chickens, omelettes, sandwiches; boiled and poached eggs; boiled ham; beef-steak, coffee, chocolate, toast and butter—our fine ladies who visit here between their shopping calls, their visitations or their millineryings, are not likely to go hungry for want of a substantial lunch, any more than their lords and masters down town, who bolt beef and potatoes at Brown's or even dine at Delmonico's. If you take a sly glance at the plates of these delicate customers, or listen a moment to the low-voiced orders entrusted confidentially to the waiters, you will see that ladies have appetites and stomachs as well as the rest of creation. Indeed, we have sometimes thought that Othello must have been troubled with the dyspepsia and envious of the digestion of the gentle Desdemona, when he exclaimed—

> ————————oh curse of marriage,
> That we can call these delicate creatures ours,
> And not their appetites!

The great bulk of the company here is too correct and commonplace to require much notice—for, however commendable and admirable we all admit decorous virtue to be, yet it is certain that it lacks those piquant peculiarities requisite to popularity. Of the few women and many men whom we have known who were really popular, scarcely one had a whole armor. Fat wives of lean financiers, speculators and tradesmen—we beg pardon, merchant princes—flaunting in scarlet, yellow, blue and green, whose pride is in their cashmeres and carriages, and whose flirtations are limited to disputes with the clerks at Beck's or Stewart's—these form the staple of the guests. Here and there, however, are a couple of tender doves sweetening the cream of courtship with Vanilla, or giving a relish to the curdled sentiment of matrimony with lemon essence. Yonder are a middle-aged man and woman in deep and earnest conversation. They are evidently man and wife—though not *each other's*! Should their legitimate spouses suddenly make their appearance, there would be white lips and fearful hearts! They made an appointment at the *soirée* last evening to meet here by accident at noon to-day and discuss an ice-cream with Lafayette cake and other confectionery. Broadway is not very far from Mercer street, and there is a dress-maker living in a large, fine house, with whom the lady has sometimes a great deal of business—and, curiously enough, a dentist's sign is also on the front door, which doubtless accounts satisfactorily for the gentleman being seen going in there, as we have often heard him complain of the tooth-ache. How conveniently civilization arranges every thing!

There is a distinguished member of the literati, with a lady at his side, and a light moustache on his lip. The lady has written some exquisite verses for private circulation, and one or two of them, by mere accident, have found their way into the magazine. She was sincerely annoyed at the circumstance—for she has plenty of money, an indulgent husband not given to jealousy, and an unexceptionable position in society. She has plenty of talent and genius to become an eminent blue-stocking, if she chose—but that would upset all her calculations and plans in life. She loves the society of literary men, and could not exist amid the vulgar inanities of mercantile and "fast" men. But if she herself were to become publicly distinguished, her game would be up at once—as she would never stoop to mingle in the miserable jealousies and envies and contentions of literary life. She couldn't do it. As it is, she manages very comfortably—solacing herself for being bored by husband and friends and the tiresome "set" to which she belongs by secret correspondence and stolen interviews with some man of genius—whom she changes, "by mutual consent," at least every six months. Some unsophisticated reader may be shocked at this—but it is a very mild form of the hypocrisy which pervades the fashionable ranks of society; innocence itself compared with many terrible and heart-breaking secrets that might be revealed.

Do you see yonder tall and graceful woman, seated in all the pride of cold dignity with her husband?—yes, he *is* her husband, although he appears quite insignificant beside her. At home she has so well taught him to know his place, that he does not forget the lesson, even sometimes when she would escape mortification if he would not remember it. He looks inquiringly and deferentially into his wife's face, as if ready to start at a moment's warning on any errand she may have for him to do. This is a journalist of some distinction, who at forty married a beautiful woman of twenty-five, whom of course he worshiped. She was ignorant and selfish, though with natural shrewdness enough to hide all deficiencies from her enamored lover's eyes, and to appear to him as something little short of a goddess. Gradually, however, he found that the divinity he had set up was only in his own brain; but he had given himself too entirely to his delusion ever to recover from it, although he knew that he was deceived. His spirit once broken by the pertinacious selfishness of his vulgar-souled partner, he never even struggled in the toils—he had no heart to do it—but went on and on, day after day, toiling and racking his brain all to pieces, to minister as far as he was able to her discontented and imperious wants. He had long ago given up the idea of inspiring her with gratitude or even content. She received whatever he could earn for her, as a matter of course, sometimes in haughty silence, but more frequently with querulous and bitter complaints that it was no more. During the years they have lived irreproachably together—for she is a very moral and conscientious woman!—her mind has been greatly smoothed and developed by contact with that of her husband, but her heart remains the same—cold, impassive, unbending, demanding every thing as a *right*, conceding nothing. To look at her and her husband as they go along Broadway, you would take her for a frigate under full sail, with her cutter in tow. There—she has sent him to Beck's where she has left her parasol; and when he returns and finds a handsome young "friend of the family" seated by his wife's side, he is not a bit jealous, and invites him to dinner with a very sincere cordiality, which the young gentleman accepts with demonstrations of the most unbounded respect. Indeed the scene is quite touching!

But we must leave off character-painting and return to generals. This isn't by any means the only ice-creamery in New York—nor even the only "fashionable" one. Come with us through Leonard street and so along into Pearl, where we can cross over into Chatham Square. There's an ice-cream establishment here that goes by steam! What thinks Bobus of that? Why of course that all the ice-cream made here must be warm!

There is quite a different set of customers at these tables from those we left in Broadway. To reach the saloon, too, we go up a flight of steps—broad and easy, to be sure, yet a flight of steps, notwithstanding; and as such, except in case of a millinery establishment or a shawl loft, of course not to be tolerated in "good society." Underneath our "Patent Steam Ice-Cream Saloon" is a feather-bed warehouse, or something of that kind, which bears off a good two-thirds of the rent. But the "saloon" is quite as spacious, quite as airy and quite as handsomely "got up" as the more exclusive establishment in Broadway. The company, although the bonnets are a little too short and worn rather far back on the head for strict beauty, and shawls and dresses, ribbons and trimmings, may be a little exuberant in color and arrangement, are generally better looking than on the other side of town. There is of course a great deal of humbug and pretense about the superior beauty of the lower classes, opposed as well to the science of human physiology as it is to logic, good sense and actual observation. As a general rule, the "ultimates" of form and feature correspond pretty closely to the station, occupation, mental development and mode of life of their possessor. The helot has the face of a helot, whatever it might be capable of becoming in a few generations of advancing culture; and the snob, the vulgarian, the ignoramus and the outlaw, each carries his name written not only in his face but in every limb and gesture, every movement of his body.

But the company at the Patent Steam Ice-Cream Saloon are neither helots nor shelots, but the wives and daughters of the substantial tradesmen, mechanics and artizans of the city, the great middle class, whose aspirations, reaching the full standard of well-to-do content, wisely fall short of that snobbish longing after social notoriety which so many of their class mistake for exclusiveness and aristocracy. They live easily, but are not ashamed to work and work well. They visit and make feasts and festivals, and have holidays and nights sacred to pleasure. They eat well, sleep well, digest well and have easy consciences and no envy. It is no wonder that, under these circumstances, they are in good condition, and rosy and comfortable. They may not be skilled in French or crochet-work—may not even know a *cadenza* from a *primo basso*—yet they have minds and hearts keen to appreciate and quick to feel; and they are altogether a pleasant sight, this glorious autumn afternoon, sitting at these handsome tables, every matron attended by a "little horde" of hungry expectants, clinging full of hope and confidence to mama's knee—hope that they will get now and then a spoonful of the delicious Patent Steam Ice-Cream, (which after all, dear reader, is *not* warm,)—and confidence that their reasonable expectations will not be disappointed.

There was in old times another ice-creamery which we would have liked right well to show you—but alas! its days and nights are long since over. The American Institute doles out its sermons and squash-seed samples on the spot where once the cream traveled briskly from arbor to arbor, and the "garden" re-echoed to the sounds of hilarity. Who of our readers remembers—or rather, who does not remember— "Contoit's Garden?" Can we ever forget that cream— soft-boiled egg sweetened with brown sugar!—and those iron spoons, which the negro waiter chuckled conventionally over as he deposited your egg-glass of "refreshments" upon the little table—as much as to say, "steal that if you dare!" For many years Contoit's was the great place in Broadway, and was patronized by all the aristocracy, like Taylor's or Thompson & Weller's now. Then it was said to be suspicious; and at last the evenings were monopolized by a class of visitors who generally brought their "spoons" (and very soft ones they mostly were,) along with them. At last, "respectable" people did not like to be seen going there at all, any time of day—and finally the whole concern suddenly disappeared and a great five-story building took its place, like the shifting of scenes in a play: and then everybody wondered for a few days, and talked about the growth of the city, and so forgot all about Contoit and his ice-cream which was not ice-cream, and iron spoons that nobody would carry off wrapped up by mistake in his handkerchief.

There is no lack of ice-cream shops of a lower grade than those of which we have been speaking—where, although the company is not "picked," the pockets of the unwary visitor generally are—and where assignations are made and all other sorts of nefarious traffic carried on. But we have determined that our first "streak" of sunshine shall be unobscured by a cloud; and we will leave all these places—at any rate for the present. We have had—reader, may we speak for you as ourself?—a delightful and not uninteresting ramble; and having discussed the harmonious and refreshing bill of fare at the College Hotel—Sanderson is a poet and his dinners are lyrics with epigrams of dessert[10]—we will renew our tramps by misty gas-light.

10. This is a plug for Foster's landlord. The College Hotel, on Murray Street a block west of Broadway and the City Hall Park, was operated in 1850 by A. A. Sanderson. Foster is listed as a resident of the hotel in *Rode's New York City Directory, for 1850–1851.*

No. IX

The Dance-House

*Pete Williams's, or Dickens's Place—The House
and Cave in Water Street—A Literal
Description—Curious Facts about the
Life of Prostitutes*

It is an especially dark and muggy night, and we could not
wish for a more favorable opportunity of visiting the celebrated dance-house of Pete Williams, known ever since the
visit of a distinguished foreigner to this country, as "Dickens's Place."[11] The old building was burnt down or gutted in
a fire some three or four years ago; but so popular a resort
as this could not remain long unbuilt, and in a few months
it resumed its wonted aspect—though perhaps a trifle
cheerfuler—and reechoed its wonted sounds of festive jolli-
fication. You may have read recently in the newspapers—for
since the telegraph has taken the news out of the inkstands
of the editors, they are turning their attention to all sorts of

11. Charles Dickens described this or a very similar establishment in his *American Notes for General Circulation* (London, 1842),
a highly critical book that won him few friends in the United
States.

abstruse and aesthetic subjects—long and dreary disserta-
tions on architecture, from which you learned exactly all
the writers knew—nothing. But however extensive may have
been your reading or observation on the subject, it would
puzzle you to find an appropriate designation for the style
of architecture in which Dickens's Place is built. The outside
is of boards, discolored in various places and mismatched—
as if they had been gathered together from the remnants of
some pig-pen wrecked in a barn-yard. Jack-plane nor ruler
never violated their mottled surfaces, and as to grooving
and smooth-edging, they are as innocent of it as a wrangling
couple. The door is fastened with a wooden pin stuck in a
hole by the side, like a country stable—although on occasion a stout padlock stands sentry over the premises. But it
is a gala night, and the door is invitingly open—the faithful
pin hanging to its post by a string. We pay a shilling at the
door and enter. No tickets nor presentations are required.
No master of ceremonies tortures you with inconvenient
questions, nor director of the floor struts round with all the
women in the room under his wing, doling them out, one by
one, as he sees fit. You are here—you pay your shilling at
the door—and you are "hunk."

It is Saturday night, and the company begins assembling
early, for Saturday night is a grand time for thieves, loafers,
prostitutes and rowdies, as well as for honest, hard-working
people. Already the room—a large, desolate-looking place,
with white-washed walls garnished with wooden benches—
is half full of men and women, among whom the latter at
this hour predominate. Later there will be pretty nearly a
numerical equilibrium established—for the "friends of the
house" are out in all directions picking up recruits.

In the middle of one side of the room a shammy platform
is erected, with a trembling railing, and this is the "orchestra" of the establishment. Sometimes a single black fiddler
answers the purpose; but on Saturday nights the music
turns out strong, and the house entertains, in addition, a
trumpet and a bass drum. With these instruments you may

imagine that the music at Dickens's Place is of no ordinary
kind. You cannot, however, begin to imagine *what* it is. You
cannot *see* the red-hot knitting-needles spirted out by the
red-faced trumpeter, who looks precisely as if he were blowing glass, which needles aforesaid penetrating the tympa-
num, pierce through and through your brain without
remorse. Nor can you perceive the frightful mechanical con-
tortions of the bass-drummer as he sweats and deals his
blows on every side, in all violation of the laws of rhythm,
like a man beating a baulky mule and showering his blows
upon the unfortunate animal, now on this side, now on that.
If you could, it would be unnecessary for us to write.

Probably three quarters of the women assembled here,
and who frequent this place, are negresses, of various
shades and colors. And the truth compels us to say that, on
the whole, they are more tidy and presentable—or rather
less horribly disgusting—than their white companions.
Such bleared-eyed, idiotic, beastly wretches as these latter it
is difficult to imagine and impossible to describe. The orchestra have taken their places, ready to begin. The "bar" is
crowded by motley and thirsty souls, refreshing themselves
for the severe exercises about to commence, and the ladies
are all agog for the fun to commence. Each gentleman, by a
simultaneous and apparently preconcerted movement, now
"drawrs" his "chawr" of tobacco, and depositing it carefully
in his trowsers pocket, flings his arms about his buxom in-
amorata and salutes her whisky-breathing lips with a chaste
kiss, which extracts a scream of delight from the delicate
creature, something between the whoop of an Indian and
the neighing of a horse. And now the orchestra strikes up
"Cooney in de Holler" and the company "cavorts to places."
Having taken their positions and saluted each other with the
most ludicrous exaggeration of ceremony, the dance proceeds for a few moments in tolerable order. But soon the excitement grows—the dancers begin contorting their bodies
and accelerating their movements, accompanied with shouts
of laughter and yells of encouragement and applause, until

all observance of the figure is forgotten and every one leaps, stamps, screams and hurras on his or her own hook. Affairs are now at their height. The black leader of the orchestra increases the momentum of his elbow and calls out the figure in convulsive efforts to be heard, until shining streams of perspiration roll in cascades down his ebony face; the dancers, now wild with excitement, like Ned Buntline at Astor Place,[12] leap frantically about like howling dervishes, clasp their partners in their arms, and at length conclude the dance in hot confusion and disorder. As soon as things have cooled off a little each cavalier walks up to the bar, pays his shilling for the dance, and the floor is cleared for a new set; and so goes on the night.

In one corner of the dancing-hall is a door leading to a little apartment furnished with some wooden benches and a deal table, answering the compound purposes of committee-room, dressing-and-shawl-room, banquet-hall, and some others of which the muse says nothing. Cold cuts can be had here at almost any price, cash on the nail, and champagne made of very superior pink turnip-juice is kept ready for the upper crust whenever the fun grows fast and furious and those with money have reached the "damn-the-expense stage of excitement."

Beside the b'hoys, members of rowdy clubs and those who "run" with the engines, the dance-house is a favorite resort with sailors ashore, who almost invariably, with that improvidence which marks their character, come with all the money they possess in the world in their pockets, and of course are generally robbed by their partners, whose profession combines theft with something a great deal more infamous. Not unfrequently worse tricks than mere robbery are practised upon these good-natured and unsophisticated

12. Ned Buntline was a leader of the Bowery crowd that marched to the Astor Place Opera House on the evening of May 10, 1849, to protest the continuing performances of the English actor William Macready. Twenty-two people were killed by militia fire in the riot that ensued.

creatures. Being well plied with poisoned liquor, the old hag who happens to be his partner commences making the most outrageous demonstrations of love and tenderness, which end in a proposal of immediate marriage! This startling proposition jumps with the adventurous and excited temper of Jack, exactly. He takes a fresh quid, splices the main-brace, and a magistrate (sometimes a *real* one!) appears, who performs the ceremony and poor Jack is by the enlightened laws of New York the legal husband, protecter and defender of a miserable, rum-and-disease-eaten harridan. The next morning, with the fumes of the liquor dissipated but its sickening poison remaining, he slowly recalls the history of the night and finds that he has, as usual, made a "——— fool of himself." But he hasn't yet begun to be aware of the extent of his folly: for when his vessel is ready to go to sea, and the poor husband, half dead with the wifely hardships he has endured on land, looks forward with joy to the moment when he shall find himself at the belaying-pin or yard with no drunken wife at his elbow—lo! comes a warrant summoning him to satisfy the law that he will either stay on shore or give security for the maintenance of his wife and family, under penalty of a prosecution for abandonment! Of course, he knows nothing how to act; and it depends entirely upon the lawyer or the magistrate into whose hands he may fall whether he is let off by giving an order on his owners for the whole or only half of his next three year's wages. Used up, probably diseased, and completely chap-fallen, Jack resumes his station before the mast, and sees his native land sink under the blue wave with a fervent hope that the next solid place he exchanges for the deck of his vessel, will be the bottom of the sea.

It is quite usual for fights of the most desperate character to occur between the sailors and negroes, or rowdies, who frequent Dickens's Place, and sometimes whole squadrons of the police are called in before the disturbance can be quelled. The rowdies are generally armed with pistols or slung-shot, and every sailor carries his junk-knife—so that, what with these dangerous weapons and the rattling of the policemen's "bills" upon the heads and bones of the rioters, the dance-house occasionally gets up scenes of glorious excitement. Sometimes the rowdies get the worst of it—but the victims are usually the sailors, or outsiders who incautiously venture in without proper protection.

It would be scarcely fair to dismiss so important an "institution," (if the American Art-Union will pardon us for presuming to use a word to which they seem to claim exclusive right,) as Dickens's Place, without a few words respecting its landlord and proprietor. Pete Williams, Esq. is then a middle-aged, well-to-do, coal-black negro, who has made an immense amount of money from the profits of his dance-house—which, unfortunately, he regularly gambles away at the sweat-cloth or the roulette-table as fast as it comes in. He glories in being a bachelor—although there are something under a dozen "yellow-boys" in the neighborhood who have a very strong resemblance to Pete, and for whom he appears to entertain a particular fondness—frequently supplying them with sacks of candy, penny worths of peanuts, and other similar luxuries for the most part enjoyed only in dreams by the juvenile population of the Points. Pete is a great admirer of the drama, and is in fact a first-rate amateur and critic of things theatrical. Whenever there is anything "high" going on at either of the theaters, you may be sure Pete is there; and although we never heard it positively asserted that he furnished theatrical criticisms to the newspapers, yet from the tone and peculiar collocation observable in many of them, we should not be at all surprised to hear that they were the product of his classic pen. He of course abominates Macready but "hollers" on Forrest and goes his death for "our Charlotte," whom he always prophesied would turn out some pumpkins and nothing else![13] He delights in the Ravels and luxuriates over the ballet. He has

13. It was the bitter rivalry between Macready and the American actor Edwin Forrest—a rivalry that quickly took on strong nationalist overtones—that precipitated the Astor Place riot of May 10, 1849. "Our Charlotte" was the American actress Charlotte Cushman, who is discussed in the next chapter.

been heard to express opinions very much in favor of Miss Mary Taylor's *Marie* in "the Child of the Regiment," (why not translate it "female child of the Regiment," by way of perspicuity?)—and it is even whispered that he has been seen burrowing like a beaver round the back seats of the amphitheater at Astor Place. Such is a brief description of Pete Williams and Dickens's Place. We trust that our readers will not draw "oderous" comparisons between our humble and unpretending statement of facts and the elaborate and artistic picture of the place given by Dickens after a single visit. We both have written to the same end—to interest the reader: but while the great artist has summoned the aid of all his well-prepared colors to fascinate the imagination with harmonious hues, graceful proportions and startling contrasts, the unambitious reporter contents himself with sketching human nature as it is and as all may see it.

While on the subject of the dance-house, we may as well give a brief description of a terrible place of the kind formerly existing in Water street, near Cherry, but which is now happily broken up. The entrance to this den was through a front cellar, occupied as a regular sailors' and thieves' eating-house and groggery, and which to the stranger or the casual visitor presented no other appearances than might legitimately belong to such a concern. The low ceiling, the dirty bar with its rows of bottles and platoons of tumblers, its dingy cigar-boxes and attenuated lemons,—the gruff and phthisicky bar-keeper who dealt out the damnable poison at three cents a glass, without ever winking or looking his customer in the face,—these were the only things that arrested the attention. But he who understood the secrets of this abominable hole opened a little low door at one end of the bar, and immediately found himself in a long, narrow passage, entirely dark and not wide enough for two persons to walk abreast nor high enough for one to go upright. Traversing this passage for some fifty or sixty feet you came to another door, which,—if you knew the trick of it,—opened to your hand, and you issued into an open court surrounded on all sides by a high and unscalable wall of boards, surmounted with a thick *cheveaux-de-frise* of long and sharp iron spikes. Going straight across the yard, you encountered another door at which you were admitted upon giving the proper kind of knock; and stumbling down a dark flight of stairs, still another door opened and admitted you into the principal hall or dancing saloon. This was a room probably forty by sixty feet in extent, entirely underground and being overbuilt in its whole extent by a stable. Thus guarded, and removed from the street, no sounds uttered in this impregnable cavern ever by any possibility reached the upper air; but all—whether groans or laughter, the obscene blasphemy of drunken prostitution, the howl of the ruined gamester, or the prayer of the doomed victim beneath the ravisher's brutal grasp,—died where they were born and were never heard of more. A wire attached to a little bell behind the door ran across the yard and along the dark passage alluded to, issuing from the wall of the front cellar within a foot of the bar-keeper's head. Whenever any threatening demonstrations, either from rowdies or police, were made outside, the bell tinkled—the three doors guarding the cavern end of the passage were securely barred—and, if affairs were judged sufficiently imminent, a concealed trapdoor, opening into a corner of the stable, let out the parties in the cavern, who immediately went to bed in the various chambers and sleeping-rooms of the building above ground, and not a trace of the night's doings was discoverable. The trap, however, was seldom and cautiously used, for it was the very key to the whole establishment—a secret which, once known by one too many, rendered all the other precautions useless. But the secret was carefully kept—as was that, also, of the hanging trap under the floor of the barroom in front of the door leading to the dark passage. Beneath the floor at this spot was a pit some eight or ten feet in depth and partly filled with water. By jerking away a timber supporter, attached to a rope, the other end of which was fastened within convenient reach of the bar-keeper's

hand, the whole floor in that corner of the room was converted into a nicely-balanced trap, which a few pounds
weight would instantly upset, precipitating whomsoever
was upon it into the pit below—precisely as we used to
catch rats in our grandmother's soap barrel, by hanging
half the barrel-head on a pivot and sprinkling the edges
with cheese. But these secrets, as we said, were dangerous
and carefully kept; indeed, they were never known until the
final capture and suppression of this infamous establishment. So narrow and dark was the passage-way leading
back from the cellar that a single resolute man, armed with
billy or slung-shot, could have defended it against all the
police in the city, killing them one after another as fast as
they came out.

The above-ground building in front of the stable was occupied by the tenant of the premises and his wife as a regular brothel, and from fifteen to twenty girls, inveigled when
drunk or taken while destitute and starving, were always
kept for the use of the customers. Immediately upon coming
into the house they were charged five dollars a week, each,
for board, and supplied with clothes, knick-knacks, false
jewelry, whisky, medical attendance, &c. &c. at such rates
as the landlord and his tender-hearted help-meet thought
fit. Of course, in a few days every one of them was irrevoca-
bly in debt to her landlord, and eventually became absolutely his property—wearing his clothes, eating his food,
drinking his liquor and living in his house. The front door of
the premises was always kept locked, and no girl was ever
permitted under any circumstances to go out unless accompanied by the landlady to keep watch of her and prevent her
from running away; whatever they received from their
sleeping companions was immediately handed over to the
landlady; and if any suspicions of foul play in keeping a portion of it back were excited, a strict search was at once
made. If the suspected one were found guilty she was taken
to the cave, her back stripped to the skin, and then the
many-stranded thong blushed blood as it descended upon

its hellish work, and the shrieks of the poor victim died ere they reached the air and were heard alone of heaven.

But now for the principal hall itself, and the horrid orgies which it nightly witnessed. Among the various resources for filling the den with victims the most ordinary and the most useful were the ships of war and other vessels arriving in port—the sailors from which were decoyed into the oyster-cellar and thence to the cave. Once there, their fate was sealed. Two roulette tables and two sweat-cloths occupied the four corners of the room, while a bar was rigged up on one side and an orchestra on the other. The walls were lined with benches upon which were seated the girls of the establishment, stripped to the last point of decency and ready to commence the dance. The rest can be conceived. It was merely a repetition of what we have described at Dickens's Place—except that at the latter there is little gambling. So profitable did the proprietor of this nefarious hole in Water street find his trade that he was enabled to retire in two years, with a clear profit of over thirty thousand dollars. He now keeps a rendezvous and sailors' boarding-house on the East River, and his name is good for any amount to which he chooses to subscribe it. He pays all his debts promptly—for aught we know rents a pew in some fashionable church—and is, altogether, as times go, a very respectable man.

There are many dance-houses in and about New York—some better and none worse than those we have described. Among them the German dance-houses in West and Washington streets deserve especial mention, as do also the "check-apron balls," the "flotilla balls," and several others—not omitting by any means the splendid affairs which come off every now and then at the various fashionable fancy houses. But the night is far spent and we must take another occasion to group together these various temples to the light-footed muse Terpsichore,—whom we pray, meanwhile, to inspire our dreams.

No. X

Theaters and Public Amusements

*Miss Charlotte Cushman—Epitaph in Prose on
Old Drury—The Third Tiers—Mager's Saloon
in Elizabeth Street—The Dutch Drama and
Shilling Concerts—The Italian Opera—Max
Maretzek and His White Neckcloth—The
Aristocracy of New York—The Picture Galleries*

Miss Cushman is in town! The excitement is what the grandiloquent newspapers call "tremendous." The rush to the
box-office to secure seats is also "tremendous"—so is the
applause with which she is nightly greeted by "large and
enthusiastic audiences"—so are the "efforts she makes to
rescue the drama from its degraded position"—and so likewise are the puffing and panting criticisms with which she
is every morning overwhelmed—and, let us hope, at least
amused. In fact, everything about her is either tremendous,
terrific or magnificent. The way she eats her breakfast is
tragic in the extreme, especially to the comestibles within
her reach. The tenderest lamb cutlet shudders in terror as
her fork approaches the dish where it reposes, and the

boiled eggs palpitate to their inmost depth at every flourish of her spoon. She is the rage. Gentlemen reproduce the color of her favorite mulberry morning gown in their scarfs and cravats—ladies emulate each other in exactly copying the motion of her hips as she walks the stage in *Rosalind*, and newsboys gather in curious knots in Anthony street to watch her as she passes in and out at the stage door. Sub-editors of scrubby little papers grow furious in their impotent eulogies of everything she says and does, from the first preparatory "hem!" of her entrance to the final movement of her embroidered handkerchief as she soothes the tragedy-startled rouge upon her cheek and bows her adieus. The stage-manager for the first time in his life grows civil at the morning rehearsal, and the treasurer extends to her the "little trifle" of her salary, with an air of profound awe. For once even the codfish aristocracy bend from their velvet ottomans and damask-lined carriages, and cards and invitations to dinner pour upon the favored child of Thespis, in a hospitable snow-storm of polished pasteboard.

And who, then, *is* Miss Cushman? That rarest and most worship-worthy of all God's created beings—a woman of genius. Do we complain, then, of the homage that is paid to her? Heaven defend us from such heresy to the religion of intellect! No! If we might add one dew-drop to the fresh laurel that cools the fevered brow of the enchantress; if we could contribute one throb to the glorious pride that swells her breast—our homage should not be wanting; for we, too, have bowed before the divinity that speaks through her wondrous voice and eyes and makes itself manifest in every movement of her Pythonic form. But the paths of the courted and brilliant actress and the plodding slave of the inkstand are wide apart—their spheres do not meet nor mingle. For him Fame but flutters her wing disdainfully as she sweeps by—or if he sometimes pluck a feather, it becomes but a common goose-quill in his fingers.

But the strangest part of the business is that four or five years ago, this same woman—then in the full strength of mind and body with which youth once and once only en-

dows us—with all her genius more powerful and active than
now; and wanting in nothing she now possesses except some
taming down and artistic polish, the very things our audiences care least about—played the same characters night after night which now so electrify the town, to meager
audiences and inappreciative journalists. Now and then a
box-office criticism at ten cents a line made its appearance
in her behalf, and here and there a true and discriminating
friend formed a band of hopeful and trusting supporters.
But it was up-hill work; and many a time the poor girl, conscious of her own powers and ready to quarrel with destiny,
must have well-nigh fainted on her weary way. But in a lucky
hour she went abroad—received the stamp of foreign appro-
bation—and returns to her countrymen an empress, nod-
ding but to be obeyed, smiling but to be worshiped. Here is a
a lesson, oh ye obscure ones! Get ye to your closets—read
your Bibles—learn that a prophet is not without honor save
in his own country—then take a deck-passage for Liverpool,
and come back never or come back in triumph. Tom Thumb
and Christy, Catlin and Cushman—here is the head of that
successful category, of which may you speedily form the tail!

Would you learn the fate of earthly institutions? Go to the
tumbling dead-walls of the Park Theater—the Drury of
America—which so long held up its head in decrepitude and
decay, subsisting but on its former glory, and see what is
written there. You will perhaps, after scanning its calicoed
surface, reply, "Steamer Ali—Sugar-Coat—and Plantaloons
for—the Great Anaconda—Whig Nominations—Panorama
of Principles—Democrats Rally to the—American Museum"—and so on, reading interminably from the handbills
lying like scales (or like political editors) one upon another.
No, my friend, these are but seemings. That which is really
written there is but a single word—MUTABILITY—a dread
word containing the whole history of the past. As we gaze
upon its syllables we recall the scenes of joy and sorrow,
mirth and agony, which here so oft have passed in mimic
procession—now as real as the solemn and life-and-death

business of actual life transpiring side by side with them. We recall the actors who here have strutted their little hour upon the stage—Cooper, Kemble, Kean, Booth, Tree and Wallack—the kings and queens, princes, knights and fairies, who have not flitted more fleetly than their real counterparts beyond the theater—and we seem thus to surround ourselves with the cloudy past, from out whose mists look forth long gone but once familiar faces. Even those whom the grave has not yet claimed—where are they, and how has Mutability set her crumbling seal upon them! Booth! Ah, worse than dead—than hissed and damned! Thy brain, long smouldering with the ill-pent fires of madness, has at length eaten itself away, and thou art—what? Kemble! Last but not least noble of thy great house! In thee, the drama yet has hope. Thy father's name once more restored to thee, it is impossible thou should'st not once more seek the glorious arena where all the honors that render it immortal were won. Tea with the literati—a basket of flowers—a deal table—and an open book: is the daughter of the tragic Muse content with these? And Placide and Wheatley, Barrett and Vernon, and thou good and faithful Thomas Barry and imperturbable Blake—where are ye all? Faded, scattered, gone—never more to be reunited in the same cast until the great Stage Manager calls you for rehearsal in some spiritual Old Drury in the Elysian Fields. It is true that the noble Broadway, with its handsome balcony and modern front, its plenitude of lamps and palatial entrances—its damask sofas and golden chandeliers—fills the eye like a beautiful picture and gratifies every desire of comfort and repose when we would be amused. Yet, after all, we never pass the old Park walls, standing grimly defended by troops of pauper peddlers and thieving beggars, and letting the sunshine or the moonlight through its windows and wide crannies, like a dismantled fort, without a sigh and a keen memory of the past.

But stay! This is rhapsody—and we are cast for plain straight-forward description. We must pull the string of our safety-valve and get down smoothly into our own proper stratum. It is set down in our part that we are to speak of things as they are. Let us hasten to say, then, that the Broadway, now the leading theater in America, is in many respects worthy of this distinction—though this is by no means admitting that it is free from deficiencies. While such artists as Henry Placide, George Barrett, Chippendale and Mrs. Vernon, Murdoch and Jamieson, Mrs. Mason and young Wheatley, are still in their prime and to be had for the asking, why is it that they are permitted to waste themselves upon minor establishments, where worse acting would better please, when the principal theater in the richest city on the continent, the grand focus of art, literature and fashion, the absolute metropolis of twenty millions of people, so sadly needs their presence? It is not managerial parsimony, we are well aware, that dictates this. Perhaps it is that curse of the fine arts, which keeps them contemptible and their disciples beggars—professional jealousy.

There is another strong and valid objection to the Broadway Theater—which, truly, it shares with all the others in the country, but which is especially reprehensible in an establishment which claims to be, and in fact really is, far superior in every respect to all its cotemporaries.

It is true that thick walls and wide stair-cases separate the public entrance from that for abandoned women: yet it is nevertheless true that one-quarter of the entire house is set apart exclusively for the use of the latter, in which they nightly and publicly drive their sickening trade. Within a few feet and under the same roof where our virtuous matrons with their tender offspring are seated, are momently enacting scenes of cold-blooded depravity enough to make the heart of humanity shudder. Painted, diseased, drunken women, bargaining themselves away to obscene and foul-faced ruffians, for so much an hour—drinking, blasphemy, fighting, rioting—such are the accompaniments, the antithesis, would we might add, to what is transpiring on the stage. This is the greatest and most obstinately-persisted-in

outrage to public sense and public decency of which the age
furnishes any example. And public opinion has itself at last
felt and determined to resent the insult. This is the reason
why our theaters are nearly deserted on ordinary occasions,
save by dead-heads, rowdies and whoremongers. The respectable and virtuous public will not visit an assignation-
house, even though it be called a theater, unless impelled
thither in fashionable crowds by some extraordinary genius
like Miss Cushman, to keep each other in countenance and
render homage to the enchantress of the hour.

Of the other theaters little need be said. Each has its
characteristic, which may be summed up in few words. The
Bowery is the representative of that immense and important
class of our population, inhabiting the Sahara of the East,
and living—somehow—from day to day and week to week—
upon the labor of their hands. The butcher-boy, the mechanic with his boisterous family—the b'hoy in red flannel
shirt-sleeves and cone-shaped trowsers—the shop-woman,
the sewing and folding and press-room girl, the straw-
braider, the type-rubber, the map-colorer, the paper-box and
flower maker, the g'hal, in short, in all her various aspects
and phases—with a liberal sprinkling of under-crust blacklegs and fancy men—these make up the great staple of Bowery audiences. The style of acting that prevails here may be
conceived from this catalogue of the audience—but it never
can be described. The loud and threatening noises from the
pit, which heaves continually in wild and sullen tumult, like
a red-flannel sea agitated by some lurid storm— the shuffling and stamping of innumerable feet in the lobbies— the
unrepressed exuberance of talking, the laughing, children-
nursing, baby-quieting, orange-sucking, peanut-eating, lem-
onade-with-a-stick-in-it-drinking unconventionality of the
"dress circle"—the roaring crush and clamor of the tobacco-
chewing, great-coat-wearing second tier—the yells and
screams, the shuddering oaths and obscene songs, tumbling
down from the third tier—mingling with the convulsive
howls and spasmodic bellowings of the actors on the stage—

such are the elements from which, were we Hogarth, Hood, Doyle, Leach, and Gavarni compressed into one, we might attempt to create a picture of the Bowery Theater.

The Chatham Theater is smaller, but on the same plan, with the addition to its audiences of the elite of the Jewish population, who frequent it regularly and whose gaily-dressed women form one of the most conspicuous—not to say handsomest—features of the audience. The newsboys, too, are death on the Chatham, as well as the regular b'hoys and rowdies. From this rich soil has sprung the "Mose" of Chanfrau, which, with the negro of Rice, form almost the only original dramatic embodiments of character ever produced in the new world.[14]

The Olympic has made a fortune for its manager—himself a comedian of considerable talent—by adhering to burlesque and broad fun, with now and then an attempt at serious opera, which, fortunately for the fortunes of the house, the audience very naturally always mistake for as good burlesque as the best of it, and so laugh where they ought, operatically speaking, to cry bravo! and crack peanuts when they should be splitting white kids. Burton's is an establishment of precisely similar character, although the truly artistic delineations of Mr. Burton himself form a permanent attraction of a high order at this theater.[15]

There remains only Niblo's—a most remarkable illustration of what ordinary means used with extraordinary judgment will effect. The rope-dancing and comic pantomime of the Ravels, with a just respectable comedietta company two nights in the week—these are the staples with which Mr. Niblo nightly fills his house, winter and summer, year after year. The secret of it is very simple—no woman is admitted

14. Francis Chanfrau created the character of Mose the Bowery b'hoy in Benjamin Baker's *A Glance at New York in 1848*. Thomas D. Rice's creation was the black-face minstrel character Jim Crow.

15. William E. Burton, complimented here, was the man whose signature Foster forged on at least two promissory notes before being arrested and sent to jail in January of 1855. See the Introduction.

at this house, under any pretext, unless accompanied by a gentleman. The consequence is that rowdies avoid the house, or, if they visit it, have no inducement for misbehaving—and respectable and quiet people freely come, with their wives and children, sure of being neither shocked by obscenity nor frightened by violence. The performances, too, are always good, piquantly selected, and run off easily, so that if you go there you may safely calculate on being amused instead of bored.

We said Niblo's was our last theater. Strictly speaking, we were right—but there are innumerable other places of evening amusement well worth describing. Among the most disreputable is a hole called the Franklin Theater, where "model artists" and similar disgusting exhibitions, elsewhere sufficiently noticed, are nightly carried on, for the benefit of half a hundred impotent and dilapidated old lechers and twice as many precociously prurient boys. One of the most remarkable public resorts, however, in the city, has never been noticed in print, and is totally unknown out of its own circle of patrons, except by the police. This is "Mager's Concert Hall," in Elizabeth street, near Grand. It is an immense room on the second floor, elaborately and gaudily painted in fresco, with scenes from the Dutch mythology (at least they are not from any other) in which naked goddesses, grim knights, terrific monsters and American eagles, are like Shelley's immortal combatants—"Feather and scale inextricably blended." The floor, on ordinary occasions, is filled with rough tables and wooden benches, and partly across one end runs a balconied platform by way of orchestra. Every Sunday night takes place at this establishment a grand German and English concert, vocal and instrumental. Several female singers, with those marvelous guttural alternating voices resembling the compound creaking of a dry grindstone, or the cry of a guinea-hen, are regularly engaged here, and perform in both German and English. The orchestra consists of a gigantic seraphina, two violins, a flute and a fagotto, all played by Germans, and of course played well.

These concerts are regularly attended by the respectable German men and women residing in the city, to the number of from twelve to seventeen hundred. In pleasant weather the audience seldom falls below fifteen hundred. The price of admission is one shilling—which, we believe, but are not certain, as we have never happened to be dry when visiting Mager's, includes a drink of Rhine wine or a swig of bierisch. At any rate there are immense quantities of these liquids phlegmatically engulphed in the Germanesque oesophagi of the visitors, both male and female. Every thing, however, is carried on in excellent order and there are very seldom any disturbances here. The audience are not at all nice, and are easily pleased—and in fact the performances themselves, so far at least as the instrumental music is concerned, are very respectable.

Next the orchestra a pretty large stage, with proscenium drop-curtain and scenery, all in order, is constructed, at which during the week regular dramatic performances take place by a company of German actors, who are regarded by their audiences as the Macreadys and Cushmans of their time. As to their merits we cannot undertake to speak critically—being as innocent of German as of petty larceny. We will say in our own behalf, however, that we entertain none but the kindest feelings toward the actors and actresses—although they have given us a great many remarkably hard words.

Sometimes in the dancing season this immense hall is put to worse purposes than those we have thus far enumerated—being rented out to disreputable women for grand public balls and flare-ups, in the "high faluting style." Of these, however, we shall speak in another chapter.

But we must not forget, among our places of public amusements, the Astor Place Opera-House—the resort of our exclusively aristocratic Upper Ten Thousand—and the Picture-Galleries, of which latter New-York has a very creditable share, for a new country. The Italian Opera, that costly and precious luxury of the heart and mind, is now in its third season, which, like third efforts at any thing, promises to be abundantly successful. Indeed, we do not see how it can very well fail, so long as Max Maretzek, the Napoleon of managers and the Alexander of conductors, is in command, with his spotless white neckcloth and wielding his jewel-tipped baton. Even before the opening of the season the subscription exceeded the actual expenses, and all the subscribers manifested a settled determination to *make* the Opera successful, at all hazards. This is all right and gratifying, as the amphitheater with its two-shilling admittance affords an opportunity of listening to good music to a large class of population, who, in other countries, are entirely shut out from the enjoyment of such luxuries—and even "fashionable young men about town" are not slow in availing themselves of it. This truly democratic characteristic of the Astor Place Opera-House makes it a great favorite with the intelligent and ambitious among the great middle class, who nightly fill the spacious amphitheater, and form by no means the least important portion of the audience.

The Astor Place Opera-House is admitted by persons of taste, both native and foreign, to be one of the most elegant and comfortable theaters in the world. Its internal arrangements, the gay and airy effect of its white and gilt open lattice-work, the richness of the crimson velvet sofas and chairs, the luxurious hangings of the private boxes, and the flood of gas-light shed from the magnificent chandelier and numerous other points about the house, furnish a *coup d'oeil* of beauty it would be difficult to surpass. When this picture is filled out with the lovely forms and faces of five or six hundred of the most beautiful women in the world, dressed *à meraviglia*, and as many distinguished looking men, the effect may be conceived. Add to these elements of delight the exquisitely balanced orchestra, pouring out a golden sea of harmony, upon whose voluptuous undulations the voices of the singers float in melody, and the scene becomes one of fairy-like enchantment.

The company of the present year is in many respects the best that has yet appeared in America; the new tenor, Signor Forti, being especially worthy of notice as a true classic artist, whose entire performance, although marred occasionally by some trifling faults, should be carefully studied as a model by all who would learn either to sing or to enjoy good singing. His style, we are told, strongly resembles that of Mario—so pure, so tender, so full of power and breadth, when required, but above all so equal, so finished and so finely graded. Altogether, we may now safely congratulate Brother Jonathan upon having at length permanently established in his metropolis the choicest and most expensive luxury which civilization has yet produced.

Another very popular feature of our public amusements is picture-seeing; and in this respect it is really incredible the progress we have made and the advantages with which we are provided. To say nothing of the American Art-Union, which does great good in a certain way, by breaking up the soil whence will grow in time a taste for the beautiful, there are in New York several permanent galleries where a large number of real pictures may be seen. The most conspicuous and valuable of these are Mr. Nye's very precious collection of genuine paintings by the old masters, the International Art-Union and the Düsseldorf galleries.

Of Mr. Nye's collection, in the Lyceum Building, we almost hesitate to speak as we feel, lest we be accused of undue partiality. Common justice, however, demands that we should rank it as by far the most interesting and valuable gallery of old pictures ever in the western hemisphere. It contains nearly one hundred and fifty paintings by all the most celebrated artists of the fifteenth and sixteenth centuries, when Painting was at the meridian of its glory and its disciples were the friends of monarchs and the protégés of princes. A single picture by Titian—the Martyrdom of St. Lawrence—has won many and many an hour of rapt devotions from us—while amid the soft splendors shed around by the immortal pencils of Raphael, Murillo, and the other great masters of the divine art, life and its perplexing realities have often been forgotten in sweet and delicious dreams. Our testimony can add nothing to the estimation in which this gallery is held by artists and connoisseurs; but so far as it may be worth any thing, it is very cheerfully given. We have taken great pains to ascertain the truth; and from our knowledge of Mr. Nye himself and the entirely patriotic and unselfish motives which induced him to expend nearly a quarter of a million of dollars in the purchase of this gallery, we do not hesitate to assert our full belief that every picture in this gallery is exactly what it is stated to be in the catalogue. To test the matter fully, the proprietor has offered to submit the paintings in detail to the judgment of some thorough European judge, and to forfeit every one of them which is decided to be other than it is represented, on condition that those pronounced genuine shall be purchased at a fair valuation for the purpose of forming the nucleus of a great national gallery and school of art.

We learn that a negotiation is now pending to transfer these paintings to the Smithsonian Institute, for which purpose several distinguished members of our National Legislature have volunteered to ask an appropriation from Congress. Another suggestion is, that Congress should make a grant of public lands for the purpose of founding a National School of Art, of which the invaluable gallery of Mr. Nye would form a noble beginning. It is surely time that our country should begin to see whether she has not other duties to perform than the mere development of her physical resources. Nations, like men, have brains as well as bodies.

Another laudable and very promising effort to increase and refine public taste in this country, by the introduction of pictures of a high order of merit, has been recently made by the managers of the International Art-Union, whose splendid gallery is the very next door below the Lyceum, and is constantly filled with crowds of admiring visitors. Scheffer, Delaroche, Waldmüller, Gendron, Landelle, Court, Schlessinger, and many other European artists of lesser note have contributed their *chefs-d'oeuvre* to adorn the walls of this institution, and its gallery is the only place in America where anything like an idea can be gathered of the paintings of the modern French school,—a school which, whatever may be its defects, possesses innumerable excellences which the artists of every other country should study and imitate.

The plan and conduct of this institution are extremely liberal, and it is not strange that they have already commended it to a wide popularity. The managers, an extensive print-publishing house in Paris—to whose enterprise we are indebted for engravings of all the great pictures of the day, American as well as European—assumed the entire outlay and responsibility of establishing the institution—advancing the necessary funds to throw open a gallery of fine paintings before a single subscriber was obtained. Another popular feature of this institution is that beside distributing gratuitously a large number of pictures throughout the country, it provides for sending at least one American student of painting to Europe to study two years under the best masters, all at the expense of the institution. These new and public-spirited features of the International have given it immense popularity, and its gallery is constantly full, while its subscription-books are rapidly filling up. Already, in the first year of its existence it has come to be regarded as one of our permanent and most valuable public institutions. It is a great favorite with all the artists and ladies, and its influence upon public taste cannot be otherwise than greatly beneficial.

It is really quite refreshing to drop in at either of our picture-galleries, of an afternoon or evening, and watch the crowds of well-dressed and intelligent ladies and gentlemen who come to view the pictures and converse about art. Sometimes, as we have elsewhere hinted, meetings of another and more tender nature occur, of which we of course have too much politeness as well as good nature to seek to become witnesses. We are satisfied that in the presence of the beautiful nothing impure could possibly emanate from any heart worth the saving.

No. XI

The Light Fantastic Toe

*Dancing in New York—Extra Doings—The
Grand Ball at Castle Hastings—Another of the
Same Sort, Only a Little More So—Flotilla
Balls, &c. &c.*

New York is undoubtedly the greatest place for dancing in
all Anglo-Saxondom. Nowhere else, within the empire of
that

——grunting guttural
Which we're obliged to hiss and spit and sputter all,

has the light-toed goddess so many and such enthusiastic
worshipers as in this staid old Dutch settlement of Gotham.
There seems to be something in the intermixture of Puritan
and Knickerbocker blood which gives peculiar activity to
the heels and elasticity to the toes. No sooner is cold
weather established and the city comfortably covered with
its November counterpane of buckwheat cakes than the
spirit of dancing escapes from her summer confinement,
and commences cutting up her "shines" in every part of the
city. In the height of the season there are at least a dozen

large public balls given in New York every night. Going up Broadway, home from our midnight toil at the morning paper, the Apollo, the Minerva, the Chinese Assembly, the Coliseum, the we know not what saloons, stream light and music into the air, while sleepy cabmen watch below. In other quarters of the town similar places are similarly crowded with dancers. The company frequenting these parties comprise nearly all classes of our population, except the Snobbish Ten Thousand who affect aristocracy and are so uncertain of their position that they dare not bring it into general society for fear of losing it. The great staple for the winter balls are the military and fire companies, the annual Fireman's Ball, Dodworth's Band Ball, Tammany Hall New-Year Festival, and several other established "institutions." These have been frequently described, and indeed present nothing very particular except the ordinary affairs of dancing, flirting and suppering, which every body can imagine if not practice for himself.

But there are another variety or two of New York balls which never have been described, and of which ordinary and orderly people, who go to bed virtuously at ten o'clock, have no possible idea. These are the affairs most fit for our purpose—which is, simply, to go over as little ground as has been trodden before us, and to turn up to the light as much of the unploughed sod of metropolitan life, as we can.

Let us imagine a modern-built three-story house of the largest class, three parlors deep, and furnished throughout in a style of costly and tasteful magnificence. The carpets are Wilton, the sofas and chairs, ottomans, lounges, &c. &c. are of purple velvet, with crimson and rose-colored hangings—the walls are hung with pretty fair pictures, in handsome gilt frames, and the whole is brilliantly lighted with gas. Then imagine these rooms filled with a company of something over one hundred women, some of them very good-looking and all magnificently dressed, and a corresponding number of men, embracing all the aristocratic bloods and "fast men" about town—personages whose entrance into the proudest drawing-rooms Above Bleecker makes the hearts of mother and daughter pant with hope and fear. An orchestra of superb musicians, exquisitely proportioned and directed by one of the most celebrated *maîtres de danse* in the city, is ready, and the company are about to take their places, and commence the grand business of the night. But first a word about this party:

This is "Castle Hastings"—the residence of one of the most dashing and distinguished courtezans in the metropolis—the Aspasia of the nineteenth century—who, abandoning herself openly and avowedly to the pursuits of pleasure and power, has brilliantly fulfilled every aspiration which the heart of an ambitious woman without principle can entertain. Her intellect is keen and shrewd, her habits temperate, and her will perfectly controlling. She never forgets herself—never deals in sentiment nor hypocrisy—and always avows frankly her business and her objects. She has amassed a large fortune, and conducts her establishment upon strictly "correct" principles. If it is not virtuous, it is at least decorous; and if, as says a wise and honest magistrate, whose firmness and frankness have won him the admiration of all good men, prostitution be really a "necessary evil," the "Empress Kate" deserves well of the community. However, we do not write either to palliate or condemn—only to describe.

The ball to which we have alluded took place at this well-known establishment only a few weeks ago, and was probably the most perfect affair of the kind ever got up on this side the water. Indeed it would have done honor to the most aristocratic libertine circles of Paris, London or Vienna. It was originally intended for a masquerade affair—but such things being strictly prohibited by law, and the Mercury who edits the "Scorpion," having given notice that he intended to be present with his "unrivaled corps" of reporters,—the big bugs who had accepted invitations and were making preparations to be present in full masquerade costume, *à la Louis Quinze*, became frightened and backed out. The affair, therefore, assumed the shape of an ordinary dress-ball, and the "Empress"—who is not the woman to be foiled in anything she undertakes—pushed on the preparations with great spirit. Cards of invitation were regularly issued to all the upper crust fancy and sporting-men, bloods, fast men, &c. &c. and requisitions made upon all the fashionable "bowers of beauty," "temples of love," &c. &c. to furnish their quota of ladies. The "Castle" itself was magnificently represented by "Marchioness D'Orsay," "Mary Queen of Scots," the "Princess Jenny," "Lady Anna Morris," "the Jewess," &c. &c. beside the Empress Kate herself—while among the visitors were to be recognized nearly every courtezan in town celebrated for wit, beauty or accomplishments.

The ladies had been provided by Kate, and none others were admitted; while the Empress herself took her station at the reconnoitering-grate in the door, to watch that no improper character—in short, none but "gentlemen"—should be admitted. At eleven o'clock, the company being assembled, the orchestra struck up and dancing went on vigorously,—everything being conducted with the strictest propriety,—until one, when the party adjourned to the various boudoirs, dressing-rooms, &c. &c. on the upper floors, where we shall be excused from following them. In about an hour the whole party reassembled in the lower saloon, where meanwhile had been laid a magnificent *souper de minuit*, by one of our most fashionable and aristocratic French confectioners. The table was lavishly and expensively furnished, with plate and crystal, and of course the viands and wines were of the costliest and most *recherché* description. But all this innumerable newspaper descriptions have rendered too familiar "to the meanest capacity" to be dwelt upon. At three o'clock the rooms were again cleared for dancing; and daylight saw the gay disciples of the Paphian goddess, jaded and haggard with the fierce pleasures of the night, flee like ghosts from the presence of the fresh and chaste Aurora.

A few nights after this grand affair, another ball, on a more free and easy style, but in which many of the same personages principally figured, took place at "Mager's Saloon," in Elizabeth street—which place we have already described as being the locale of the shilling concerts and Dutch theatricals mentioned under our dramatic head. Here all restraint was in a great measure laid aside, and the reckless Cyprians and their excited cavaliers gave loose reins to their prurient tastes and manners; and amid noisy riot and confusion, drunkenness and profanity, the scene toward morning degenerated to a mere orgy, little better—save that the actors in it were better-dressed and better-looking—than the nightly revel at Dickens's Place. At "Castle Hastings" vice and licentiousness wore their holiday masks, new painted and trimly cut after the fashion of virtue and respectability; but at "Mager's" the uncomfortable mask was thrown aside for freer breathing, and they stalked forth in all their naked and disgusting deformity. The inevitable, irresistible tendency of unchasteness, as well as of all other forms of dissipation, is to degenerate the creature made in God's image to the likeness of a brute. Each form of dissipation has its peculiar type in the animal kingdom. Drunkenness and licentiousness find their appropriate model or "ultimate" in the hog and goat; but we very much doubt whether either hog or goat would not find himself astonished if he could be for a moment endowed with sensibility and consciousness, and permitted to visit the scenes where his human prototypes are disporting themselves.

Beside the regular Cyprianic balls, at least one of which takes place every night, in some quarter of the city, there are innumerable dancing parties on the tapis—we couldn't truly say on the carpet—in all seasons. In the winter there are "check-apron balls" and "high-flyer stampedes" at the Red House, at Palmo's, and at the various public houses "on the road." At these the company generally consists, for the most part, of the real "b'hoys" and "g'hals" of Bowery and the East End—of the better class of journeymen butchers, mechanics and artizans generally, the firemen, and in short the whole Upper Ten Thousand of the world of Red Flannel-dom, attended by the folding-girls and seamstresses; the milliners' apprentices, the shop-girls, the "supesses" from the Bowery and Chatham theaters, and all unmarried womanhood from the Bowery to the Dry Dock. These are noisy, boisterous and "high" affairs altogether—so much so that it would be extremely dangerous for any one to interfere in any way with the jollities of the evening, or to attempt to repress the exuberant voices or spirits of the company. Sometimes an effeminate snob libertine from the fancy dry-goods counter, the aristocratic counting-house or the lawyer's office, ventures into these entertainments to see what he can pick up quietly. But there are sharp eyes upon him, and he had better look well to his "antecedents," as our friend Louis Napoleon calls them. The g'hals themselves despise him, and the b'hoys are little inclined to disguise the open contempt and hatred he inspires. Should he become at all demonstrative in his attention to any of the ladies, his chances for a pictorial pair of eyes are very much superior to those of a subscriber to the American Art-Union for drawing a picture.[16]

The "flotilla ball" is an immense favorite in the summer, and the number of these excursions and dances which take place every season on our waters is almost incredible. They are in every respect similar to the check-apron festivals, save that they take place on board the steamboat instead of in the dancing-room. Many of these water excursions are got up with much taste and good order, the company judiciously selected, and are really delightful entertainments. At all events they are favorite amusements with a class of population forming one of our most decided and interesting national characteristics, and as such very properly claim our attention.

16. The American Art-Union, mentioned several times earlier, used funds raised through subscription to purchase oil paintings and statuary. At the end of each year these artworks were distributed among the subscribers by lottery. Carl Bode, in *The Anatomy of American Popular Culture* (Berkeley, 1959), has calculated the odds of winning an artwork in this lottery at nineteen to one (p. 62).

No. XII

Mose and Lize

The Philosophy of the B'hoy—Ditto of the
G'hal—Lize and the Fashionable Lady—The
Target Excursion—The Fireman—Lize at
Work—Lize at Her Toilette—Materials for a
New Literature

Who are the b'hoys and g'hals of New York? The answer to
this question, if it could be completely efficient, would be
one of the most interesting essays on human nature ever
written. Innumerable are the attempts of writers of all
grades and calibres—including Mr. Cornelius Mathews and
ourselves—to adequately describe these original and strictly
American developments of human character. In no other
country could Mose or Lize exist a day, without undergoing
such radical transformation as would completely destroy
their identity. There are the great middle classes in all other
countries—but in none other does any branch of them display any thing like the peculiar and distinguishing at-
tributes of the American b'hoy and g'hal. All through our
own country, however, the type is found in abundance, but
very slightly modified by location and surrounding circum-

stances. The b'hoy of the Bowery, the rowdy of Philadelphia, the Hoosier of the Mississippi, the trapper of the Rocky Mountains, and the gold-hunter of California are so much alike that an unpracticed hand could not distinguish one from the other; while the "Lize" of the Chatham Theater and the belle of a Wisconsin ball-room are absolutely identical, and might change places without any body being the wiser. Not even Mose himself would be likely to suspect the substitution.

The secret and key of the entire class of characters represented by Mose and Sykesey in New York and by Davy Crockett and the "Yaller-Flower of the Forest" on our whole western and southwestern frontier, (extending and including any where from the Mississippi to the Pacific,) is just this— *free development to Anglo-Saxon nature.*

The elements of the Anglo-American character exist, in greater or less perfection, in several European countries, but so thoroughly repressed by poverty and the paralyzing influence of even the best of monarchical governments that it is only in America that they have shown of what they are capable. There can be no doubt that, thus far, the Anglo-American is the highest and most perfect specimen of the human being—low enough and imperfect, it must be confessed, when compared with a lofty ideal of man as the noblest of God's creatures, yet high and perfect to a gratifying extent when contrasted to the peasants, serfs and slaves of Europe. In the boisterous roughness, the rude manners and the profanity of the b'hoy there is little, truly, to elicit our admiration. But his cheerful and patient performance of the labor to which he is allotted and by which he lives—his constancy and faithfulness to his domestic duties and responsibilities—his open abhorrence of all "nonsense"—the hearty manner in which he stands up on all occasions for his friend, and especially his indomitable devotion to fair play—bespeak for him and his future destiny our warmest sympathies and our highest hopes. There is at last a reasonable prospect that a race of full-grown men and women shall have a fair chance to see what faculties and capacities God has implanted in them, and how far they can develop and improve the talent that has been given to them without other driving or other restriction than such as they choose to impose upon themselves.

For our own part we confess that we have not only hope but confidence in the "b'hoy." We see in those very traits which we are sometimes almost inclined to consider intolerable, the mere exuberant and undisciplined activity of qualities the most useful and noble. His hatred of the self-styled "aristocracy"—what is that but an exaggeration of a virtuous contempt for coxcombry, affectation, sham and snobbery? For well he knows that the only aristocracy in such a country as his is composed of its men of genius and intellectual power. He meets and mingles with, at political assemblages, superior minds whose possessors stand high before the world and whose names carry with them a wide and almost immeasurable influence: and he sees them dressed like himself and totally divested of pretension and exclusiveness. He is on intimate terms with men like Walsh and Leggett,[17] whom he knows to be far superior in every respect to the shallow-pated, milk-hearted sucklings of foppery and fashion. How can he fail, under these circumstances, to imbibe a thorough dislike of an aristocracy he believes to be absolutely his inferiors—who possess no natural nor political rights over himself—and whose one solitary point of distinction is that they have more money than he? Every thing about him gives the lie to the pretensions of the aristocracy—and yet he sees that by the mere accident or perhaps dishonesty or oppression and defrauding his class which has enabled them to amass a little money, they live in ostentatious idleness and ease,—producing nothing

17. William Leggett, as assistant editor of William Cullen Bryant's *New York Evening Post* between 1829 and 1836, vigorously articulated the radical Democratic themes of equal rights and anti-monopoly. He died in 1839, just as Mike Walsh was emerging as a radical leader in New York City.

yet enjoying all,—while he produces all and enjoys nothing. Is it not natural that all this should rankle in his heart until he becomes impatient, unjust and reckless, and sometimes even is led to wreak personal vengeance upon the obnoxious class? Understand us—we do not *defend* this; nor do we contend that a wrong, however great, can be a justification for another wrong. But is it not *natural*? And why need we look farther for the causes of that deep-seated hostility to the "codfish aristocracy" which rolls its carriage-wheels over his toes and raises a cloud of dust in his eyes?

But the virtues of the b'hoy are by no means all of a negative character. Look for a moment at our Fire Department, which owes so much of its real efficiency to this class of men, whose sturdy frames, unyielding sinews and reckless daring in the hour of danger, when stoutest hearts are appalled with sudden calamity, save hundreds of lives and millions of property—lives and property, too, in which they have no direct nor personal interest, and for saving which they do not expect even thanks. We never hear of a rowdy fight or a fireman's riot without immediately picturing the men engaged in it, working like Titans hour after hour at the brakes, standing knee-deep in ice and mud, with perhaps icicles freezing from their fingers and a calcined wall toppling just above their heads—or marking their companions scaling dizzy and tottering ladders resting their upper rounds in burning seas of flame. Yonder we see one standing fearlessly upon the very verge of a five-story roof, chopping deliberately away at some wooden spout it is desirable to sever, while the treacherous flames crawl like fiery serpents out at the window-casing, down the shingles, and at length grown bolder, come to lick his very feet. So absorbed is he in his perilous occupation that he has not heard the cries of warning which the crowd below have been sending up through the smoky din of the conflagration. In a moment more the roof is all on fire, the air has lost its last particle of vitality and can no more be breathed. Too late he discovers his peril; and, blinded by smoke, suffocated and choking with the hot air, he strikes out at random for the window whence he issued, now framed with glowing flame. For a moment his heart sinks, as he sees before him his horrible but inevitable fate. But in another he rallies—recalls the half-remembered fragments of a prayer his mother taught him, long, long ago—sends a look, a kiss and a blessing after "Lize," who perhaps even then is dreaming of him in her tidy little garret bed-room—and disappears forever. This is no fancy sketch, but dire and terrible reality—and what but a lofty impulse, a truly noble and humane instinct, an ambition purer and higher than that of the greatest warrior that ever lived, can impel these daring men to such sacrifices and to brave such imminent dangers? Who among the pampered and sneering apes of fashion, who set themselves up for the exclusive nobility of this republic, would do as much—or a tithe as much—for their fellow-creatures?

The governing sentiment, pride and passion of the b'hoy is independence—that he can do as he pleases and is able, under all circumstances, to take care of himself. He abhors dependence, obligation, and exaggerates the feeling of self-reliance so much as to appear, on the surface, rude and boorish. But the appeal of helplessness or the cry of suffering unlocks his heart at once, whence all manner of good and tender and magnanimous qualities leap out. The b'hoy can stand anything but affectation—on that he has no mercy; and should he even find a fop or a coxcomb inabsolute distress, we fear his first impulse would be to laugh at him.

In his amusements, as in his food and clothes, the b'hoy isn't particularly nice as to their quality, so that they are "rich and racy," and that there is plenty of them. We have already seen the b'hoy at the theater, the ball, and in his various haunts and lounging-places. He is especially fond of the bar-room and the engine-house, always on the look-out for a fire, a fight or a frolic, and seldom long without one or the other of these commodities "on hand." Perhaps, however, if we were called upon to select the one thing in which above all others the b'hoy delights, we should name the target excursion. With his trim-fitting black panties, "sixty inches round the bottom," and his fire-new red flannel shirt, his gun jauntingly carried at a "support" and the periphery of his straight-brimmed hat cutting the plane of the ecliptic at an angle of twenty-three degrees twenty-eight minutes—with his spotless white belt across his manly chest, a splendid band of music in front, the inevitable negro with the target behind, and Lize smiling and clapping her hands in admiration from the window—who so proud and happy as he? Talk of your kings and emperors and generals and conquerors, whose glory is but the foul mist rising from the groans and sufferings of millions—what are they to the joyous, riotous, rollicking, good-humored b'hoy strutting home from the field of his bloodless prowess, the riddled target borne proudly in the van, and his eye and chest dilated with innocent conquest! And then the welcome home from the faithful Lize—the stout embrace, the hearty smack—the recounting of all the incidents of the day—these are all strong and piquant characteristics, a single glance at which would go farther than pages of description. Perhaps a contrast between the b'hoy and the Broadway dandy, which we were lately cognizant of, will assist the imaginations of such of our readers as have not seen the elephant.

"Do tell me all about your fine parade with the Hoosah troop yethterday, Mither Thmith," lisped a young lady of the Upper Ten to a dandy Hussar, the other evening at a party in the Fifth avenue.

"Oh I assure you, we had a most chawming time, my deah madam—perfectly chawming."

On the same evening Mose returned from a grand fireman's parade and target-excursion, and was met by Lize at the door.

"Well hoss, what kind of a time'd ye hev—say?"

"Well now yer'd better *bleeve* we hed a gallus time! Give us a buss, old gal! Guess I seen ye lookin' out er ther winder this morning—*I* did."

"Oh git out—*you Mose!*"

If Mose is most perfectly himself at a target-excursion, Lize never feels herself at home but at the theater or the dance. She is an industrious, patient, unenvious creature— or if not quite unenvious, at least less afflicted with envy, that most disgusting form of selfishness, than any other class of woman-kind. She is perfectly willing to work for a living, works hard and cheerfully, as any day laborer or journeyman mechanic of the other sex. She rises before the sun, tidies up herself and afterward her little room—swallows her frugal breakfast in a hurry, puts a still more frugal dinner in her little tin kettle (they call 'em pails in Yankeeland,) and starts off to her daily labor in the press-room, the cap-sewing or the book-folding establishment, as happy and care-free as a bird. Perhaps she deviates a block or two from her direct route to exchange a smile and a word with Sykesey or with Mose, and make an appointment for a steamboat excursion, a sleigh-ride or a visit to the Bowery to see Jim Wallack in Romeo and Lester in the favorite Dan Keyser de Bassoon. From six to six o'clock she works steadily, with little gossip and no interruption, save the hour from twelve to one devoted to dinner. Then the tongues of herself and her companions are suddenly let loose and fly as merrily and noisily as a flock of magpies. Gossip, scandal, "sells" and laughter are the piquant sauces of the homely dinner; and punctually at one every plump mouth is wiped carefully and sealed hermetically, and every hand is again busy with the monotonous, never-ending daily toil. Exactly at six o'clock this great female industrial school, in which the scholars never learn anything, is let out, and its inmates pour into the streets, being joined by hundreds of others from similar establishments, and all forming a continuous procession which fills Nassau street, and turning away up Chatham and the Bowery, loses itself gradually in the innumerable side-streets leading thence into the unknown regions of Proletaireism in the East End.

The g'hal is as independent in her tastes and habits as Mose himself. Her very walk has a swing of mischief and defiance in it, and the tones of her voice are loud, hearty and free. Her dress is "high," and its various ingredients are gotten together in utter defiance of those conventional laws of harmony and taste imposed by Madame Lawson and the French mantua-makers of Broadway. The dress and the shawl are not called upon by any rule recognized in these "diggins" to have any particular degree of correspondence or relationship in color—indeed, a light pink contrasting with a deep blue, a bright yellow with a brighter red, and a green with a dashing purple or maroon, are among the startling contrasts which Lize considers "some pumpkins" and Mose swears is "gallus!" But the bonnet!—that is the crowning achievement of the out-door adornment of the full-rigged g'hal. It is of various materials at different times— though without any special regard to the season—but we believe that white chip and fancy straws are the favorite patterns. The outside is trimmed with a perfect exuberance of flowers and feathers, and gigantic bows and long streamers of tri-colored ribbons give the finishing touch to a hat which, resting on the back of the head, extends its front circumference just round from ear to ear across the top of the forehead, leaving the face entirely exposed, and the eyes at full liberty to see what is going on in every direction.

The newest invention in the costume of the g'hal is a fascinating article of outside gear, termed by some a "polka," but generally known as a "monkey-jacket." It is cut like a gentleman's tight sack to fit the back and shoulders smoothly, and reaches halfway down the thigh. When neatly cut and fitting to the figure of a plump, healthy and elastic-limbed g'hal, with the full-skirted dress swelling out voluptuously from beneath it and undulating like a balloon, it certainly has a very exhilarating appearance. Attempts have been made to introduce this piquant garment into more western regions—but thus far without any very marked success. It is true that once in a while an unusually fresh well-formed donzella of Above Bleecker ventures into the street of a morning encased in her bewitching polka; but if mama discovers it the young lady is sure of receiving a severe lecture on the proper distinction between some folks and some people—concluding with a fearful warning against the dangers of overstepping the barrier which separates persons of "position in society" from the mere common vulgar herd.

Thus we have slightly and faintly sketched the character of the b'hoy and the g'hal—the most original and interesting phase of human nature yet developed by American society and civilization. We cannot of course be expected in a sketch like this to follow our characters into their private and daily lives—to develop their motives and methods of action in detail and to depict their life-drama as it flows along in its strong but turbulent course. This is the task, not of the sketcher but of the novelist or the dramatist. To both these classes of writers the b'hoy and the g'hal, and the great middle class of free life under a republic of which they are the types and representatives, afford an inexhaustible and almost untrodden field, with a rich and certain harvest. With the exception of the single drama in which Mr. Chanfrau, slight as is its plot and meager and commonplace as are its incidents, has been able by the force of his genius to confer a new character upon the stage, nothing has been adequately done to begin imparting to our literature the original and rich wealth lying latent in the life and history of Mose and Lize. Nor would it be easy to designate, at the present moment, the pen that is to perform this inestimable service to our country's literature.

No. XIII

The Dog-Watch

*Thieves and Burners "About"—Doing a
Countrydian—A Scene Underground—Model
Artists in Dishabille—A Night's
Experiences—Winding Up of Mr. Green's
Adventures—Night in the Tombs*

Mr. Zerubbabel Green, eldest son and hope of Deacon
Hezekiah Green, and Thankful Green, his wife, all of
Stephentown, New York state, arrived in the city last
evening by the Albany boat, on his first visit to town, for the
express purpose of seeing the world and knocking about a
little; for since Zadock Pratt, the Stephentown tanner, has
turned out a great man, they don't see why the son of Deacon Green shouldn't try his hand in the same direction.

The young Zerubbabel, fixed up in his smartest black
fulled-cloth coat and trowsers, with a particularly streaked
and short-waisted vest, the stripes running cater-cornered
and meeting in the middle, and his old bell-crowned hat
brushed as smooth as a mink, had been attended as far as
Greenbush by dad and the old woman. The parting on the
horse-boat which was to convey Zerubbabel over tew Albany

where the 'Lida was waiting to take him down tew York, was touching in the extreme. But our pen refuses to paint such agonizing scenes, and so we permit our modest muse to draw the curtain. Suffice it to say, that the 'Lida, freighted with its precious burden, arrived safely at the wharf, foot of Robinson street, and Zerubbabel narrowly escaping from the hands of the barbarian tribes of cabmen and hotel runners, baggage-smashers and pickpockets who thronged the landing, fortunately encountered a real gentleman, with a beautiful blue and crimson scarf and a great gold guard-chain, who politely offered his assistance. Zerubbabel had heard a good deal about the Upper Ten Thousand; and knowing that his townsman, Zadock Pratt, lived at the New York Hotel, he took it for granted that his own arrival in the metropolis had been calculated on, and that this real handsome and superfine gentleman had been deputed on the part of the aristocracy to give him a proper reception and see to his things. The stranger was excessively polite— rescued Zerubbabel's hair trunk from the hands of a pagan cabman, his carpet-bag from a porter, and took his umbrella and an extra pair of boots for bad weather, under his own arm; and piling Zerubbabel and himself, together with all the traps, into a cab, they drove off to the ——— Hotel.

After supper, the stranger proposed to Zerubbabel that they should start out for the purpose of going through a course of sprouts. Zerubbabel didn't know exactly what that meant; but presuming that it had some relation to the new primy donny, or some other upper-crust fixings, got his hat and sallied out arm in arm with his obliging and attentive companion. First they stopped at Sherwood's and took a drink, Zerubbabel being much affected by the naked Venus behind the bar, and quite dazzled by the magnificence of everything about him. Then they visited the Broadway Theater, where Mme. Monplaisir was exhibiting her voluptuous proportions to an enraptured audience. This almost took poor Zerubbabel's breath away; but at the end of the first act they adjourned to the Arbor and took another drink, which considerably revived him. He was soon, however, shocked worse than ever, by being led into the back room, where, in a cool green recess, lay a magnificent woman, as naked as she was born. Zerubbabel at first absolutely screeched with modesty, but being assured by his friend that it was only a picture, he felt comforted, and swanned to man if he didn't think it was a live critter. From this place they returned to the theater, but now went up to the third tier, where were a great many beautiful ladies, splendidly dressed, with whom Zerubbabel's friend seemed to be upon the most intimate terms. Zerubbabel had seen on the wall of the stairway below that this was the entrance to the "Family Circle," and these he supposed were the ladies of the real aristocracy. He was gazing round in a state of complete bewilderment—his head swimming and his eyes dazzling with all the strange sights he had seen and the liquor he had drunk—when he saw his friend approach with a lady. The stranger whispered in his ear,

"Your name—I want to introduce you to the Countess of Astoria."

"Green—Zerubbabel Green," gasped our hero—"the Countess! Whew! You don't say so?"

"Mr. Green," said the stranger, bowing low, "I have the honor to present you to the Countess of Astoria."

Zerubbabel dropped his hat, stammered, blushed, and looked sheepish.

"Don't you think, Mr. Green," observed the Countess, "that we had better take a little refreshment?"

"Sartainly, ma'am—that is, I've no occasion, I thank you—but jest as you say."

"This way," said the polite stranger, with a bow.

"What'll your ladyship hev?" inquired Zerubbabel.

"Oh, I'm not particler, I'll take a brandy toddy."

Zerubbabel looked aghast. But as brandy toddy was the fashionable drink, he took a brandy toddy too—and so did the stranger—of course Mr. Green insisting on paying for all.

The Countess now proposed that they should call her carriage, and invited Mr. Green to go home with her.

"No you don't, Moll!" whispered the stranger—"this is *my* job," and politely bowing his adieus, he took Mr. Green by the arm and led him down stairs.

"But why didn't you let me go home with her ladyship?"

"Oh, she belongs to a slow set—horrible dull and stupid. We'll have something worth two of that before morning. What say you to a turn on the Five Points and round? I know the Chief of Police like a book, and he'll accompany us, and see that nobody takes any liberties with us."

"Good—I'm ready."

"Have you got much money about you?"

"Tew hundred and seventy-five dollars, all in York money."

"Well—I've a considerable sum myself. We had better deposit our pocket-books with the Chief, for fear of accidents—because then the city is responsible if any thing is missing. Here we are at his office. I'll call him out."

The stranger left him a moment, and almost immediately returned with a third party.

"Your Honor," said he, "my friend Green, here, and myself, wish to take a turn through the city and see what's going on; but as we've got a little money that we don't care about losing, we wish to deposit our pocket-books with you, in your official capacity, so that the city will be responsible if any thing occurs."

"Certainly, gentlemen,—certainly, Mr. Browning. Any thing I can do for you or your friend is at your service. Shall I give you receipts for the pocket-books?"

"No, that's not important—we shall be back again in the course of an hour or two. Just deposit them in the safe, and then come with us. We want your company."

His Honor disappeared with the pocket-books, and in a few moments returned; when the whole party set off on their expedition.

Passing the Tombs, they entered the regions of the Points and soon brought up in the suspicious anchorage of Cow Bay. Here, diving down a dark stairway, they entered a dimly-lighted cellar, filled with little stalls, several of which contained customers, feeding upon shilling stews. The air of the room was thick and difficult to be breathed.

"We must call for something to drink, just as a matter of form," whispered the stranger to Green, "and I haven't a cent of change."

"Nor I either—what shall we do? It won't do to ask His Honor, I spose?"

"Oh no, that would be too mean."

"Wal, dang it, here goes!" exclaimed the poor victim, after a moment's hesitation. "Come out here, old seventy-six!" and unbuttoning his herring-bone waistcoat, he fumbled with a strap and drew out a buckskin belt from under his shirt. It was well stuffed. His Honor and our polite stranger exchanged a glance of joyful intelligence. The prize was richer than they had dreamed.

The liquor was called for and drank, at least by Green— the poisoned stuff taking almost instant hold upon his already half drunken brain, and reducing him to a state of reckless, oblivious insanity.

"Come ahead, old fellers!" he shouted, as he doubled up his belt and carelessly thrust it into his trowsers pocket. "Come ahead! I'll show you that Old Stephentown ain't afeard. Do you happen to know the Honorable Zadock Pratt?"

"Know him? To be sure I do—and a glorious fellow he is."

"Rather guess he is—and I'm Deacon Green's son, next door neighbor, tew Stephentown."

"My dear Green, let us embrace—you are from this moment my sworn friend and brother;" and the Chief of Police opened his arms and suffered the maudlin green-horn to blubber upon his bosom.

Recovering themselves from this little display of the bright and tender side of human nature, the stranger whispered to the man behind the bar, and then led the party through a low door, and into an adjoining cellar. Here a sight met the astonished Green, which totally upset the few remains of common sense in his bewildered noddle, and left him entirely at the mercy of his companions. The middle of the low, smoky room was occupied by a party of dancers engaged in the mysteries of a cotillion, the music being furnished by a negro fiddler, mounted on a barrel in one corner. The dancers, however, are the principal objects of interest. They are both black and white, and are distributed with some little regard to the laws of mathematical proportion—two of the four women are black and two white; while the partners of the latter are two shiny buck negroes, and of the others a couple of drunken sailors. The ladies are not dressed in the strictest ball-room costume, one of the negresses being merely in her chemise, and one of the white women absolutely stark naked. There are several bunks round the sides of the room, from which the occupants have been aroused in a drunken hurry, to partake of this midnight orgy, and have evidently found the process of dressing altogether too slow for the occasion. As for the gentlemen, they are furious with the excitement of the dance, and whirl intertwined about in such swift evolutions that it is almost impossible to distinguish one from the other. The entrance of our party has not served to take their attention from the amusement in which they are absorbed, and they seem every moment to grow more and more animated. At length one of the negroes trips, either accidentally or by design, and falling, the whole party tumble over him in a heap, and roll indiscriminately upon the floor, amid such yells, screams and laughter as would mock the saturnalia of hell. The music stops; and gathering themselves together, the dancers walk up to the bar, (there is no room in the Five Points, however small, without its bar,) take a drink all round, and retire exhausted to their bunks.

Our hero and his friends left this den, and again issued into the street. The gentleman who was personating the Chief of Police "for this night only," now complained of being hungry; and Mr. Browning, saying he knew where was a first-rate place to get a good snack of oysters, piloted the party to a notorious thieves' oyster-cellar, of rather better appearance than most of the establishments in that quarter, where they ensconced themselves in one of the little stalls and ordered "four stews," with brandy and water. In the next stall was a party engaged in eating, and who were laughing and talking very loudly. They appeared to be absorbed in a good-natured controversy on some subject that greatly interested them, and about which they were proposing to bet.

"I'll lay five dollars that I can do it," said one.

"Well, Jack, I don't want your money, because you are a good fellow, and pretty d——d drunk, any how."

"That's none of your business. Will you bet?"

"Why, if you insist upon it, I"—

Here they were interrupted by our friend Browning and Mr. Green, who had been watching them for a moment or two.

"I say, gentlemen," observed Mr. Browning, "I hope you won't consider it an intrusion, but I'd like to bet a trifle on this game. This," he continued in a whisper to Zerubbabel, "is the celebrated game of thimble-rig. Follow my example and we'll fix them finally." Then turning to the gentleman with the thimbles under his hand, he continued:

"Now, sir, I will bet you a hundred dollars that, you let me place these thimbles, and I can tell you under which one the little black thing is."

"Done!" said the fellow.

"Done!" said Mr. Browning, putting his hand into his pocket.

"Oh," said he, suddenly remembering, "I left my pocket-book at the Chief's office. Green, my boy, lend me a hundred till we get back."

"To be sure," said Green; and he felt for his precious belt—now in one pocket, now in another, then in all at once—then fumbled in his bosom, where he usually wore it. He was evidently forgetful of what he had done with it. "Dang it," said he, at length—"where is it?"

"Oh, now I remember," said Mr. Browning, "you gave it to the Chief, with the pocket-book. But I'll call him, and make sure. Your Honor, didn't Mr. Green give you his money-belt as well as his pocket-book, to take care of for him?"

"To be sure he did, sir. They are both safely locked up in the City Treasury."

"Never mind, let's put up our watches—I'm sure of winning."

"Come, stranger," said the man with the thimbles, tauntingly, "do you back out and treat?"

"Not exactly. But we've left our money in the City Treasury, to be taken care of for us. However, we'll lay both our watches against your hundred dollars, and His Honor the Chief of Police, who is in the next box, shall hold the stakes. Is that satisfactory?"

"All right—go ahead!"

The Chief was called—Mr. Browning's dashing gold lever with fifteen jewels, and Mr. Green's more modest but substantial silver one, were handed over, together with a hundred dollar bill from the thimble man.

"Now, then, look sharp—are you ready?"

"Yes—ready."

"Now you see it, now you don't see it, and now where's the little joker?"

"It's under that one by his right hand, isn't it?" whispered the stranger to Green.

"Of course it is—I seed him put it there, slyly like," returned Green, in the same tone.

"Here it is," said Browning, laying his hand on the rigger's arm, while with the other he raised the thimble.

There was nothing under it!

"That's cheatin'!" at length exclaimed Zerubbabel, almost blubbering.

"What's that you say!" exclaimed the rigger.

"Yes, it *is* cheating, sir," quietly retorted Mr. Browning.

"Take that, damn you, and that!" shouted the rigger, rising and striking at Browning fiercely.

The row instantly became general, and Zerubbabel was knocked over and trampled upon, before the Chief could interfere. The room swam round—a deathly sickness came over him like a shudder—sparks flew from his eyes, and he knew no more.

When he awoke, he was lying cold, stiff and bloody, in the gutter, and two men were lifting at his head and heels. He was but half conscious, and suffered them to mount him on a wheel-barrow and trundle him away, without showing a sign of life.

"D'ye think he's dead?" asked one.

"Don't know—if he is, we've got to take him to the dead-house, that's all."

"I ain't dead, gentlemen," at length Zerubbabel managed to whine out—"where are you taking me? where am I?"

"Oh, you'll find out soon enough. We're only a going to give you a more comfortable bed than the paving-stones of Cow Bay."

In a few minutes the whole party arrived at the Tombs, where Zerubbabel, thrust into a dark and dreary hall, was left to find a place among the many who were lying along its walls, and to recall at his leisure the process of being put through a course of sprouts. Gradually his senses returned to him; and although feeling wretchedly, and firmly persuaded he was about to die, he remembered dimly everything that had happened, and came at length to the melancholy, the awful conclusion, that he was in jail.

A solitary gas-light, half turned down, burned in a corner behind the high door of this vast hall, throwing flickering gleams and shadows like ghosts along the walls—now bringing into sight and now hiding entirely the forms of the sleepers. There may have been fifty, or perhaps a hundred, gathered by the industrious policemen during the night, from the gutters and entries of houses, and shoved in to this general receptacle, like dead bodies into a Potter's Field in time of pestilence. They were all of the lower classes, as whenever a *gentleman*, with good clothes and money in his

pockets, happens to get drunk and lie down in the streets—
and such things do happen in the best regulated cities—the
polite guardian of the hour takes private and especial care
of him: and who shall blame the discriminating policeman
for thus performing his functions? Who would act differently? Nobody who would accept the office of night watch-
man.

Perhaps half the inmates in Loafers' Hall are women—
yes, reader, women. If you are incredulous call at the Tombs
any night and satisfy yourself of the truth. There you will
see them—as Mr. Zerubbabel Green saw them—though we
trust not with his awful head-ache. As he stretched out his
bruised and stiffened limbs, raised his well-pummeled head
and tried to penetrate the gloom of the mysterious place, he
thought—poor unsophisticated youth—he thought that he
was dead, and had waked up among the demons who were
henceforth to be his companions. Gradually, however, his
silly senses returned to him, and one by one the events of
the night rose dim and vague in memory's horizon. His departure from home; his arrival in New York; his dashing acquaintance of the Upper Ten Thousand, and the strange,
bewildering adventures of the evening; and then his
money—not only pocket-book but belt. Had he deposited
them with the Chief of Police, and were they indeed all safe?
If yes, he was indifferent to the rest. His head would stop
aching, and his bruises would heal—he would recover his
money, get on board the boat and go right home to Stephentown as fast as he could get there, and never leave it again
as long as he lived. Oh how his head ached! and his heart
too! He actually groaned and moaned in the excess of his
agony, both mental and physical.

At length came daylight—dreary, drizzling and dismal.
Zerubbabel was dragged from the hall, with its other inmates, and carried before the magistrate. When it came his
turn to be examined, the policeman gave in his brief and
pregnant testimony—found drunk at two o'clock in the gutter in Cow Bay—and the magistrate was about to dismiss

him to the cells, when Zerubbabel raised his hands and begged to be heard, in a tone so heart-broken and piteous that even the sympathies of the sleepy magistrate were touched, and he ordered the poor fellow to speak. Interrupted by sobs and tearful blubberings, so full of abject wretchedness as to repress all sense of the ludicrous, he told his story. It was some time before he could be made to understand how he—he, Zerubbabel Green, one of the cutest chaps at a dicker or a wrestling match in all Stephentown—had been so utterly, so completely taken in and sold at the first offer. He was discharged from custody, and a policeman set on the trail of the villains who had got his money and watch. The last we heard of him was that he had returned to Stephentown—how, we don't know—and, there being a Methodist revival going on in the neighborhood, had manifested the most unequivocal symptoms of being under concern of mind. Once, however, when the class-leader inquired of him if he felt any change, he put his hand in his pocket, then in his breast, and replied bitterly—"No! that gosh-blamed Chief of Police has got every cent!"

No. XIV

Saturday Night

*The Weekly Holiday—The
Markets—Washington Market—The Old
Woman's Basket and Dilemma—Catharine
Market—The Poor*

Saturday night is—if our emerald-colored friends will excuse the bull—the poor man's holiday. During the rest of the
week every one is engaged earnestly at his or her regular
occupation—the mechanic at his bench, the laborer with his
hod, the rag-picker with hook and bag, the beggar at his corner. Even the children of the poor are hard workers, notwithstanding their apparently riotous idleness. The little
bare-footed girl watches the sky for rain, and when everybody else feels gloomy and uncomfortable, she is as merry
as a clover-field to see the shower come down, and hies to
her crossing as blithely as a bee to the horse-chesnuts in
midsummer bloom. The boys, too, all find employment—or
employ themselves in trying. But Saturday night is poverty's saturnalia. The laborer trudges home with his week's
pittance, stepping lightly, and his heart swelling with happiness at the thought of the comfort he is about to confer upon

his family. The newsboy relaxes his cry and gives his over-worked lungs repose, while he dances forth in insane glee, "bound to have a first-rate spree." The pale seamstress and the buxom folding-girl, the humble housewife, the ragged pauper, the tidy, the wretched, the handsome, the de-praved—all welcome the approach of Saturday night.

For an instructive and comprehensive glimpse of Satur-day night, let us take a turn through the Markets. Here there is a regular congestion and as in the individual man the stomach is the center of commotion, so in the "grand man" or city, the market is the great focus of interest. He who lives at ease upon his income—or his landlady—scolds if the steak be a thought muscular or the eggs a shade too old—whose whole household experience consists in going to bed, breakfasting, dining, supping and sleeping again—can scarcely form to himself any conception of the importance of Saturday night to that large class of our population who go to market but once a week. To them, the return of that time is waited for with hopeful stomachs, half fed during all the week with what remains from the last supply and what can be "picked up" from day to day, here, there, and every-where. We know it is a melancholy thing to say, and still more melancholy to think of, that a couple of hundred thou-sand people in a single city—and those, too, who work the hardest and longest, and in labors the most repulsive, which ought therefore to be best rewarded—should be absolutely cramped six days in seven for something to eat. But it is sadly true. And while the clergyman, clad in purple and fine linen, faring sumptuously every day, receives princely re-wards for doing so great a labor of love as declaring to his fellow creatures the glories and beatitudes of divine faith—while the lawyer mounts to power and affluence on the madness and the crimes of society—the physician grows rich upon the pains he knows not how to alleviate, and the blunders he buries with his patients—while the merchant becomes a lord by trafficking in what he does not produce—the laborer and his family, who really hold society together by the work and cunning of their hands, are often without a dinner. This, oh critical rhetorician, is a long sentence, we know it—but it is not half so long as the six thousand years of servitude under which the working man and the working woman of the world have been struggling.

But we are here at Washington Market. What a squeeze—what a crowd! It is not here mere elbows and knees, and brawny chests and broad stout backs that you are to encounter. Now you stumble against a firkin, and now are overset by a bag. And there is a woman who has somehow—it is impossible to tell how—squeezed through between you and your next neighbor: but her basket, to which she clings with death-like tenacity, appears to be made of less elastic material than herself. It has assumed the position of a balloon, and forms a target for a score of noses pushed on from the rear. There is no chance of its coming through, that is certain; and the woman will *not* let go of it—that seems equally clear. There is nothing, therefore, for you to do but to crawl under it. As you are in the act of performing this difficult and delicate passage, a couple of salt mackerel, at the bottom of the basket, as if in sympathy for your sufferings, bedew your Leary with their briny tears, while a piece of corned-beef, with a large slice of the fat, lovingly reposes on your coat-collar. You at length regain your feet and ascertain that you have been kneeling in a basket of stale eggs, to the imminent ruin of your new black pants. The Irish huckster-woman who owns them, seeing this wholesale destruction of her brood of incipient chickens, pours out a volley of abuse upon your devoted dead, and loudly demands full compensation for her irreparable loss. You gladly pay whatever she requires; and by dint of pulling and squeezing, and being pulled and squeezed, we at length make our way through the lower walk, past the butter and cheese stands, and stalls for carcasses of dead hogs and sheep, now ancle-deep in mud, and so on to the fish-market. If you are any thing of an amateur in smells, you surely may here be gratified to your nose's content. But don't tread on that pile of eels, for they are slippery fellows and would be very likely to bring you "down upon 'em!" And see there! A fine green lobster has caught your foot in his pinchers and will be through the leather directly. You will find him the closest friend you ever had—he'll stick like a burr.

Washington Market, however, is nothing to its rival on the other side of the city—Catharine Market. Here is New York life in one of its most active and demonstrative phases. So many attempts have been made to describe the class frequenting here—all of them producing but the merest shadow of the original—that we should despair of success were we to attempt the dangerous ground. Imagine all the coarseness, all the shameless filth, all the squalor and brutality from which you have escaped, and then conceive, steeped to the lips in it, a population made reckless by ignorance, want and vice, and utterly regardless of public opinion, or even unconscious of its existence. Then you will have some faint idea of the many who frequent Catharine Market of a Saturday night. To be sure we do not mean to say that there are not many respectable, well-to-do people who come there; we speak entirely of the lower stratum of its customers. The truth is, that the condition, both moral and physical, in which such a city as New York permits its poor to exist, is utterly disgraceful—not to the poor, for they deserve only our deepest pity, but to the community—the powerful, enlightened, wealthy community—which permits its unfortunate children, who know nothing but how to work, to become thus horribly degraded. Are the public weary of hearing this repeated? But it must be repeated and reiterated, until government and the wealthy know and feel its truth, and see clearly their bounden duty to that portion of their fellow creatures who are not able, in the sharp and selfish competition of keener brains, to take care of themselves.

Saturday night is a great time at all the cheap theaters and places of public amusement and brings out, in all their gaudy plumage, the plump and noisy birds of the Bowery and the region round about. Theater, Museum, Christy's, garden, concert and ball-room, are ever crowded and gay on Saturday evenings, and their proprietors are sure of making up handsomely for a bad week. The Chatham street and Bowery shops, too, and those crying near the water, on both sides of the city, are thronged with customers on Saturday night; and in short, the whole world of middle and lower life turn out to trade and enjoy themselves, to see and to be seen.

No. XV

The City at Day-Light

*The Station House—The Tombs—The
Battery—Loafers—The Daylight
Market—Morning, Sunrise and Farewell*

Our task is ended. The thousands of twinkling gas-lights
which have thus far dimly lighted our steps, have one by one
expired, leaving only here and there a feeble ray struggling
amid the thick gray morning fog that soon will melt into
daylight. The sleepy policeman has gone his last round, and
turned in at the station-house for his morning snooze—
leaving the city entirely unwatched at the very hour of night
when it most requires his vigilance and care. By his side,
piled up on broad wooden benches, divaning the damp and
dreary cells, sleep the human swine, both male and female,
who have during the night been rescued from the gutter. One,
in the agony of awakening, and to escape the red-hot devils
whom delirium tremens whirled in myriads upon his track,
has cut his throat from ear to ear, and lies struggling his last
amid the little pool of blood, while his drowzy bench-fellow,
disturbed by his spasms, swears a sleepy oath, and inquires
why the h—— he can't lie still, and not be waking up his
neighbors. The burglar with his gang, engaged in some desperate adventure, at which they have been working undis-

turbed all night, now venture safely forth with their booty and their tools, gliding swiftly through the dreary streets to their dens, to sleep till the day is past, and darkness once more tempts forth the human owl to seek his prey. The bloated night-walker, who has no regular place even to sleep, and who lives by pacing the purlieus of the Points or Water street all night, and enticing drunken negroes, sailors or loafers into two-shilling bed-houses, or even less convenient places, has made her last desperate foray for the night, and cowers, shivering and yawning with cold and sleep, under the protection of some friendly stoop or unfinished building. At the Tombs the morning roll is about commencing, and by the dim light of his dark lantern, policeman after policeman brings in the report of his watch, and deposits the culprits along the sticky and oozy benches. The magistrate, with spectacle on nose, deciphers by instinct the mis-spelled returns, and consigns the miserable wretches one after another to the welcome cells, to be thence despatched to the Penitentiary, the Hospital, or Potter's Field—either fate a glorious relief from all they have been able to accomplish for themselves unaided in the world. The news-carrier issues from the reeking steam-pit, where the ceaseless panting of the city's brain gives forth its myriads of sibylline leaves, to bring pleasure and despair, ruin and recreation to the countless thousands of the city. The bill-poster with his mountain of startling wonderment on his shoulder and gigantic paste-bucket in hand, anoints carefully the ends of brick-piles and the dead-walls wherever he can encounter them, and then proceeds to ornament them with gay-printed sheets of paper, eruptive with the eulogistic lies of their authors, and uttering more marvels of art and artists than the realm of the Beautiful has power to conceive or entertain.

The homeless loafers on the Battery have outslept the watching of the stars, winking at their pale echoes in the placid waters. Perhaps they have been dreaming, these wretched and ragged loafers, of the green fields and happy days of childhood, when they slept nightly guarded by a mother's love, and their days were watched over by a father's protecting care. The cold breath of October wakes them now to the dreary and desolate reality of their fate, dreary and desolate as the yellow and blood-stained leaves that are floating flake-like from the trees, and caught up by the winds in mad play. They are not so fortunate as their brother-loafers of the gutters, who are given a night's lodging—such as it is, to be sure—but at least under cover; and are perhaps sent for thirty or sixty days to the Penitentiary, where they eat and sleep comfortably, and work lightly. Truly it is very properly considered a special favor by the vagabonds of civilization to be arrested and taken care of at the expense of the community. Certainly it is the duty of the community to do this; but it is a question whether if it were done a little more magnanimously and a little less squalidly—a little more willingly and a little less as if it were reluctantly wrung from it in sheerest necessity and self-defense—the chances of securing the pauper's gratitude, and thus perhaps even reaching his self-respect, would be greatly promoted.

But daylight strengthens and the morn comes on apace. Already the streets begin to fill with their crowds of business people of all sorts, hastening to their various avocations, while the sons and daughters of luxury slumber off the effects of their late hours and dissipation. One by one the shops begin to open their glass eyes, and the sleepy clerks crawl yawning round the counters, making the preliminary arrangements for the business of the day. The cry of the newsboys begins to be heard, and a stir is perceptible about the hotels and steamboat landings, ferries and railroad depots. Phoebus, that prince of omnibus drivers, has mounted his box and cracks his fiery whip, scattering streams of sunshine upon the earth; while the other lines gradually make their appearance, slowly emerging from the side-streets and waiting for full fares before they will start down Broadway in earnest. They come, however, thicker and thicker, and soon the welcome "all full, driver!" is heard from three or four impatient passengers, speaking at once—

the door is pulled to with a slam—the driver casts an inquiring look down the little six-pence trap at his back, gazes ruefully as Alexander round because there are no more seats to fill, and at last dashes Jehu-like down the street. A few minutes ago his only object in life seemed to be to get over the ground as slowly as possible. He walked his wide-ribbed horses, stopped at every corner, trying to convince himself that the gentlemen coming leisurely down Eighth street, had beckoned him for a ride, and made believe deaf whenever either of the unfortunates he had already caged, implored him to go ahead. Now you would imagine that he was old Boreas himself in chase of a runaway wind. He dashes over the back of Russ pavement in front of the New York Hotel like a boat gliding over the surf, and then plunges heavily into the rolling, tumbling sea of cobble-stone hillocks which form the ground-swell of Broadway.

Another scene of great activity in the daylight city is the market. Indeed long before daylight the boats and carts of countrymen and hucksters begin to arrive and to make arrangements for a favorable display in the morning. The remnants of yesterday's withered remainder are skillfully mixed with the freshness of the morning's store—tubs, baskets and buckets are replenished and made to look sweet and new—stale eggs are carefully turned and fresh ones placed on top—and all the tricks of trade by whose permission we eat and drink, are set a-going. The coffee-and-pie-stands are already crowded with their hungry customers, while many are reduced to the hardship of resorting to the oyster-boats and swallowing the delicate natives naked as they were born, or else go entirely without a breakfast—and such is the degrading force of habit that we have seen many who absolutely grew fat upon this diet and seemed utterly unconscious of the misery they were compelled to suffer!

Thus fades the night, and thus begins the day; and so, turning off the gas, we raise our hot brow and weary eyes from off the page, and commending our labors to the hospitality of your affections, bid farewell!

New York by Daylight

Selections from

New York in Slices

and

Fifteen Minutes Around New York

A General Dash
at the Ferries
(from *Fifteen Minutes Around New York*)

Hurra! There goes the bell! Give us the change—run—jump—dash—here we are! Thanks to a quick eye, a pair of tolerably long, if not handsome legs, and considerable practice in the sharp work of getting about and around New York. A greenhorn, or a Philadelphian, or anybody from those provincial places, would have now been paddling about in that involuntary salt water swimming-bath shut in by the slip. Imagine, for a moment, our venerable and respected cotemporary (that's the respectable word for neighbor, we believe,) of the *City Item*, in such a scrape. He would never say another word against New York—never!

But the fact is, we needn't have been in so terrible a hurry. We could very profitably have spent five minutes of our sacred fifteen, in the passengers' room. Suppose we step ashore, and wait for the next boat?

The first person who enters the room, after ourselves, is a lady. She is dressed in one of those chocolate-colored, unrevealing, linen-and-cotton out-door night-gowns, which the Genius of Ugliness has just invented, and is chuckling over as one of his most successful achievements. A shirred barege

bonnet of a similar hue, with a thick green veil—that national symbol of propriety and virtue in this country—carefully conceals her features. Still, as she walks, the
voluptuous undulations of the form, so seductively painted
by Balzac, in his Madame Marneffe, disclose the young
woman, full of life and animal spirits. Pretty, too, she doubtless is. But why that "envious veil?" as somebody calls it.
There is no sun, and the day is stewingly warm—regular
fricasee weather. She must be nearly suffocated under that
thick face-counterpane.

"Madame, we really must beg to suggest that—"

"What would you suggest to that lady, sir?"

"That—ehem!—it is a remarkably fine day, sir. What!
Harry, my boy—is it you? Why, where the mischief are you
bound?"

"Sh—!"

"Oh, I see—all right."

Here comes a thin, intellectual-looking woman, of thirty-
five. Nothing old-maidish about her—rather on the strong-
minded womanish order. She is thin, but not meagre; looks
as if she worked hard, and still knew how to enjoy life in her
own independent way. That is a music-teacher. She has for
years supported her father, mother and younger brothers, by
teaching the piano. She also composes a waltz or a polka
now and then, and writes tolerable articles for a soi-disant
American musical journal. She gets up at six o'clock in the
morning, and spends ten hours every day in giving lessons
at the houses of her—patients, we had almost said. What an
unheard-of amount of stupidity she must encounter in the
course of the year! What scores of "interesting young ladies"
who don't know the difference between A flat and a diapa-
son, and whose fingers are incapable of learning the distance from tonic to sub-dominant—to whom 3–4 time
possesses no marked difference from 6–8, and who never
could see the use of those tiresome flats and sharps! And yet

our musical old maid has managed to preserve her temper and her complexion. What a wife she would have made!

Mose and Lize, with a party of very particular friends, have just burst through the toll-house, very much like, as we may imagine, the Goths entered Rome. They—our Bowery friends, and not the Goths—are laughing and shouting with fun. Mose carries his coat on one arm, and a huge basket in the other hand, at which he now and then glances in a most expressive manner. The thing is clear—a pic-nic is coming off —and there'll be "high" doings before that party gets home.

Here is a nervous old gentleman, who is always afraid of being too late, and looks into the room timidly, as much as to ask, humbly, whether anybody has any objection to his going over in the next boat. He advertised yesterday morning in the Herald for a wife—and, fearful that somebody would be sure to recognise him in New York, made the rendezvous in Greenwood Cemetery. If he knew that the fair one whom he expects to meet, and who has written to him in such tender terms, is a pocket-book dropper, a "burner," a "watch-stuffer"—in short, a genteel swindler, who has laid himself out for a big haul, our nervous and timid friend would take the first stage up town, and remain in bed and on a diet of herb-tea for a fortnight. The probabilities, even, are that he would marry his landlady.

Closely following the nervous man, is a lady whom you at once recognise for an Englishwoman. She is not in the least handsome, but there is a solidity and reality about her, a sincerity of purpose and character, an absence of that shop-window-iveness of now-a-days,—a real, substantial, business-like air, which announces unmistakeably the English wife and mother. We know her well. She is the wife of an English officer, sent over to this country to make some observations upon steam marine. They stop, of course, at the Clarendon; but the five children and the governess could not be permitted to stay in a hotel: it was altogether too much opposed to English ideas. They are established in

Brooklyn, and the mother goes every day, and mind you, *walks*, although it is so easy to ride, walks from the Clarendon to the South Ferry, and from the foot of Atlantic street, a mile and a half, to her children's temporary home. Her American friends at the hotel—thin-chested, crinolined and dyspeptic, done up in orange-colored organdies and Virginia-fence lace collars that don't go below the hem of the dress, are astonished at her temerity in taking those daily walks, and "wouldn't do it for the world." In fact, they consider it quite vulgar; and can't at all see the necessity of walking when there are so many omnibuses! Our English-woman, however, is sound and healthy-colored—enjoys the exercise—has strong and hearty children, and, in her green-striped de laine dress and brown bonnet, is one of the most contented creatures in existence.

But the boat is in—we must be off.

Stop! Let us wait for that graceful and majestic woman, who walks down as deliberately as if she were Cleopatra, and the "Passaic" were her pleasure-bark, so magnificently upholstered by Shakespeare. She is veiled, but in that be-witching, fascinating, odalisquish sort of way so seldom achieved by an Anglo-Saxon, on either side of the water. Who is she?

Lend us your ear: That is THE LADY IN BLACK. Her history and adventures were well known, some years ago, and she was for the usual period the object of one of those unac-countable moral spasms known as a "New York excite-ment." She was, among other trifles, accused of murdering her husband, and stood her trial unblenchingly. She was ac-quitted, and soon after sunk from public attention. She now lives a retired, if not a virtuous life, and may be frequently seen going home or coming into the city, spreading her lures for any old victim with a sugary tooth, who may happen to encounter her on the ferry boat. If that heart could write its experience, its thoughts, its sensations, what a record it would be! What a veil would be lifted from the mystery of the life of woman!

And now, we should like to know why it is that people will not and cannot wait quietly until the passengers who have just come over, have time to get off, and out of the way? Everybody knows that the boat won't go until the passengers are aboard—that it is safely chained up to the wharf, and that the bell will ring in season to give them plenty of time. Still, as soon as the boat appears in sight, the waiting crowd collects on the verge of the wharf, waiting its arrival with intense anxiety; and the instant it touches, a general rush and scramble takes place to get on board—of course, embarrassing, delaying, corn-smashing, and generally upsetting the comers ashore. The consequence is, that what might be so easily, naturally and conveniently achieved, is transformed into a regular battle between two opposing hosts, armed with umbrellas, baskets, bundles, and babies. The loss on both sides is of course tremendous; and the whole business of crossing a ferry is thus voluntarily rendered one of the most atrocious "little miseries" to which metropolitan human nature is liable.

At last we are on board again. A large fat woman, who jumped at the last moment, basket and all, has fallen short and gone down. However, she considerately threw the basket on board, and its beets, sausages, and doughnuts are scattered all about. No doubt they will be collected, with the rest of the "remains," by the deck hands, and sent home; so that Mr. Theophilus Squiggins, of Myrtle avenue, although he may have a cold wife, will have a warm dinner.

True, we are not exactly a lady—although we were very near one last evening at the opera—but still we shall take the liberty of going into the "ladies' cabin," where, stuck up in that Fourieristic arm-chair extending all round the cabin, are quite as many trowsers as petticoats. The "gentlemen's cabin" is only occupied by negroes, blackguards and smokers—a practical definition of the word gentleman, for which we beg leave to say we are in no way responsible.

Well—over we go, gliding swiftly as a dream, and gulping down great mouthfuls of fresh sea air, enough to supply the city deficit of oxygen for the remainder of the day. The lovely panorama of the river and bay passes before us—we squeeze ourselves in among the posts and pier-heads of the shore—the bell rings—the usual desperate fight to "effect a landing" takes place—and our fifteen minutes, as well as ourselves, are "over."

Racing down the Avenue.

The Mock Auctions

(from *New York in Slices*)

We hope our country acquaintance, Mr. Greenhorn, will excuse us when we tell him we don't sympathize much with
his loss in buying a splendid gold watch for fifteen dollars,
and a casket of diamonds for eighteen-pence a piece. If he
supposed (as he protests) that they were genuine, he must
have known that they were stolen, to be sold at any such
price; and he has allowed his appetite for a sharp bargain to
get the upper hand of his honesty as well as his usual
shrewdness. We tell him plainly, then, that his intention was
to avail himself of somebody's being robbed. If he has got
bitten, who is to pity him?

Notwithstanding that we don't sympathize with Mr.
Greenhorn, we condemn the villany of Mr. Funk, as roundly
as the roundest. He is infinitely less respectable than the
burglar or the blackleg, and deserves a severer punishment.
There are rascalities enough, Heaven knows, in trade, in the
best of streets, and under the most virtuous auspices. From
the heavy importer of Water-street to the three-penny re-
tailer on the corner, lies are told every day enough to place
anybody who *had* a soul in extreme jeopardy. But the Peter
Funk is the sublime of mercantile swindling—the result of
the commercial principle carried to its ultimates. The thing

he does upon a scale of magnificent falsehood and impudence, is done by the dealer in diluted brandies and damaged calicoes upon a smaller scale, in a more sneaking manner. Mr. Funk sells our friend Greenhorn a pinchbeck watch for gold, and real glass beads set in pewter for diamonds. Well—what then? The respectable house of Wiggins & Winkle sells us, yes *us*, the veritable writer of these "Slices," a catty-box of real Souchong, into which has been mixed ten or a dozen pounds of Bohea, and a basket of champagne which they know to be galvanized cider, and which cost them ten cents a gallon. Our wife buys a new frock at Blinkum's, which she is assured is the real French chintz, warranted fast colors, and which, after the first washing, looks like the fag-end of a consumptive rainbow. In fact, he or she who *buys* any thing anywhere, must keep a sharp lookout. Let a person take a thousand dollars and start down Broadway, buying at every shop and paying whatever is asked, without question or hesitation, and how much do you think his purchases would be actually worth by the time his money gave out? And yet, the shopkeepers are honest and respectable—have pews in church, and have two gowns, and everything tidy and comfortable.

Peter Funk is a gentleman of extensive connections, and has establishments in various parts of the city besides Chatham street and Lower Broadway. You may find the red flag of Peter Funkism flying in Pearl-street and other "heavy" quarters, where it is generally supposed that transactions are *bona fide* and dealers responsible. There are pinchbeck and glass beads in many other kinds of goods besides watches and breastpins. The country merchant, who buys from a sample, and takes the "invoice" measurement, (forged in the back office,) is frequently amazed upon opening his bales, to discover that he has bought a pig in the poke—that his splendid English prints have become metamorphosed into cheap domestics, and that his woad-dyed French broadcloth smells horribly of logwood. In truth, the whole auction system, although there are of course individ-

"Peter Funk"

ual exceptions, is false and hollow, conducted upon a wrong basis, and depending for its profits upon the shrewdness of those who sell and the gullibility of those who buy.

The organization of the mock auctions is complete, and each shop is the centre of a conspiracy against the pockets of the community, requiring six or eight accomplices to carry on business successfully. Besides the auctioneer and his clerk there are the outsiders, who always attend the sale and bid on every thing that is offered—making bargains by the score, each one of which according to their own story, ought to enrich them. Men are employed by the day to stand outside the counter to act as false bidders. We have seen men in the mock-auction rooms in Broadway within the last few days, whom we have known to be engaged in the same business for ten years. They are generally men of middle age and of honest looks. Then there is the "respectable jeweller" round the corner or across the way, to whom the doubtful or hesitating are referred as to the genuineness of the article for sale, and who is always ready to give a favorable answer. This is done, too, very safely; for in the case of a gold watch, for instance, the Peter Funk, whom Mr. Greenhorn takes to be a rival bidder, takes you to the jeweller and exhibits a *real* gold watch for his inspection. The verdict is of course favorable; and, on the way back, the watches are dexterously exchanged in the outside pocket of the Funk, and you go on bidding for what you now suppose you *know* to be a genuine lever, Tobias make, full jewelled. So with the articles of jewelry—pencils, rings, breastpins, necklaces, &c. &c. The whole arrangement is perfect, and such an air of earnestness and sincerity is preserved by the accomplices on the outside of the counter, that an inexperienced stranger cannot fail to be taken in.

But the peculiar feature of this business is, that the poor dupe never knows *how many* articles he is buying. For instance, the auctioneer holds up a card containing a dozen or two of small articles, and asks, "How much a-piece, gentlemen, for these splendid gold pencil-cases, very heavy, and warranted eighteen carats. The last of an immense stock from a Broadway establishment, just become bankrupt, and sold under the orders of the Sheriff. How much for these magnificent pencils, breastpins, and bracelets?" The Funks make a small bid, which he receives with virtuous indignation, and perhaps ventures to inquire whether they think the articles were stolen. Upon this another Funk bids a higher sum, and the greenhorn begins to think that here is indeed a chance for a splendid bargain. At length he bids, and his fate is sealed. After playing him a little, as Frank Forrester would play a trout, down goes the hammer, and the fortunate purchaser, who supposes he has bid off two dozen articles, is taken into the back room to settle and receive his goods. Here an immense box of all sorts of trash, from a pair of scissors to a shirt-button, is produced, and he learns, to his consternation, that he has purchased seven or eight hundred pieces at twenty-five cents a piece; and a bill for a couple of hundred dollars is presented to him. If he remonstrates, the clerk is inflexible; and if he attempts to leave the place, he is forcibly withheld—a Funk is called in, who passes himself off for an officer, and he is threatened with immediate arrest for "obtaining goods under false pretences." Alarmed and dumbfounded, he pays over all the money he has about him and is kindly permitted to take his purchase—leaving his watch in pledge that he will return and settle the balance of the bill. With his load of rubbish tied up in his pocket-handkerchief, he makes his escape; and, entering the first jeweller's shop he encounters, is politely told, with a well-bred shrug of pity, that his whole cargo isn't worth five dollars. But then the lesson he has learned, if he only knows how to profit by it, will stand him well in stead for the money he has thrown away.

Let all strangers remember, once for all, that there is no establishment in the city where real watches and valuable jewelry are sold at auction. Such goods have always a nearly fixed and intrinsic value; and can neither be bought nor sold at any great reduction from the standard price. Whoever offers them thus is a swindler or a thief. Either he has stolen what he sells, or else the articles he offers are nothing but paste and galvanized pewter, and are utterly worthless. By following this plain direction, the stranger in New York will save his money and avoid being obliged to regard himself as a fool and a spooney.

If anybody would like to know why these shops are not suppressed by law, he must ask the "proper authorities"—if he can find them. It is none of our business. We expose the various devices which exist openly in the Metropolis, whose express and only business it is to defraud the unwary. If the authorities, who are perfectly cognizant of their existence, would do as much to suppress them, the evil would soon be abated.

We hope, while on this subject, we shall be pardoned for a few profitable speculations—things not often made by editors of newspapers. While passing these mock-auction establishments, and wondering for the hundred-thousandth time at the gullibility of human nature, we have sometimes asked ourselves what would be the result if all the mock auctions in the community were at once to be exposed? The sleek-fed proselytist with his mock religion; the virtuous lady leaving her splendid mansion "above Bleecker" to meet her paramour in Church-street; the respectable merchant or professional man spending his time and his income at the gambling-house or the brothel; the demagogue dealing out his pernicious slang and mock patriotism to gaping fools; the mercenary editor selling his columns to the interest or the institution that would pay him best; the financier originating falsehoods to facilitate his extensive operations and swell his profits; the painted harlot making merchandise of her mock blushes and impoisoned charms; the lawyer selling his genius and learning to well-fed oppression—would it not be a sight worth seeing? and after contemplating it should we not be ready to exclaim, "The whole world is but one vast Mock Auction!"

The Eating-Houses

(from *New York in Slices*)

"Beefsteakandtatersvegetábesnumbertwenty —In*jin*hardand sparrowgrassnumbérsixteen!" "Waiter! Waiter! WA-Y-TER!" "Comingsir"—while the rascal's *going* as fast as he can! "*Is* that beef killed for my porterhouse steak I ordered last week?" "Readynminitsir, comingsir, dreklysir—twonsixpence, biledamand cabbage shillin, ricepudn sixpnce, eighteen-pence—at the barf you please—lobstaucensammingnumberfour—yes sir!" Imagine a continuous stream of such sounds as these, about the size of the Croton river, flowing through the banks of clattering plates and clashing knives and forks, perfumed with the steam from a mammoth kitchen, roasting, boiling, baking, frying, beneath the floor—crowds of animals with a pair of jaws apiece, wagging in emulation of the one wielded with such terrific effect by SAMSON—and the thermometer which has become ashamed of itself and hides away behind a mountain of hats in the corner, melting up *by degrees* to boiling heat—and you will have some notion of a New York eating-house. We once undertook to count these establishments in the lower part of the City, but got surfeited on the smell of fried grease before we got half through the first street, and were obliged to go home in a cab. We believe, however, that there can't be less than a hundred of them within half a mile of the Exchange. They are too important a "slice" of New York to be overlooked, and strangers who stop curiosity-hunting after they have climbed the big clock-case at the head of Wall-street, haven't seen half the sights.

A New York eating-house at high tide is a scene which would well repay the labors of an antiquarian or a panoramist, if its spirit and details could be but half preserved. Every thing is done differently in New York from anywhere else—but in eating the difference is more striking than in any other branch of human economy. A thorough-bred diner-down-town will look at a bill of fare, order his dinner, and bolt it and himself, and be engaged in putting off a lot of goods upon a greenhorn, while you are getting your napkin fixed over your nankeens (we think the cotton article preferable) and deciding whether you will take ox-tail or mock-turtle. A regular down-towner surveys the kitchen with his nose as he comes up-stairs—selects his dish by intuition, and swallows it by steam and the electro-galvanic battery. As to digesting it, that is none of his business. He has paid all liabilities to his stomach, and that is all he knows or cares about the matter. The stomach must manage its own affairs—he is not in that "line."

Not less than thirty thousand persons engaged in mercantile or financial affairs, dine at eating-houses every day. The work commences punctually at twelve; and from that hour until three or four the havoc is immense and incessant. Taylor at Buena Vista was nothing to it. They sweep every thing—not a fragment is left. The fare is generally bad enough—not nearly equal to that which the cook at the Home above Bleecker saves for the beggars, (generally her own thirteen cousins, "just come over.") It is really wonderful how men of refined tastes and pampered habits, who at home are as fastidious as luxury and a delicate appetite can make them, find it in their hearts—or stomachs either—to gorge such disgusting masses of stringy meat and tepid veg-

etables, and to go about their business again under the fond
delusion that they have dined. But "custom," they say, does
wonders; and it seems that the fear of losing it makes our
merchant-princes willing to put up with and put down
warm swill in lieu of soup, perspiring joints for delicate *en-
trées*, and corn meal and molasses instead of *meringues à la
creme à la rose.*

There are three distinct classes of eating-houses, and each
has its model or type. Linnaeus would probably classify
them as Sweenyorum, Browniverous, and Delmonican. The
Sweenyorum is but an extension downward of the Browniverous, which we have already described. The chief difference to be noted between the two is, that while at Brown's
the waiters *actually do* pass by you within hail now and
then, at Sweeney's no such phenomenon ever by any possibility occurs. The room is laid out like the floor of a church,
with tables and benches for four, in place of pews. Along the
aisles (of Greece, if you judge by the smell) are ranged at
"stated" intervals, the attentive waiters, who receive the
dishes, small plate sixpnce, large plate shillin, as they are
cut off the by man at the helm, and distribute them on either side, with surprising dexterity and precision. Sometimes a nice bit of rosegoose, tender, may be seen flying
down the aisle, without its original wings, followed closely
in playful sport by a small plate bilebeef, vegetables, until
both arrive at their destination; when goose leaps lightly in
front of a poet of the Sunday press, who ordered it probably
through a commendable preference for a brother of the
quill; while the fat and lazy beef dumps itself down with
perfect resignation before the "monstrous jaws" of one of
the b'hoys, who has just come from a fire in 49th-street, and
is hungry, *some!*

At Brown's we get a bill of fare, with the "extras" all honestly marked off and priced at the margin. But at Sweeney's
we save our sixpence and dispense with superfluities. The
bill of fare is delivered by a man at the door, regularly engaged for that purpose and is as follows:

Biledlamancapersors.
Rosebeefrosegoorosemuttonantaters—
Biledamancabbage, vegetables—
Walkinsirtakaseatsir.

This is certainly clear and distinct as General Taylor's political opinions, and does away with a great deal of lying in print, to which bills of fare as well as newspapers are too much addicted. The Sweeney, or sixpenny cut, is frequented by a more diversified set of customers than either of the others. It is not impossible to see, here, Professor Bush dining cheek-by-jowl with a hod-man off duty, nor to find a black-leg from Park-row seated opposite the police-officer whose manifest destiny it will be one of these days to take him to quod—unless he should happen to have money enough about him to pay for being let go. The editor, the author, the young lawyer, the publisher, the ice-cream man round the corner, the poor physician on his way to patients who don't pay, the young student of divinity learning humility at six shillings a week; the journeyman printer on a batter, and afraid to go home to his wife before he gets sober; in short, all classes who go to make up the great middle stripe of population, concentrate and commingle at Sweeney's. Yet all these varied elements never effervesce into any thing in the slightest degree resembling a disturbance; for eating is a serious business—especially when you have but sixpence and no idea whether the next one has been coined.

It is true that Sweeney's "is emphatically a sixpenny eating-house"—but you must take care what you are about, or you may as well have dined at the Astor.—Unless you know how it is done, you will be nicely done yourself. If you indulge in a second piece of bread, a pickle, a bit of cheese, &c., &c., your bill will be summed up to you something after this fashion:—"Clamsoup sixpnce, rosebeef large, shilln, roastchikn eighteen, extra bread three, butter sixpnce, pickle sixpnce, pudn sixpnce, cheese three, claret (logwood and water alumized) two shilln—seven shilln." If you wish to dine cheaply, be contented with a cheap dinner. Call simply for a small plate of roast beef mixed, (this means mashed turnips and potatoes in equal quantities.) After you have eaten this frugal dish,—and it is as much as any one really *needs* for dinner,—you may send for "bread, hard," drink a tumbler of cool Croton, pay one shilling for the whole, and go about your business like a refreshed and sensible man.

There is still another class of eating-houses, which deserve honorable mention—the cake and coffee shops, of which "Butter-cake Dick's" is a favorable sample.—The chief merit of these establishments is that they are kept open all night, and that hungry Editors or belated idlers can get a plate of biscuits with a lump of butter in the belly for three cents, and a cup of coffee for as much more—or he can regale himself on pumpkin pie at four cents the quarter-section, with a cup of Croton, fresh from the hydrant, gratis. The principal supporters of these luxurious establishments, however, are the firemen and the upper circles of the newsboys, who have made a good business during the day, or have succeeded in pummeling some smaller boy and taking his pennies from him. Here, ranged on wooden benches, the butter-cakes and coffee spread ostentatiously before them, and their intelligent faces supported in the crotch of their joined hands, these autocrats of the press, and the b'hoys, discuss the grave questions as to whether Fourteen *was* at the fire in Front-street first, or whether it is all gas. Here also are decided in advance the relative merits and speed of the boats entered for the next regatta, and points of great pith and moment in the science of the Ring are definitively settled. As midnight comes and passes, the firemen, those children of the dark, gather from unimaginable places, and soon a panorama of red shirts and brown faces lines the walls and fills the whole area of the little cellar. They are generally far more moderate than politicians and less noisy than gentlemen. At the first tingle of the fire-bell they leap like crouching greyhounds, and are in an instant darting through the street towards their respective engine-houses—whence they emerge dragging their ponderous machines behind them, ready to work like Titans all night and all day, exposing themselves to every peril of life and limb, and performing incredible feats of daring strength to save the property of people who know nothing about them, care nothing for them, and perhaps will scarcely take the trouble to thank them.

But of all this by itself. The type of eating-house of which we have not spoken is the expensive and aristocratic *restaurant* of which Delmonico's is the only complete specimen in the United States—and this, we have it on the authority of travelled epicures, is equal in every respect, in its appointments and attendance as well as the quality and execution of its dishes, to any similar establishment in Paris itself. We have not left ourselves room in this number to speak in detail of this famous *restaurant*, nor of its *habitués*. It well deserves, however, a separate notice; and a look through its well-filled yet not crowded saloons, and into its admirable *cuisine* will enable us to pass an hour very profitably— besides obtaining a dinner which, as a work of art, ranks with a picture by Huntingdon, a poem by Willis, or a statue by Powers—a dinner which is not merely a quantity of food deposited in the stomach, but is in every sense and to all the senses a great work of art.

Wall Street and the
Merchants' Exchange
(from *Fifteen Minutes Around New York*)

The stock sales are over. The little group, consisting of some two score of the initiated, who understood the mysterious jargon going on within the inner red-canopied sanctuary of the Exchange, and a few wondering outsiders, who knew no more of it than did the Epicurean of the mysteries of Isis, that daily takes its place around the chancel railings of this crimson-canopied altar of Mammon, have dispersed. The loud-mouthed auctioneer, selling most picturesque and romantically situated village lots, country residences, villas, mansions—in fact, castellated palaces, surrounded by century old parks, stocked with deer and pheasants—have all bawled themselves hoarse and gone to their underground dens to count their honestly earned gains of the morning. The members of the "third board" are snooping about "the street," picking up items here and there of what has really been going on during the morning among the big bugs; who is "short," who is "lame," who has been "cornered," and what is whispered about among the knowing ones as the programme for to-morrow.

It is a quarter past two o'clock. There is an apparent lull in the street—but it is only apparent. The forty-five minutes between this time and three o'clock contrive to crowd themselves with more anxiety, solicitude, hope, fear, despair, and mental agony than was ever got together in any other three-quarters of an hour since the last moments of the flood.

From our look-out behind this titanic granite column, let us look abroad upon the street. The sun pours down his streams of red hot light upon the step and sidewalk. The Custom House gleams like an immense live coal at white heat, and the banks that contain this deep-flowing current of Wall street, with their sombre hues of dirty greys and hot, smouldering browns, throw back the sunshine with livid beams that suffocate the very air. Still, through this gasping atmosphere, hurry, with silent, shuffling step, throngs of men, old, young, well dressed and untidy, fat, lean, tall, short—all different, yet all alike, with that expression of uniform anxiety, which, to the knowing observer, is as unmistakable as the aspect of a counterfeit bill to a broker. Up and down the steep steps of the banks, which at every few paces dip themselves in the current—in and out at softly-swinging green baize doors, that turn as noiselessly as the gates over which is written in the vision of the immortal Italian, "Let those abandon hope who enter here"—plunging down into the innumerable caves that line the street and lie below the level of the walk: see them go. Would not a rational being, stationed here for the first time, and knowing nothing of the great game of money-making which absorbs the faculties of the present age—would he not conclude that some gigantic lunatic asylum had been let loose, and that its inmates were rushing about in disgust with their newly-found freedom, trying to find their quiet and sombre cells again?

But let them go—the rabble of the street: while we turn our attention within, and see what is going on in this beautiful Rotunda, with its marble walls, and graceful Corinthian columns, upon which those composite capitals have *not* been placed. The in-comers here are, for the most part, evidently of the mercantile old fogy class. They pause to blow, at every three or four paces, as they hoist their heavy and unwieldy persons slowly and toilingly up the granite steps. The Shaving Cream man lifts his hat with involuntary respect, as they pass by. They are evidently themselves the shaving cream of our financial aristocracy. Heaven help those who are so unlucky as to be shaved by them!

Within the Rotunda you only see a crowd of commonplace people, winding in and out, grouping themselves together, pairing off, and talking in a low voice in some corner, or against a pillar—and you hear a confused, perpetual murmur, like the swarming of bees, or the voice of the sea in a calm. The lofty panels of the dome catch and reverberate every sound, sending it back with increased force, upon the ear, until the accumulation of these whisperings and low talkings, becomes thunderous in your ear, and almost crazes you.

If you listen to what is said, here, unless you are initiated, you will learn very little that will guide you in forming an opinion of what is going on. Half phrases, broken sentences, mysterious gestures and signs—these form the staple of what is doing here. If you have not the key, you might as well be an attendant upon the worship at a Chinese temple to Josh (not Silsbee), and chop sticks.

Here, at this hour, daily congregate the real, bona fide, no-mistake magnates of our financial and commercial aristocracy. Having taken their two shilling dinner at Brown's, or their cut of pie and coffee (or perhaps even something stronger), at the Verandah, they meet here to discuss the commercial news of the day—the prices of exchange, money and produce—and to play the great game of gambling, which leads to respectability and success, or to disaster, bankruptcy and ruin.

> Treason is ne'er successful; what's the reason?
> When 'tis successful, 'tis no longer treason.

Hudibras, nor any other satirist of human nature, ever wrote anything truer than that; and it applies with especial force to the Merchants' Exchange of New York. The hours devoted to the brokers and avowed speculators are a different affair. But at this particular hour of the day—this "High Change," as it is called *par excellence*—the millionaires and magnates of the city—those men whose slightest remarks uttered on 'Change are greedily recorded by the commercial reporters and trumpeted forth the next morning as if the Delphian oracle had spoken, meet here, and in whispers, shrugs and inuendoes, decide prices, fortunes and destinies, which ramify through every rank of society, and effect, for good or evil, the whole movement and life of the community. It is they who get up or suppress panics—who cause money to be "light" or "easy"—and whose decisions, formed upon their own personal and private gambling interests, settle the question whether the country is to be prosperous or unfortunate.

Yonder, prowling about like a cat at midnight, among the tiles and chimneys, is a commercial reporter, the "money market man" of a daily paper. If ears were ever useful, his are so. Each one of these somewhat ungraceful auricular appendages, opened to its fullest extent, is drinking in the whispered, broken, ejaculatory conversations going on around him. With the electric apprehension only to be acquired by such a life of experience as his, he gathers into the focus of his brain, all the different rays of intelligence, news and thought, floating about, in this gold-impregnated atmosphere. When he leaves the Rotunda, which will not be till the "last cat is hung," he will linger down the steps and along the walk in the vicinity, to catch some laggard millionaire by the button, and try to worm out of him the secret of some "transaction" in flour, or grain, or what not, that has not "transpired." Then off he rushes to the telegraph office, to put his Southern and Western correspondents in possession of the important secret that "20,000 barrels flour were sold to-day, at an advance of 6d on yesterday's quotations—to be delivered next week." The same astounding intelligence is repeated in the evening editions of his own paper, and in sundry correspondences which he keeps up with journals out of the city. These apparently insignificant facts are what regulate and control the whole movement of society and decide those other all-important questions, whether madame is to have a new carriage and mademoiselle a new lover, who is only to be caught in a point-lace net stretched over a palpitating bosom (swelling with vanity, not love); or whether the old Brougham and the old Harry are to do until the next favorable turn in the market.

The fatal hour of three is chiming from the spire of Trinity—that beautiful, pure and holy monument of art, rising like an exhalation from the fiery dust of the city, and looking solemnly down upon the clamor and crowd of Wall street. The banks have already their shutters closed, though now and then some belated customer steals out from the door and rushes wildly off with a bit of paper in his hand, which he savagely crushes up in his fingers, lest it should escape his grasp and have to be taken up over again tomorrow. The street grows rapidly vague and silent—footsteps echo but rarely along the pavement—the omnibuses cease to stop at the head of the street to wait for passengers—the clock points to ten minutes after three, and Wall street has locked up and gone home. What a time we have been lingering here! We have consumed almost the other three-quarters of an hour which we had wrenched from the business of the day, for our visit to Wall street.

But we must not quit this important and interesting quarter of New York without some grave and profitable reflections. Who, then, are these favored and powerful individuals who exert this immense control over society and the world? What they *were*, we will say nothing about: as to who and what they *are*, go to Jullien's or Ole Bull's, or Sontag's, and you will see. They are the patrons of the Opera—the hope of Art in this country and this age: and the beauty of it is, that they know as much of painting, of statuary, of architecture, and the belles lettres, as of music. They are quite as familiar with Shakespeare and Milton, Shelley and Tennyson, Byron and Coleridge, as with Rossini and Meyerbeer. There is no conceivable subject of poetry, art or literature, upon which they will not pronounce a judgment with the authority of a critic and the prolixity of an amateur. They have that which is so much better than knowledge, or study, or experience, or brains, or in fact, than anything but money—they have position; and that position they have obtained and can only keep because of their *money*. No one cares to dispute with them their claims to fashion and exclusiveness. No one dares to exhibit the ludicrous mockery of their pretensions to elegance and social eminence. No one dares lay bare the lie upon which they live, nor to hold them up for what they are. No one dares question them, as they stride insolently through the temple of fashion and good society, or march disdainfully and with flying colors to their velvet-cushioned pew in Grace Church. While all know the truth, yet they pass unquestioned. Why is this? Because the great majority of their neighbors are as bad as themselves, and dare not for their lives agitate the question of an investigation into the title deeds of those who hold within their grasp the lordly domains of aristocracy and fashion. The few who might safely challenge these vulgar pretenders, shrink with instinctive disgust from the thankless task; while of the great struggling, fighting, straining world below them, each hopes to receive, at some remote period, the favor of a smile of recognition from these misshapen images that the demon of snob democracy sets up in the niches of the beautiful and the great.

Let us return from our long and interesting detour to Wall street and the purlieus of the Exchange. Let us watch the process by which the fortunes are accumulated that enable their possessors thus to lord it over the world, and climb to these places of eminence and distinction which should be reserved alone to the wise, the brilliant and the good. We will not descend to the particulars of the various transactions which go to make up the sum of that profession known as trade. Suffice it to say, that the foundation of it all, the secret of success, the key to wealth and power, is the cautious over-reaching of the neighbor. So long as the merchant or the speculator maintains untarnished that conventional honor which thieves find it absolutely necessary to enforce in the division of their plunder; so long as his bank account is good and his credit untainted in "the street," no matter how savagely he may oppress the poor man within his power—no matter how many hearts he may have wrung with anguish, how many lips may turn white with hunger, how many desperate souls driven to crime, how many milk-white virgin bosoms be given to the polluting touch of lust, for money to buy bread—how many fellow beings may be wholly crushed and made forever desperate by the iron grasp of this man, he is still respectable, "one of the most respectable of our citizens." And should one of his beggared victims cross his path on his way to church, or entreat but a solitary penny to stave off the pangs of hunger, he would assume the indignant air of a martyr, suffering under the persecutions of an insolent and ungrateful world.

The engines and instruments by which this man works are numerous and characteristic. Sometimes he forestalls the market of a certain kind of produce, and then when his carefully concealed operations are completed, gradually expands the price in accordance with the increasing demand, until he thus gathers his thousands from the absolute necessities of the community. Sometimes he organizes a company to kindly supply the people with money, or to dig coal, or copper, or zinc, or lead, from fabulous mines, drawn carefully out on paper maps, and situated in some inaccessible Sahara amid the wild regions of New Jersey. Then he sells the stock out upon a fictitious valuation got up by incessant puffs in the leading commercial papers, and so makes a fortune, and the scheme explodes. Sometimes he discovers that the interests and honor of the nation require a railroad from

Frogtown to Tadpolopolis, and a similar operation lines his pockets at the cost of a few hundred green victims; or perhaps the commercial prosperity of the Empire State demands that a line of steamships should be established to break down all opposition, and prove that some things can be done as well as others. Straightway the newspaper pumps are put in operation, and books of subscription opened, and flaming appeals made to the patriotism of Congress for a small appropriation of a million or two, just by way of experiment, and to sustain the honor of the country. Of course the stock is subscribed and paid for by the victims, while the appropriation goes into the pockets of the shrewd capitalist, and he becomes more magnificent, more haughty and insolent than ever. Arrived at the station of the millionaire, whether in fact or in renown, it makes no difference, he has forgotten himself and all the incidents that might embarrass or humiliate him in his present position. Trace him back but a single generation, and we may find this paternal ancestor cobbling boots or hammering at a barrel; while on the maternal side, the shop-board and the goose loom in the distance, and a well-worn thimble would be the only proper seal and device for the family coat of arms.

Such is a fair and not overdrawn picture of a type of the money, shop-keeping aristocracy of the New World—a race of beings who, as a natural historian, we undertake to say, have never been equaled on the face of this earth, in all that is pompous without dignity, gaudy without magnificence, lavish without taste, and aristocratic without good manners.

The Needlewomen

(from *New York in Slices*)

The public are already in possession of abundance of statistics on the subject of female labor. Our object at present is to review things in the general, for the purpose of giving the reader a comprehensive view of the various classes into which society in the metropolis is divided. It will be sufficient, therefore, for our purposes to present in a few words the average prices paid for various kinds of needlework, at the principal and prosperous establishments.

Common cotton shirts, and flannel under-shirts, six cents each. A good seamstress can run up two of these shirts per day; and even a very swift hand, by working from sunrise to midnight, can make three; being seventy-five cents per week for the common workers, and $1.12½ for the swiftest, of course allowing nothing for holidays, sickness, accidents, being out of work, &c. &c. Good cotton shirts, with linen bosoms, neatly stitched, are made for twenty-five cents apiece. A good seamstress will make one in a day, thus earning $1.50 per week, by constant labor. Fine linen shirts with plaited bosoms, which cannot be made by the very best hands short of fifteen to eighteen hours steady work, are paid fifty cents each. An ordinary hand can make a garment of this kind in two days. Trowsers, overalls, drawers, under-shirts, &c. &c., pay a shilling apiece to the seamstress, who can make one and perhaps two a day. Cloth pantaloons, vests, &c., pay eighteen to fifty cents—very seldom the latter price; and a woman makes, on the average, about one a day. Thus, not to prolong these details, it may be stated, in a word, that the seamstress who is fortunate enough to get steady work earns from seventy-five cents to two dollars a week. Besides these, it is necessary to state that the dress-makers, or at any rate the great majority of them, get absolutely nothing for the work. The way it is managed is this: the proprietors of the large dress-making establishments receive a great number of apprentices, who remain six months for nothing, boarding themselves in the mean time, for the privilege of learning the trade. They can already sew swiftly and well, or they are not accepted. To them are given out the dresses, and they are kept constantly at work sewing (not learning any thing new) until the very day before their apprenticeship expires. Then a few hours are spent in giving them some general directions about cutting a dress, and they are discharged—there being no room for *journeywomen on wages* in an establishment where all work is done by *apprentices for nothing*. As fast as their "education" is completed they are replaced by other apprentices. And so it goes on; the dashing proprietress of the establishment growing rich and aristocratic, and the poor girls turning out upon the world to die of starvation and despair, or sell themselves to infamy.

Here then are the facts respecting a large and increasing class of our female population; and a sad enough picture they present. It is this picture which gave rise a few days since to the following eloquent outburst of feeling from a lady of our acquaintance, of whom I was soliciting information: "Is it not the strangest thing that can well be conceived, that Woman, who by the present constitution of society is made politically and socially a slave—who has no voice in the government to which she submits, in making the laws she is forced to obey—who is in short not recog-

Needlewoman.

nised by any human institution of these days as an independent individual, or as any thing apart from the necessity Man has for using or abusing her—that she is not, like other slaves whose existence is merged in their masters, even secured food, clothing, and shelter for the fleeting 'gleam between two eternities' on which glides by her pale and suffering apparition! The workwoman has indeed no rights of her own. She can be oppressed, cheated, trampled upon, until the joyous life within her becomes a dead and poisonous impulse that drives her through the world eager for the grave, or stings her into desperation and revenge. But how revenge her wrongs? She has no redress, neither in those laws she did not sanction, nor in that public opinion she cannot influence, and which regards her not. Seeing this, her gentle and tender nature at length undergoes a change. Then the feeble becomes the terrible; the weak and suffering Woman is transformed into an avenging demon. And who may wonder at her?"

In this great republican metropolis—this foregone result of the highest and best thing that civilization can do, with all our boasted "free" institutions in full bloom and life—there are thirty thousand virtuous women who have to live, die, and be buried on what they can earn with their hands. In the ranks of this class of our population, we find Woman in almost every aspect of misery, ever struggling, and faint with the burden of life. Wives and daughters of broken-down merchants and speculating politicians form a large item in this catalogue. Reduced from affluence to poverty and keen want, they are all unlearned in the great secret of yielding gracefully to the inevitable, and maintain day by day a fierce, unequal, but not doubtful contest with "cruel Fortune," until they sink beneath temptation or despair—to the brothel or the grave! A majority are borne up by pride alone from beggary, and the few who still calendar them among their acquaintances do not suspect to what strait they have been driven, until the crisis arrives and is over.

Next come the widows of tradesmen and mechanics, the
wives and daughters of those who cannot get employment,
and the wives of sick and intemperate husbands, and the
children of invalid or drunken parents. Here are to be found
some of the most patient and long-suffering, starving, toiling, heart-broken, yet courageous women that ever glorified
their Creator. Here, in miserable open garrets, utterly deprived of human hope and sympathy, and often languid and
faint from the mere want of food, these creatures show what
angels women are. Sometimes—oh! too often—the selfishness of pain and suffering, or the brutal appetite of hunger
and intemperance, makes the sick father or the drunken
mother command the pale and tender daughter to go out
into the streets, and sell herself for gold! Must it not be a life
resembling hell itself that begets such crimes as this? And
how dare we wonder and shrug our shoulders with a pious
sneer at those among these unfortunates who do not resist?

Then, too, from out their workshop windows, through the
chinks and crannies of their miserable lodgings, our poor
workers see how gayly the busy and seeming-joyous world
goes on—how every one appears to have hope in his eye and
elasticity in his step. Nor can they fail to mark among the
passing throng many women not more beautiful than themselves—whom perhaps they have well known as fellow-
workers—who go flaunting idly along in gay and costly
robes, receiving the stealthy smiles and admiration of the
lords of creation, who follow skulking after till they turn
down some dark corner, and with the outlay of a smile and a
seductive word secure their victim. They want for nothing—
they live in luxury—their white hands look fair and delicate
from want of employment—their eyes seem to sparkle with
health, and their forms are rounded and elastic with generous fare and absence of toil. Is it surprising that our poor
workers, looking out from their rags and squalid poverty
and starvation upon all this, should forget (what perhaps
they have never been informed of) the horror, the agony, the
despair, the disease, the madness, which are the inevitable

future of the courtesan? and that too many of them should,
alas! desire to be like her?

But we are trenching upon somewhat broader ground
than we had intended to occupy in these unpretending
sketches, and find ourselves in contact with that great and
terrible question, the Causes of Prostitution—a question
which none has yet had the courage to answer. Our object is
simply to present a correct view of a large and unfortunate
class of females, surrounded with all the trials and tempta-
tions which beset them—leaving the reader to draw his own
conclusions. Having done this, with what little power of
pen-limning we possess, we will take advantage of the occasion to solemnly warn young women in the country against
indulging for an instant the fatal desire of coming to the
City to seek their fortunes by labor. If they could, as we have
done, attend day after day the bar of the Police Court, or
read the secret docket of the innumerable cases of heart-
brokenness, desolation, and crime that there appear, or hear
from their own lips the history of the wretched creatures
who people the innumerable dens of infamy that abound in
the metropolis, they would learn this one frightful truth,—
that more than half the prostitutes and female criminals in
the city came here from the country to earn a living in some
honest way, and to gratify an innocent longing for a little
female finery, and a passion to "see the world." The sad
story is ever, ever the same: first destitution, then absolute
want and hunger, then turned out of doors, houseless and
homeless, or offered the dreadful alternative of prostitution.
Young Woman!—if you are indeed a real Woman, and no innate demon assuming angelic form of purity the better to
carry on hell's work on earth—mark well our warning! Stay
calmly where you are, beneath your own pure skies, and
amid the virtuous freshness of your home, no matter how
humble it may be. Work, spin, dig, till the soil—do *any thing*
virtuous that will earn you bread, and mere bread is not so
very difficult to get in the country! But as you value your
moral purity, and the welfare of your immortal soul, come

not into the city, to lose yourself in the boiling, seething caldron of licentiousness that rages forever here. If you have an intellect too active to be satisfied with the dull routine of a country life, read and improve your mind by study, and mature your heart by contemplation. If you have aspirations for the beautiful, surround yourself with flowers, and teach birds and gentle creatures to be your playmates and companions; endear yourself to all the little children in the neighborhood: conceive the grand and noble ambition, the only one worthy of Woman's soul, of rendering yourself necessary to your fellow-creatures, within the natural reach of your sphere, and of adding something to the beauty of this beautiful earth, of which God has made you the brightest and most precious blessing. Thus may you, poor and humble though you be, fill your life with a gentle joy that shall bring health and happiness to cheek and eyes, and surround your innocent pillow with celestial dreams.

A Plunge in the Swimming-Bath

(from *Fifteen Minutes Around New York*)

Plop! goes the fat man, whom we just saw waddling across the Battery, with his face red as the full moon, and his whole man appearing about to melt. He stripped in marvellous quick time, and glided into the water like a large lump of warm fat. How gratefully to him, in every pore of his body, is the cool wave, embracing him in its soft, inexorable arms, no thin man can conceive. A lean man splashes and splutters about in the water like four sticks tied together. The only wonder is, why he ever came into it. There is no use in his trying to swim—that's clear; he would inevitably break his toes or scrape his shins, or even his knees, against the bottom. He belongs to the crane species—he can only keep his head above water by wading.

But your fat, sleek, oily, contented man, like our friend who has taken the plunge, enjoys his bath with an active and positive enjoyment. The bath is his antithesis; and for the few moments it lasts, he is as much at home as if he were a very large and very clumsy fish, and, in fact, he very much reminds you strongly of a porpoise, as he goes wallowing and rolling and blowing about.

There's Dandy C——, who has been told by his physician that the swimming-bath will permanently relieve the gout and general debility brought on by his incessant and indiscreet dissipations. At any rate, the doctor is conscientious. His skill can do nothing for decayed marrows, diseased livers, disorganized kidneys, and a general atrophy produced by a premature exhaustion of all the forces of life.

Dandy unfolds himself as carefully as if he was a contribution to the Crystal Palace, and had been marked "very fragile—this side up, handle carefully." Having neatly folded his clothes, and deposited them in a safe and dry place, he cautiously dips one great toe into the water and draws back with a shudder and a "ugh! how cold it is!" Our fat friend, who is cruising lazily along shore, sees the state of things, and makes a sudden dive, which throws a barrel or two of water into the face and over the attenuated person of our roué. He gives a scream, falls back, and faints, like a fine lady. Everybody runs to the spot—nobody has any salts or French vinegar, and nobody is exactly in a state to go to the apothecary's. The fat gentleman, who has now come up, and is floating on the surface of the water, like a rich tit-bit in a bowl of turtle soup, suggests that water is a sovereign remedy for fainting away; and, it being at least the treatment nearest at hand, they all consent, and Dandy is thrust into the water. The fat man's therapeutics succeed admirably. The patient, after a few kicks and dying gasps, opens his eyes, and, taking a dismayed look of "surrounding circumstances," screams, lustily.

"Oh dear! Oh, I shall be drowned! I've got the cramp! Help me out! Murder! Mur—bbl—uble—phlubble! Ah!" and the poor fellow, overpowered with perhaps the first positive "sensation" he ever had in his life, actually disappears beneath the water. The fat gentleman, who is lying on his back, dying with laughter, reaches down and grabs Dandy by the hair, as he supposes, and up comes—a wig!

"What a fool, to go in swimming with a wig on!" exclaims the indignant and cheated fat gentleman; and, just as he is preparing to make another dive, Dandy catches him by the leg, with desperate gripe, and drags him down, down!

Things begin to look serious. The fat gentleman, roused to the highest state of muscular activity, splashes, flounders, and splatters so lustily, that it is no easy matter to approach. Dandy hangs on, like death, and with that fatuity which belongs exclusively to drowning men and men in love, makes every possible effort for his own destruction. At length, and when affairs are evidently approaching a crisis, a stalwart Californian—the bony and muscular embodiment of leanness, with a head like St. Paul, and a body like an omnibus horse—wades up to the defendants in the case, and with a jerk, throws the water-logged Dandy on dry land, and lifts the gentleman once more into the air. Dandy, however, was pretty far gone. They had to take him away in a cab; and we have heard nothing of him since.

Here is a young and dainty fellow, with a just budding moustache, and a skin as soft and white as a woman's. He is almost as modest, too, and blushes at the sight of his own legs, like a girl. We doubt whether he will finally venture to extract himself from his chemise. Yes—he is looking around fearfully; and seizing a moment when he thinks no one is watching, off it comes, and he, like a poor sinner,

> Stands shivering on the brink,
> And fears to make the plunge.

Poor, dear little fellow! He really quite reminds one of Endymion, or some such moonshine. And now he has attracted the notice of a party of *gamins*, who have been making all sorts of mischief for half an hour, splashing themselves and everybody else, ducking one another and "holding 'em under" till they grew purple in the face, and could no longer breathe, and cutting up every imaginable "shine" which it enters into the heart of boys-terous youth to conceive, or its hands to execute. We fear our Miss Nancy will fare hard with them.

He has not yet ventured into the water, but stands with his last garment in his hand, very much in the attitude of Canova's Venus. One of our *gamins* comes up softly behind him, and, ke-wash! in he goes, his shirt flying in one direction and his legs and arms sprawling towards all points of the compass. His gasping cries are stopped by shouts of laughter—and one of the tormentors cries— "Hold him under, Jim! He's a green 'un!"

What may be the sensations of this poor devil the next minute and a half, we won't undertake to say; but we should imagine they were something similar to those of poor stuttering Charles Lamb, who was ducked three times by the Brighton bath-men, before he could manage to sputter out, "I'm to b-be d-dipped—*only once!*"

Here comes an old fogy. We shouldn't wonder if he were president of a mining company, or a director of the Crystal Palace, at the very least. He enters with a grave and stately step, looking round with awful dignity upon the place, and all that it contains. The atmosphere grows grim with respect, and the very water takes a brown and muddled hue, as if something of great importance were about to happen— perhaps a water-spout! The very shad in the bay keep well over towards the Jersey shore, and the vessels at anchor wheel slowly around with the tide, and point their noses seaward, as if ready for a sudden start. Endymion scrambles out of the water, wringing his shirt, in briny despair, and his white, satin skin looking like that of a young sea-gull. Our fat friend, who has by this time gotten himself completely rehabillated, walks off, giving a look askance at the old fogy; and even the gamins themselves cower, shivering, in a crowd, and begin trying to insert themselves into their crumpled and unstarched garments. The Californian is the only one not overawed by the august presence. Wading up in front of the old fogy, and looking at him with a comical expression, he says—

"I say, old feller—give us a chor o'terbacker, will yer?"

"Tobacco, sir!" exclaims Old Fogy, Esq., aghast. "Tobacco! Do you mean to insult me?"

"Well, I shouldn't mind, old hoss! Jest you come into this here small tin pan full of water, what they calls a swimmin'-bath in these small-potatoe diggins, and ain't no objections to takin' a turn with you. Whooray! Who's afeard?"

Old Fogy looks, reflects a moment, slips on his boots and trowsers, and muttering something about the "encroachments of democracy," disappears.

Now for the ladies' department.

A Quarter of an Hour
Under an Awning
(from *Fifteen Minutes Around New York*)

Six o'clock and down-town—and a thick grey blanket
spreading out all over the north and west. Broadway is a
dense and turbid stream of people, flowing upwards. Men,
women, children and little niggers, rush wildly up the side-
walk, hurrying to escape the coming shower—while here
and there prudent old gentlemen, (they are not nearly in the
same proportion as the wise virgins spoken of in Scripture,)
pick their way leisurely along, with their umbrellas ready
for use, and a quiet chuckle of self-complacency on their
faces.

The rain has not yet come down—but it *will* come, and
speedily. The question now is, "can we get home before it
comes?" It is worth trying, at any rate—so, here goes for a
dash into the struggling current. What enormous strides the
women take, with their beautiful silks and fresh summer
muslins wabbled up ingloriously about their ancles! They go
like a quarter horse down the back stretch—passing everything on the road, and determined to pull up ahead of the
party. It's no use—we can't keep up such a killing pace; and
besides, here comes the rain, in drops as big as eggs. We

drop behind and take our stand under the awning at Chambers street, waiting for an omnibus.

Under an awning in Broadway—waiting for a stage in a rapid rain-dash—at half-past six o'clock! There's a situation! and one which, if it could be fairly presented on the stage (we don't mean the omnibus) would draw the whole town after it. Here they come, gathering from all directions, crowding in beyond the line of rain, reaching over each other's shoulders, and making frantic signs to every omnibus that passes—while the drivers, shaking the big rain-drops from their flapped hats with a most triumphant negative, splash on, leaving our awning congregation momentarily growing larger and more desperate.

"Oh, good gracious me!" suddenly exclaims a lady in the centre of this *extempore* mass-meeting, who wears a brilliant lilac bonnet, a green and orange silk dress, and flesh-colored silk stockings (easy to be seen) and lavender-colored boots. "Oh, my goody gracious! there's a hole in it and its all a-running down my back—and, oh my bonnet! it'll be clean spoilt!"

"Hush, my dear—don't make a row; you shall have another."

"Mhmh! I know I shall have another—but who knows whether I can get another such one as this?"

"I trust in Providence, my love, that you cannot. You certainly can't do worse."

Snicker, giggle, he, he, he! from the crowd, *sotto voce.*

"Brute!"

"Darling!"

Here's a stage at last, the driver of which has pulled up. What a rush! There's a man getting out. Help him out—pull him out—quick! hurry! Twenty umbrellas make a desperate dash at the vacated place—one would almost think it was a vacant situation in the Custom House. No use! Off they go—four on the top, two on each side of the driver—two on the steps, and fifteen inside—twenty-two in all; as we do live by bread, 'tis true! And the discomfited nineteen, drenched and desperate, sneak back to the awning—which, by the way, is no longer much of a protection, except that it changes the shower without into a series of sporadic water-spouts, which pour down in steady streams on our devoted heads. The lilac bonnet is wilted long ago, and it now looks as if it had been a sugar bonnet, and all the extras had melted and run away. The owner would evidently like to follow its example; but the "brute" who paid for the bonnet looks at the fallen and smashed-up wreck with evident admiration—a sentiment he never entertained for it in the days of its pristine grandeur.

Dinner was to be on the table precisely at six—and Jemima strictly enjoined it upon us to be punctual, as she and the girls were going out. Of course they can't go out such a night as this—but then, there are Jemimas, and Jemimas and punctuality are blessings.

Don't it come down *beautiful!* and just at this hour, too, of all others in the twenty-four! By the time one gets home thoroughly wet through, the storm without will have exhausted its fury, which will be transferred within. Who wonders at Caudle's untimely end? The stages rattle by in an incessant procession—every one apparently more crowded than the last: the drivers no longer deign even to look towards our melancholy and stranded group, cowering like the last of a shipwreck, trying in vain to shelter themselves under the lee of the wave-washed deck.

We have an idea—let us take a seat in a down-town stage, and so stick to it till it returns. Lilac bonnet has just cast loose, with her convoy, and both are scudding under bare poles for the railcar, where they hope for better luck. Deluded mortals! The cars are all full and running over with down-towners, who had jumped on board to secure seats going up. A carriage of course is not be had—or, if it were, you would have to pay a week's salary for half-an-hour's use of it. No—there is but one alternative to waiting—and that is, wading. Lilac bonnet won't do either! She's evidently making up her mind to faint: that unsuccessful trip to the railroad, and the return, have proved too much for her. There—

LIMITED TO TWELVE

Inside an omnibus.

she's off! Carry her into Rushton's, give her some ether or chloroform, establish her in an elegant attitude against that Windsor Soap box, and then run out and give "all the particulars" to that shark of a reporter who has been dodging in and out of the crowd during the whole affair.

"Police! police! My pocket's picked! Where's the police?" bawls a stout, red-faced man, running from one to another and exclaiming piteously, "Oh, do give it to me—for God's sake give it back to me!" At last he accosts a flashy, stylish-looking gentleman, with a brilliant cravat and oily whiskers and moustache. The "gent" frowns sublimely at him—"Damme, sir, do you think I've got your dirty pocket-book?"

"How did you know it was a pocket-book? He didn't say what it was," remarks the astute reporter, who is rather up to snuff.

"That's him—hold him fast—I knows him!" exclaims a policeman, at this moment coming up—(he must have rained down!) "How are ye, my covey? Come, tip—tain't no use—I knows yer of old, I does."

Our magnificent gentleman wilts instantly—as rapidly as the lilac bonnet. The policeman produces the pocket-book, from Whisker's outside pocket—he all the while protesting, like the lover in Washington, that he hasn't the least idea how it got there. He begs the officer to step aside, and he thinks he can convince him, &c., &c. The proprietor of the restored pocket-book looks pleased—almost grateful. After fumbling for a long time in his trowsers pocket, he drags out a very smooth quarter, and hopes the policeman will accept it, although, as a general rule, he is opposed to paying public servants for the performance of their duty. Policeman stares—and puts tongue in his cheek. Old gentleman wonders what that means—but he pockets the slighted quarter with evident satisfaction. Reporter takes a note, and, picking up an umbrella which the owner had leaned, dripping, against the fire-plug, scampers off. Owner dumb with consternation, gesticulates violently in language which a member of the Deaf and Dumb Asylum would immediately interpret into—"Here, you—rascal, bring back my umbrella!" Owner has a new hat, and the umbrella is an old one: "A new hat on the head is better than an old umbrella across the street."

Here's a young physician, without a carriage—just getting into practice—has been running all day—only half an hour for dinner—last chance gone. He must evidently either go hungry or neglect a patient. An errand boy leans yonder against the wall. He don't care—not he—if it rains till midnight. Here a small actor and his wife come creeping like drowned rats out of a stage, each with a bundle of the night's finery under the arm. They look very little like the comedy countess and strutting man of fashion they are to become in a few moments.

But at last there seems to be a lull—the mud-drops plop up less fiercely from the Russ—and, as if everything were about to come right at once, here is the very omnibus for which we have been waiting. Our meeting under the awning has dispersed like a conclave at Tammany Hall, after the lights are turned off. The lilac bonnet has disappeared with its good-natured husband; Don Magnificio Whiskers has paired off with the policeman; the owner of the new hat and the lost umbrella is staring vacantly in the direction where the reporter made his rapid exit; and the red-faced financier and ourself start for the omnibus. We are not malicious—but all's fair in omnibus riding; and a sly trip of our respectable antagonist, quite by accident, lays him sprawling in the mud; we mount the steps in triumph, and hurra for home, a wet welcome, and a cold dinner!

Sunday in New York

(from *New York in Slices*)

A strong man in action stopping to take breath—a racehorse panting between the heats—a ship pausing ere it plunges headlong down the mountain of the storm, and leaps on her course—are faint figures to indicate the abrupt and absolute repose that overtakes the metropolis every seventh day. In other places the contrast between Sunday and weekday is not so striking—for, although the quiet may be as complete, yet the noise and tumult are not so great, and the effect of the contrast, which here absolutely startles one, is wanting. If one fall asleep on a railroad, the stopping of the cars will be pretty sure to wake him; so the New Yorker becomes so accustomed to the ceaseless, the incredible din of Broadway—into whose rushing river-bath of dust and clamor every one dips at least twice a day—that the sudden, solemn, absolute silence of the Sabbath comes upon him like a sweet shock, rousing into activity his higher and more contemplative faculties, and laying, for a time, the fierce and remorseless spirit of Business that during all the week has been dragging him about by the hair.

In the narrow streets and alleys down-town, where usually the rattle of drays drowns out consciousness itself from your brain, and the sidewalks are piled hill-high with boxes, bales, and bundles, now the footfall echoes and re-echoes loudly on the smooth-worn flag, and the long lines of lofty warehouses extend with the prospect unbroken by drays or merchandise. In Wall-street, late so fiercely crowded, and struggling each man as if for life, all is still as death or the desert. The Dog-man has disappeared from the Custom-house steps—the doomed Canary birds no longer draw up their miniature wheelbarrows of seeds—the Shaving Cream man has smoothed himself out of sight—the innumerable shaving-shops down cellar have closed their cavernous jaws—and the Rotunda is as empty as Judge ———'s hat when his head is in it. The whole lower part of the City, where usually one would think, from the noise and hubbub, that the continent was running through a funnel, and this was the spout, is now as silent and lonely as a city of the olden time deserted centuries ago by its inhabitants, and left to the winds and sands of the desert.

But in Broadway the Sabbath contrast is perhaps even greater than in the great marts of trade and commerce. The pavement is as still as if an omnibus had never rattled over it, and the bewildered sunshine goes stumbling along trying to find some accustomed plate-glass window through which to look in upon pretty goods and prettier ladies. Before the palace-stores of fashion no liveried carriages are waiting, and on the walk nothing is seen but the unbent shadows of the lamp-posts. The roar and crash of the omnibuses is hushed, and the dust lies unsprinkled by the inevitable watering-pot on wheels, or whirls away in little suffocating eddies, whither and where it will. The Large Roasted Italian Chesnut Man has taken in his warming-pan and furnace, and the little girls who sell fancy windmills on Stewart's steps are, we hope, at Sunday-School learning their lessons.

In Chatham-street and the Bowery there is a little more life, but the change is still very great and gratifying, as an unmistakable evidence of the general regard in which Sunday is held by all classes of our population. There are, we know, a few loafers and rowdies who gather about the Five

Points and the Hook, on the wharves, and in the grog-cellars
of the by-streets, who neither know nor care whether it is
Sunday or not. But they are not apparent. Their haunts are
for the most part underground, and they do not mar the
general serenity of a New York Sabbath. In the Bowery and
Chatham-street, too, the absence of the omnibuses is very
grateful; and we are sincerely sorry to hear that efforts are
making to get some of the lines, both in Broadway and the
Bowery, to run on Sunday. We trust that there is, if not real
morality, at least regard enough for the physical welfare of
mankind among our citizens to promptly frown down any
such attempts as these. The omnibus proprietors themselves, we are sure, do not wish to run their vehicles on the
Sabbath; for the increased wear and tear of carriages, waste
of horse-flesh, &c., would more than overbalance the gains.
Besides, it would be cruel and oppressive in no slight degree
to compel the worthy and some of them Christian men now
engaged in omnibus driving to either run on Sunday or lose
their situations. They are most of them men of families, and
their wives find it no easy matter to get along with the six
dollars a week which their husbands earn: but if they were
to work *every* day they would soon break down or die, and
thus leave their families destitute. The seventh day of rest is
an indispensable necessity of all laboring men—and especially those so constantly employed, and in all sorts of
weathers, as the omnibus-driver. Let the Sabbath ever be sacred to rest.

If Broadway is the great artery of New York, through
which all the blood and bloods of town must course,
Nassau-street and its environments may be called its brain,
pulsating ever with the beating of a printing-engine, and
throwing off innumerable nerves, in the shape of newsboys,
to the rest of the system. But on Sunday even this is still. It
is true that the *Sun* and *Herald*, and perhaps some other papers, issue extras when a steamer arrives on Sunday, even if
there be not an item of news, and they are frequently cried
in the very front of the churches during divine service. We

of *The Tribune* never do this, and our office is never open on Sunday. Early every Sabbath morning, too, the voices of Sunday-paper newsboys are loud and incessant for two or three hours. Most of the newspaper offices, however, are, like *The Tribune*, closed on Sabbath; and we believe that public opinion will eventually compel all others to follow the example. Indeed, this public opinion is rapidly becoming aware of the great fact that the Sabbath is a physical as well as spiritual necessity to the world, and that, were it not for its blessed intervals of rest and recuperation, thousands of persons whose occupations are uncommonly arduous or exhausting would either die or become insane before the prime of their years. The united and unequivocal testimony of physicians, physiologists, philosophers, magistrates, and legislators, has been so widely diffused over the world by the benevolent labors of the American Tract Society and other religious institutions, that all classes of the community are becoming familiar with them. And should these lines fall into the hands of any man, woman, or child who has not yet become convinced that life and health are deeply interested in observing the Sabbath, we would earnestly advise him or her to go to the American Tract Society's office, 150 Nassau-street, and procure "The Sabbath Manual," by Rev. Justin Edwards—one of the most perspicuous, complete, and eloquent works on the Sabbath we have ever read. They will also find peculiarly interesting, in relation to this subject, tracts 8, 20, 116, 163, 334, 336, 415, 474, and 502.

But to return to New York on Sunday. If from what we have said, you conclude that signs of life and animation are wanting throughout the Sabbath, you are greatly mistaken. We spoke of the middle of the day. But in the morning at nine o'clock, punctual as an eclipse of the moon or a man to whom you have promised money, the Sunday-School bells begin to ring from a thousand steeples—and, despite the ill-natured remarks of people who are ashamed of themselves for hating the Sabbath and its institutions, we always find it most delightful music—with more heart and soul and meaning in it than all the *caterwaulini* to which the walls of the Tabernacle have ever resounded.

Then, like troops of fairies summoned by the sound of a familiar bell, bright-faced children in their fresh and pretty Sunday gowns and jackets, swarm the streets, and take their way to Sunday-School—a place whose charm it is difficult to describe, but most beautiful to acknowledge and feel. Never in all our wide experience among children—and we have known and loved thousands of them—have we found a boy or girl accustomed to attend Sunday-School, who did not feel it a pleasure to go there, and a real misfortune to be compelled, by any unforeseen event, to stay away. Through rain and sunshine, in Summer and Winter, off they go, as happy as young lambs, and also as innocent and as beautiful—for all children are beautiful.

In another hour and a half comes church—and then, if you would see how many people New York out-of-doors *can* hold, just look out, or join the crowd, and observe, as you are gently urged along by the force of the current into which you have dropped. Such a procession of beautiful ladies and attentive cavaliers cannot be seen elsewhere nor at any other time. There, too, the staid matron leaning upon the arm of her gray-headed but still stalwart husband, as they march proudly in front of their children and grandchildren, form picturesque and pleasing groups; while here and there some fond couple, still lingering within the enchanted atmosphere of the honeymoon, move stealthily along, their faces beaming with happiness. And how different the aspect and bearing of the throng from the rude crowds that rush and jostle each other on the walk in weekdays! Surely it is a blessed thing that the calm, love-inspiring Sabbath comes once a week to reunite the scattered family, and gather up the broken links of domestic affection, that sweetest and most blessed tie of earth. It is difficult not to believe that, without the Sabbath, society would inevitably retrograde to barbarism.

As soon as evening sets in, the City undergoes a change sudden and great as magic. Broadway, which all day save church-hours has been so lonely and deserted, now swarms with a dense crowd of men and women who do not, through the week, find leisure for a promenade. The great bulk of them are servant-girls, with their beaux and brothers, lovers and friends, who wait eagerly through the whole week for the setting of the Sabbath sun, that they may rush into the streets, and for a few hours enjoy the luxury of being free to do as they please. The bookfolders, the seamstresses, the fly-girls, the type-rubbers, the straw-braiders,—all the working girls from all parts of the City and every occupation,—have also found their sweethearts, and are out for a promenade in Broadway. They look fresher and walk more eagerly, and with far more energy and *aplomb* than the weekday loungers and idlers in our fashionable thoroughfare; and every face wears an expression of determination to make the most of the brief hour of recreation which is permitted to all classes. The sidewalk gives out new echoes—unaccustomed dialects break their necks against the unheeding window-shutters of the closed shops, and Broadway is no longer but a continuation, a suburb, of the Bowery. Far into the night thousands of footsteps patter upon the pavement, and the hum of mingling voices comes over the ledge of our far-up window like the music of the distant surf. At length, one by one, the few lights along the street disappear—the noise of falling feet grows more and more interrupted—conversation and strange bursts of laughter come less frequently and then cease entirely—the moonlight streams cold and glistening across the flag-stones—midnight sounds echoingly from steeple to steeple—and Sunday in New York is over.

Compositor:	BookMasters, Inc.
Text:	10/13 Aster
Display:	Aster
Printer:	BookCrafters
Binder:	BookCrafters